First Life

WENDY MUTTON

DEMPSTER STREET
PUBLISHING

Editor: Elizabeth Visser

Cover Art: Sheilla Hagedorn

LCCN 2023918371

ISBN: 979-8-9885702-1-9 (paperback)

ISBN: 979-8-9885702-0-2 (digital copy)

To Immanuel:
Jesus, your name says it all.

In loving memory of my husband John:
For his honor, courage, and constant love.

To my mother Christina Cowan Finlay:
I miss you, Mum. You left me with a love for stories and a strong belief that
all things are possible.

Chapter One

Looking Back—Seattle
Present Day

Houses have a feel. They give you the impression of safety or a sense that danger might be just outside your front window. Recollections, good and bad, stick to the walls, settle on the furniture, waiting to trigger a memory.

I grew up here. Got married here. But I wouldn't miss this place now that Mum was finally moving out. I stood in the living room surrounded by boxes crammed with the bits and pieces of her life. I tried not to look at the hardwood floor where the body had lain all those years ago. Some memories refuse to be packed away.

I struggled to shake off the ghosts. The sooner we were done, the sooner I could leave and never come back. I turned to my eighteen-year-old daughter, who had managed to pack one box in the four hours we'd been here. She handed it to me, and I froze. An old black spiral notebook lay on the bottom. It crinkled with age as I pulled it out and hugged it to me. I was holding the past in my hands.

My throat tightened with the flood of memories of sitting on my bed and writing well after I should have been asleep. The paper was yellowed and curled; my handwriting faded in spots. I sat on the couch and began looking through my find. My own words drew me in, casting their spell on me, pulling me back to 1968. I was unaware my daughter had slid in next to me until her breath brushed my cheek.

"What is that?" she asked.

"My old journal." An echo of the old fear filled my heart, but I kept my tone light. "It's about Grandma's life growing up in Scotland during World War II, about second sight and—"

I swallowed, wondering if I should say the rest. But I was the same age as Sheilla when I first heard the secret my mom had guarded for so long, when we both faced her past. I couldn't keep from stealing another glance at the floor before I looked Sheilla right in the eyes. "And about Grandma catching a serial killer."

She shook her head. "You're teasing me, right? My grandma?" Her grin faded. She reached over to touch one of the notebook pages. "What are all these loose pages stuffed in between?"

"I added my part later. The part about me and your dad."

"I want to hear the whole thing. Can you stop for a while and read it to me?" Her enthusiasm was hard to ignore.

I held up the notebook. "Look how long it would take. There's a lot to tell."

"Tell it to me then, like you're telling a story. Only, it all really happened, right?"

My mum came in from the kitchen with three cups of tea and a plate of cookies. "What's that, Wendy?" I saw the moment she recognized the notebook; she sat down hard on her rocking chair. "Oh," was all she said.

Some of our memories were still raw, close to the heart. I felt vulnerable sharing them out loud even with these dear women. But the three generations—my mom Christina, myself, and my daughter—had always been close even during teenage years. I looked into my mother's eyes and saw a kind of acceptance.

"All right, but this will take a while," I said, "so let's keep packing whether we're listening or talking. Sheilla can read it later if she wants."

Mom nodded to the pages stuffed in the front. "Looks like you go first, Wendy."

Wendy—Seattle
1968

I SHOOK my head in bewilderment. "Why did John have to break up with me on Grad Night?" It felt good to be mad at him, better than the sadness that came later. When I got home, I slammed the back door so hard it bounced back and hit my bottom. I didn't seem to care what a ruckus I was making. Tears clogged my nose as I said, "High school graduation should have been a night to celebrate."

The house was so quiet I thought everyone was in bed, but Mom's voice called to me from the kitchen.

"What's happened?"

I hadn't thought of waking her.

She stepped into the light at the end of the hall and checked her wristwatch. "You're home earlier than I expected. It's only eleven."

I couldn't get my answer past the lump in my throat. Instead, I wiped my sleeve across my eyes.

"Come on, lass, we'll have some tea, and you can tell me what a rotter John's been." I almost smiled at her words.

"Why John?"

"Easy, it's always the ones we care most about that can make us that angry."

She walked me to the kitchen table. A pile of old pictures

3

covered the surface. My vision clouded with tears that pooled under my lashes, ran down my face. Mum pulled a hankie out of her pocket and handed it over. I wiped my eyes, blew my nose, and began my complaints.

"I took in a movie with Sherry and Stephen. John was waiting by my car when we came out."

Mum looked so concerned. "You decided not to go to the grad party?"

I scrunched my face in distaste. "I don't think his friends like me and I—"

Mum answered her own question. "You don't fit in. Here, I just made a cup."

I sipped the hot tea and settled, but grief threatened to overwhelm me. "He said we were too different."

"It might be for the best."

I snapped to his defense. "John's always good with me. But his friends all drink and smoke and swear." Throughout school, people pointed out what opposites we were. I believed that worked well for us.

"He doesn't do that with you?"

Now I was impatient. "No, we've stopped hanging around with them. I felt bad about that." I didn't want him to lose his friends. Should I have pretended to be like them? I cut off that thought. "Guess we're too different. I thought, well, he was . . . that we were . . ." My face crumpled as I began to weep again.

After a minute, I took a long sip of the hot tea. "I'm so angry he chose tonight to break up." Guilt settled in as I glanced at Mom for a reaction. "I burned rubber out of the parking lot." I couldn't help a grimace. "Sherry and Stephen were with me. Guess I scared them. I heard them praying." I looked up enough to catch her scowl. "I got them home safe, and I'm sorry about frightening them."

Mum said nothing as she took a seat next to me. An old

shoebox sat open on the table. Pictures scattered haphazardly before me, and I picked up an old photograph.

"I was looking at these while I waited for you to come home," Mum said. She smiled, but her eyes were sad. "If there's one thing I've learned, it's that strength, actual strength, comes from God, but He mostly gives it to us during hard trials."

This wasn't comforting at all. I sniffed and blew my nose. I wanted to say, "Well, I'm not you." Before I could voice the thought, I realized that except for my red hair, I was a lot like her. Instead, I hiccupped a sob. "I realize you lived through the war and all that."

She stopped me. "I didn't think I was strong either. But I came through so many things—bombings, losing people I cared about." She patted my arm. "Even helped to catch a serial killer spy."

I gave her a double take. "You never told me about that."

"I've always been a little afraid to talk about it." She looked into my eyes. "You are stronger than you realize."

Already shaking my head, I said, "I'm not strong. Not at all."

Mum reached out to squeeze my hand in sympathy even though John wasn't a favorite of hers. She thought he was moody. I had to admit she was right, but she didn't know the deep attraction we had for each other, or maybe it was more one-sided than I'd imagined.

"It's always up to us if we choose to be stronger or sink into weakness." She rose. "I'll make you some toast." I always ate peanut butter toast when anything really upset me. There was comfort in her company. I sighed and looked at all the old pictures on the table. A black-and-white photograph of a young girl caught my eye. "That's you, Mum? How old?" For as long as I could remember, I had listened to her stories about growing up in Scotland during the war. I lost myself in those stories.

"Almost nine."

I teased her. "That was ages ago."

"Seems like another lifetime, over thirty years now." She

studied it with a hint of a smile. "That's my first life before I left Scotland, the year my world changed."

I turned it over to read faded writing on the back. "Christina Cowan Finlay."

"Christina, that's what my mum called me when she was put out. No, back then everyone called me Chrissy."

I moved my thumb to reveal the date. April 1936. "What were they like, your trials?"

Mum picked up another picture and spoke the way you do when you're reading from a book. Like you're watching it all before your eyes. Her words drew me away from hurt and loss.

Chapter Two

Christine—Greenock, Scotland
August 1936

I remember that year so clearly. It was the first time I heard the name Hitler. He was often in the news, and portions of his speeches played on the radio. I didn't understand German, but the sound of his voice filled me with foreboding.

That year, the eyes of the world turned to Germany. The eleventh Olympic games were coming to Berlin in August. Our papers ran pages full of stories about the athletes, and Dad never missed an opportunity to give us extra facts. He knew all about the original Olympics in Greece. My six-year-old sister Isabelle and I could listen to Dad for hours; he made everything so interesting.

We also heard stories about Hitler's hatred of Jews. The chancellor's racial policies demanded living space for the Aryan race. We listened to interviews of German Jews who fled their homes to seek asylum in other countries. One night, the radio commentator said, "A great evil is growing in Germany. Hitler is a building storm that will move outward, swallowing up innocent lives as it spreads across Europe." A shiver ran up my spine. I looked at Dad. His grim expression didn't offer me any reassurance.

Although Hitler's evil was spreading, our attention shifted away from him as disease blew in ahead of his storm and touched us even in the foothills of Scotland. The outbreak of spinal meningitis in our small Scottish town made 1936 devastating for me.

Greenock was a busy little town with shipyards and even a distillery, but life was peaceful before the meningitis. Grandma Cowan lived in a grey stone Victorian house on a hill facing the wide River Clyde. But it was only a short walk from my house on Dempster Street to her house on Wellington. Grandma was my favorite person in the world. She saw me, saw my heart.

Her home fascinated me. Everywhere you looked, treasures from the Far East filled shelves and hung on walls. A samurai sword sat on the mantle in its own stand. There were paintings of Mount Fuji, done by Grandfather himself.

Grandfather died before I was born, but Grandma told me stories about his adventures. I could see it all in my imagination. A ship's carpenter by trade, he served with the Canadian Pacific Rail Line on the Empress of Asia, a cargo and passenger ship based out of Vancouver, Canada. My mum said it was like Christmas when her father took leave from sailing to come home.

Although it was 1936 and most of our town had electricity, Grandma said she preferred the softer glow from candles and gaslights. Her house stood on a hill at the edge of town, and behind it she had a high stone wall around a beautiful garden. Beyond the wall, the Highlands rose first as foothills, wild and empty as they had been for centuries. On the weekends, my sister and I took turns going to Grandma's to dust her treasures and spend special time alone with her. Sometimes I sat on the window seat in her bedroom and watched the fishing fleet come home with a day's catch.

Even though my little sister was nearly three years younger, we were constant companions—until one sunny day in April when she came home from school with a headache and mild fever. Our regular doctor was out of town, and the young doctor taking his calls assured my mum that Isabelle would be right in a few days. But she wasn't. When he came back to check on her, he told my mum that Isabelle was pretending to be sick. I knew that wasn't like my little sister. But when the doctor ordered her sent back to school, Mum sent her.

I took her little hand in mine, and we walked to the Highlanders Academy just down the street. She was so pale it scared me. When the whistle blew, I walked her to her room.

Isabelle looked up at me with such sad eyes but managed a smile. "I'll be all right." Then she marched into class with the other first-year students.

She didn't make it an entire day. She collapsed, and they rushed her to the hospital. I was surprised when my very pregnant Aunt Jean came for me after school. She couldn't take me to see Isabelle because Isabelle had the meningitis. Instead, she took me to Grandma Cowan's. I never saw my little sister again.

The night Isabelle left this world was the same night my wee cousin Jack was born. Since my parents were at the hospital with Isabelle, I was still at Grandma Cowan's when Aunt Jean started her labor pains. With so many meningitis cases, Aunty Jean decided to stay with her mum to deliver. Grandma Cowan had given birth five times and helped with other deliveries. Grandma had me wait by the fire in her living room, but I couldn't help listening to my aunt cry out. I wrung my hands and looked toward the bedroom. I was so relieved when my Uncle Jimmy came through the door. Even before going in to his wife, he came to me.

"Chrissy, luv, I've just come from the hospital. Your mum wanted ye ta know that our wee Isabelle was too sick. She's gone to heaven." That was all, and he rushed in to Aunty. It stunned me. The house was silent. Then we heard the first cries of wee Jackie from the bedroom.

I sat alone next to the fire, trying to get warm. It was like I'd been out in the cold for a long time. I guess I sat there for a half hour staring into the flames. When I looked up, Grandma Cowan was standing there, a bundle of blankets in her arms. She bent down, handing me little Jackie. Tears flowed down my cheeks. Less than an hour old and this little life was already so precious to everyone. My heart ached as I realized I'd never see Isabelle's sweet face again, never curl up in the big bed we shared and feel the comforting warmth of her small frame next to me. It was as if God took Isabelle but left us Jackie in her place. I kissed his little forehead, wishing I could hold my little sister like this.

My Grandma sat next to me and wrapped her arms around me and wee Jackie. She whispered, "Luv, I ken this is hard." Her tears fell on my head as she snuggled us closer. "We will all miss our lassie."

I was sure I would never be happy again.

My aunts and uncles said, "Don't cry. You're almost nine and a fine, strong lass, too old to carry on. You mustn't let your mother see you crying." So, I learned to hold it in. I kept all the grief and loss locked away in my heart. Only alone in my cold bed could I let it all out and cry myself into exhaustion.

What I didn't understand was why I didn't die instead of Isabelle. She was so beautiful. I was gangly. My nose was too long and my thick, black hair too curly. There was something special about Isabelle. Everyone loved her.

I couldn't talk to my parents; they were so grief stricken. Only Grandma Cowan knew I needed to cry. In her arms, I found comfort. She heard all my questions without scolding me for thinking such thoughts. "I don't think I can do this, Gran. I'm not brave. How will I live without her?"

But Grandma said, "There now, Chrissy, you're stronger than you think. I ken that sometimes we need to grieve on our own, work things out and let God talk to our hearts. What you're needing is a guid walk."

In happier days, I spent hours exploring the hills behind

Grandma Cowan's house. Sometimes my little sister would come with me, but mostly I enjoyed wandering on my own. Not now, though. Nothing appealed to me now.

My heart was full of loss and emptiness. I didn't see how God could show me anything tromping the hills behind Grandma's house. Grandma was insistent, so I took the wee bag of snacks she gave me and looked back at her as she shooed me out of her house.

"Go ye now. Take yer jammy and a flask of water. Ye need time alone. The Highlands can gi' ye that. While yer about it, pick some flowers for your mum. It'll cheer her heart ta see something bright in her kitchen."

A short walk from my Grandma Cowan's, the land sloped upward above our town. The hills were full of early purple-and-white heather and wild rhododendrons in deep red and pink. I loved the bright yellow of the broom, now in full color. For a while I forgot to pick flowers, caught up in the wild beauty of this place.

Although the sadness was never far from my heart, Grandma was right. This solitary wandering was helping me.

A footpath traversed the grassy hill, winding around large boulders, past clumps of broom, always climbing higher. By mid-morning, I'd eaten the jammy—bread with butter and jam—that Grandma had packed. As I reached the crest of the hill, I stopped to wipe my sticky fingers on my pants and turned to look over Greenock. Despite my heavy heart, I smiled. From here, I spotted Grandma's house, my house on Dempster Street and my school, the Highlanders Academy. Only a month ago, Isabelle and I had walked to the corner and crossed Mount Pleasant Street to enter the schoolyard. I bit my lip. Never again.

I turned away from the memory to walk down the other side of the hill to my special place, a glen where an old stone tower stood in ruins. A sanctuary for me. I liked to pretend it was my castle keep. Scotland is littered with tower ruins. Not much of a watchtower, it sat below the hill, but the place was magical to me. From where I stood, a stream ran through the grass, passing the path to my secret place and winding its way toward the River Clyde. Rowan trees grew along its banks. It was still too early for the clusters of bright red berries, but the fern-like leaves still hid the tower from the casual hiker. That was one of its charms; no one but me ever came here. It was mine.

I stopped short, hearing the excited barking of a dog. I'd never seen a dog up here. I wondered if a crofter's sheep dog had gotten lost. I hurried on. Laughter floated on the breeze from my magical castle. Not a lost dog then. It sounded like children playing. I stepped across the stream, overwhelmed by the urge to play, desperately wanting to stop feeling so sad, and worrying about my mum.

As I came through the trees, I noticed a colorful red-and-yellow caravan with a rounded top and double doors. I realized it belonged to the Gypsies who came to town selling jewelry or mending pots and pans. I'd seen the way the townspeople looked at them with suspicion, even hostility. But I never understood why. They seemed carefree to me.

A pot of something that smelled delicious bubbled away over a small fire. Barefoot children flushed with fun played with their dog. A woman with long black hair that covered her shoulders and curled down her back smiled at their antics. I touched my own bobbed black hair. Mum always cut my hair short. She didn't like it messy. But I wanted to look like this lady someday. I stood there taking in the scene, wondering how these visitors found my castle.

They all looked up and saw me for the first time. I felt shy and waited to see if they were friendly. The woman motioned for me to come ahead. "Welcome," she said, and I stepped into the clearing in front of the tower but stopped when I saw a man poke his head around the far end of the wagon. He was carrying a bucket of something for his horse, but he nodded to me. His smile was friendly.

The children, a boy about my age and a girl about the age of my little sister, walked toward me, their dog in step behind them. Despite their ragged clothes, their faces were open, approachable.

"What's your name then?" asked the girl. I couldn't stop thinking how like Isabelle she looked. Afraid I might cry and ruin the moment, I bit my lip and said in a small voice, "Chrissy."

She didn't seem to notice the sadness I carried. "I'm Donka, and this is my brother Bo. Now we can play tag." Donka reached over to tag me and ran off. I stood there, startled by their invitation. Well, it was more of a command.

Bo called out, "You're supposed to chase us."

I shook bewilderment off, smiling in delight as I dropped my empty lunch sack and the flowers I'd found and ran after them. For a full hour, I abandoned my heartache and played with Bo and Donka. Then their mother called us to the fire. We sat on little three-legged stools. She handed us each a bowl of steaming stew. It tasted like heaven. I looked at Donka next to me and smiled at her cheerful face.

We chatted as we ate. "Why are ye camped here?" I asked.

Bo jerked his head up sharp. "Is this yer land, then?" His face was wary for the first time.

"Och, no, I just come here to play."

Relief softened his expression. He shrugged. "We needed a place to stay the night and followed a wagon trail off the road."

For that afternoon, Donka became my sister Isabelle. After lunch, Donka picked up my flowers, now wilted. "These won't do for yer mum. Come on, we'll get some fresh flowers." We spent another thirty minutes gathering wildflowers. When I got ready to leave, I looked at my colorful bouquet. It looked so alive and beautiful, the old bouquet faded and dead in comparison. It reminded me of how I'd felt before I found my new friends. The afternoon had been magical, and for a little while Isabelle had come as Donka to comfort me.

The sun was low in the sky, and I knew Grandma Cowan would expect me.

When I left, they waved goodbye. Bo said, "Come again."

I would never tell my mother or father about my afternoon with Bo and Donka. I knew the townspeople suspected Gypsies of stealing. I never understood why. Bo and Donka and their parents welcomed me without question. I knew I'd always be grateful for the time I spent with them. Maybe the meningitis hadn't touched them because they didn't stay in towns but in the hills and glens. Solitary places were their homes.

I went back the next day, trying to recapture the peace I'd enjoyed with the Gypsy family and to spend another secret afternoon with my little sister. I'd felt Isabelle near me as I played with Donka. I raced across the stream and through the trees to find the small glen empty.

I sat by the remnants of their cold campfire, proof I hadn't imagined it all. Dusting off my pants, I left, but halfway up the hill I looked back toward the old watchtower. For a moment I imagined Isabelle waving goodbye, but the Gypsies were gone and so was my little sister.

Wendy—Seattle
June 1968

Lost in Mom's story, I forgot my grief over John and thought of her as a child dealing with the hurt of losing her sister. My voice shook with emotion. "Oh, Mum, that's so sad."

I sipped my tea to cover my distress. The doors to all our bedrooms lined one side of the living space. My eyes wandered to my little sister's room. How would I feel if I lost Heather? I asked, "Did you ever see Donka again?"

"Other Gypsies came through town but never Donka's family."

It shocked me to see tears in her eyes. After all those years, her grief still rose to the surface. But Mum's tender smile never faltered as she added, "I like to think Donka was God's gift to me. You know, helping me say goodbye to Isabelle."

I'd never lost a loved one. Even if John and I weren't seeing each other, he was out there doing whatever he thought would be better without me. I'd been so angry with him, but at least he wasn't dead. Death's heartbreak is permanent.

Inhaling the steamy tea made it easier to breathe. How could she take my loss seriously? She'd gone through such heartache.

Then I realized she'd never once said I was overreacting. I'd had no sign she thought my grief foolish. Again, I felt grateful that she wasn't just a mom; she was a genuine friend. I changed the subject before I could feel sorry for myself again. "When did the war start?"

"Germany stayed in the news, but it was two years later before things got scary."

My emotional storm wasn't ready to blow over. I could feel sadness and loss swirling around my heart, so I teased more from Mom. If she told me stories about her life, I could keep myself from thinking about how my story might end. I asked, "You were only a child. How did you know what was happening?"

"My dad. Your Bampa is a firm believer in knowledge, all kinds. He was like that when Isabelle was alive and even more so when it was only me to listen."

Chapter Three

Christine—Greenock, Scotland
August 1938

Every night, my dad would read the paper from the comfort of his easy chair by the fire while we cleared away the dishes. One night, he read something about German Chancellor Hitler's plan to take some land.

I said a bit peevishly, "But that's in Germany, not here." People were always talking about what Germany would do next. I didn't see how that would affect us. Remembering something he'd read a few days ago, I asked, "And doesn't the PM say there'll be peace in our time?"

Dad always explained to us what the news meant. He'd been doing the same thing long before Isabelle died. It was like he wanted me to consider grander things than our own hometown or our friends.

My dad was brilliant, and deep down I was proud he explained things to me. He wanted me to live up to his expectations. With Isabelle gone, it was all up to me to make him proud, but sometimes desires got in my way.

"Chrissy, you need to understand what's happening in the world." Then he launched into his teaching mode. "Yon Hitler is a bully, but he's a canny one."

I tried not to roll my eyes. It's not that I didn't want to listen; what I wanted was to ride my bicycle before dark. I sighed as I realized this was going to take a while, so I flopped down on the footstool next to his overstuffed chair.

He continued. "Six years ago, they elected Hindenburg to his second term as president of Germany, but Hitler was the head of the Nazi party. They received quite a few votes, and they were growing in power. President Hindenburg appeased them by nominating Hitler as chancellor of Germany."

Sometimes Da could read my thoughts. I was getting lost, and he explained, "We have a prime minister and a king." I nodded for him to go on. "Hitler would be the prime minister, an' yon Hindenburg would be the king." I cocked my head and scrunched my face, trying to figure out what he meant.

"Yon Hindenburg represents the country, but Chancellor Hitler runs the government, and Hitler's man Hermann Goering presides over their parliament. They call it the Reichstag. Just after that, the Reichstag building burned down. Hitler blamed the fire on the other powerful political party, the Communists." My dad raised a finger and challenged me. "Now, Chrissy, who do you think would do such a thing?"

My eyes wandered to the window. My friends were laughing and playing outside, but when I looked up into Dad's face, he was waiting for me to speak. Times like this I wished I could learn to sidestep his questions.

"What happened next might give you a clue. Hitler encouraged Hindenburg to revoke the civil liberties of the German people to protect them and quell civil violence."

Even though I was only ten, he'd piqued my interest with his challenge, but I needed to know more. "What are civil liberties?"

"Well, your right to believe differently from your government.

The right to work where you want, go to what church you choose, that sort of thing."

I couldn't imagine someone telling me what to believe when my dad didn't. "That's a bad idea. Did Hinden-something do that?"

"Aye, he did in 1933. They called it the Reichstag Fire Decree. He said it would protect the people from the Communists. After the decree, the president died."

He had me now. I tried to puzzle it out. "Wait, are you saying Hitler burned this Reichstag place?"

"Nay then, Chrissy, he doesna have ta do it himself, but if his people burn down the building and then point a finger at his greatest competition, yon Hitler looks like a hero."

"But, Da, you don't know that he or his people did it. You only think he did, right?"

My dad gave me his signature wink. It usually meant he was pleased with me. "Things are not always as they appear, but it's not such a leap to guess how they might be." Sounds from the street faded from my consciousness as Da's face grew serious. "There were riots all over, and Hitler said it was the Communists. A lot of working people like us had their autos and even homes burned."

I stopped him by asking, "Wait, Hitler did that?"

"If you wanted the people to join the Communist party, would you do it by burning their homes or even breaking their windows?" Dad shook his head. "Then Hitler used the decree to restrict the people to a one-party government. Hitler said they made this decree to protect the people."

"But it took away their rights?"

Dad just nodded.

"And Hitler was in charge?" I stared into the flames, imagining the fires in Germany. "Then what happened?"

"He arrested anyone who disagreed with him."

"Aye, because the old president made the decree to protect the people. But it dinna do that, did it?"

"Nay then, taking away a person's rights rarely protects them. Here it gave Hitler power over them." Da winked at me again when I understood.

He was like that. He always wanted me to decide for myself. Da smiled. "Off ye go now. You still have plenty of daylight to ride bicycles wi' yer friends."

"Thanks, Da." I smiled. So he knew I was eager to get outside. I left with a thankful kiss planted on his cheek.

After that I listened whenever adults talked about the news around the world. Hitler was often the subject of conversations. People whispered about his racial policies and his greed for more territory. I didn't see how the bully of Germany mattered to us in the foothills of the Scottish Highlands.

That August, Hitler required Jews to change all non-Jewish first names to Sara if you were a girl or Israel if you were a boy. We even discussed the German notion of racial purity in class at school. No one liked the idea. Della had six younger brothers and sisters. She blurted out, "Och, if we were all called Sara, how would they know who I was calling a dunderheid?" The class laughed, but in the end none of us liked the idea of losing our names.

We talked about it after dinner, and I remember Dad said it wasn't safe to even appear Jewish. That sticks in my mind. The next day, a boy at my school said I looked like a Jew.

"And you, Albert, look like a fool." Everyone laughed at Albert's expense, but after dinner I asked, "Mum, do I look Jewish?"

She stopped clearing dishes and scowled. "What makes ye ask such a thing?"

"Oh, nothing," She didn't look away. "It's just that Albert Campbell said I looked like a Jew."

My mum put down the dish and led me to the mirror. "Ye ken we Scots are all different even if people say we all have red hair and freckles." I nodded. "It's that way with most countries. Still, Hitler says all Jews have dark hair and eyes and big noses."

I laughed, "Like Da, he has those."

"Aye, but his mam has bonnie red hair." She turned me to face the mirror. "We both have dark hair, and I have blue eyes and yours are brown. That doesna make us Jews. It makes Albert a . . ." She paused, looking for a word.

"A fool. Aye, that's what I said." Mum went back to the kitchen chuckling and shaking her head. Something occurred to me. "If I were in Germany, would they arrest me for looking Jewish?"

Mum frowned. "I don't know, maybe so, but dinna worry, that'll never happen here." I wondered if dark-eyed, dark-haired, big-nosed Germans told themselves the same thing.

Wendy—Seattle
June 15, 1968–3 a.m.

MUM PULLED a faded photograph from those scattered on the dining-room table and slid it in front of me. There she was, older than the last photo but still recognizable as my mum.

I asked, "How old were you here?"

She smiled down at the skinny girl with short black hair and enormous eyes. "Eleven, I think."

My little sister Heather was eleven, and I couldn't imagine her being so serious. "Did all those stories about Hitler scare you? Did you even understand what was happening?"

She patted my hand. "It's hard to explain. My dad's a very special person. He graduated from high school at fourteen and planned to attend the University of Glasgow. Then his father died, and he had to give up college. As oldest, it fell to him to support his mother, three brothers and sister."

"Support—you mean he got a job?"

She nodded. "He also helped raise his brothers and sister. You know, discipline, advice—everything a father would do."

"So his strength came from trials too?"

A gleam of pride lit her face. "His dream was to be a marine engineer. And eventually he became one. He worked his way through Scotts Shipyard until they saw his genius. During the war, he took every submarine built at Scotts on its shakedown cruise before it was turned over to the navy. To make sure it was seaworthy and battle ready.

"I was so proud of him. My dad spoke to me like another adult, capable of discussing world events. He expected me to understand, so I guess I did my best not to disappoint him." Mum's tone was contemplative. "Trust me, trials change you. They give you strength."

I sighed as her words reminded me that my heart was still sore from losing John. I wanted to change the subject away from reminders of my trial. I picked another picture off the pile on our kitchen table. My mum as a ten-year-old. "That's you in front of your school?"

Chapter Four

Christine—Greenock, Scotland
September 1938

Thankfully, some things never change. My school, the Highlanders Academy, was a lovely, old stone building constructed in the last century. It served Greenock's children from nursery school through high school graduation. Not a small village school. It filled almost an entire block. Large iron fences enclosed a good-sized play yard. All the rooms wrapped around a central inner courtyard where we assembled in the morning before being dismissed to our classes. This was the year I discovered something amazing about its construction. The halls echoed.

Mum enrolled me in dance lessons after Isabelle's passing. I expect she meant to take my mind off the heartache. I could lose myself in the rhythm and the sound of my steps. Tap dancing became my passion. I tapped every chance I got. In school, when everyone was in their classrooms, I'd volunteer to take any messages to the office and practice my dance steps. I knew the headmaster would scold me for tapping in the halls, but I just couldn't help myself. After all, I wore only street shoes, loud but nothing like the sharp tones of my tap shoes.

I loved the movies, especially the ones with dancing. We had a beautiful old theatre in town, the Odeon. Its domed roof and ornate stonework reminded me of an opera house. I could walk into town and see a film with my friends or occasionally with one of my grandmothers. I marveled at the tap dancing of Ann Miller in the movie *New Faces of 1937*. I watched it five times. The halls of my school became the stage, and I tapped down them to the cadence of Ann Miller. I matched her steps to the American jazz playing in my head—until I saw *Carefree* with Ginger Rogers and Fred Astaire. Then the empty halls turned into my ballroom and my taps softened, flowing with my imaginary partner. If a teacher caught me, I'd take my punishment, but I couldn't promise my feet wouldn't carry me off to some magical stage the next time. I danced through the news of Hitler's next grasp for parts of Europe.

In those days, even a child couldn't shut out the news on the radio. I kept an awareness of what was happening. Everyone did. It was the undercurrent that flowed even in Greenock. Dad shook his head at the news, reading aloud that our Prime Minister Chamberlain believed Hitler only wanted to re-unify the German people from the splintering that had happened after the last great war.

When I needed to forget all the negative news, I'd climb the hills above our town with my sketchpad and pencils to sit and draw. It was so beautiful there. In the distance, I could see the purple mountains of the Great Glens. It helped me recapture the peace the world news was tearing away. At times, my thoughts still echoed the worry in my dad's voice as he read the newspaper.

That fall, Dad brought home gas masks. They came in a metal canister with a strap, making them resemble an ugly shoulder bag. Dad sat at the kitchen table, motioning for us to join him. He opened his canister and pulled out his gas mask. "Watch me now."

Mum looked as skeptical as I felt. Dad was unshaken in his mission, determined that we should learn the proper way to wear these monstrosities.

He laid the twists of straps, goggles, and canister on the table in front of him. Then he pulled it up over his head, showing us how to put it on.

The transformation was terrifying as he slipped it on and tightened the straps. His eyes looked out from behind two bug-like goggles. His hair poked out of the straps at odd angles. The dark fabric holding it all together gathered into a breathing canister that completely covered his face. It looked as though a giant bug had swallowed my dad.

I wasn't wearing that. It was horrible, the stuff of nightmares. I heard a sharp intake of breath from Mum. I thought I saw the hint of a smile, but she put her hand to her mouth to cover it. Dad looked hideous.

He pulled it off and glared at Mum. There was no laughter in his voice as he said, "Chrissy, you're to keep this with you. It's the law an' might just save your life." He stared me in the eye and waited for me to nod. I complied, thinking, I hope to God I never have to wear that ugly thing.

I remember feeling relieved by Prime Minister Chamberlain's assurances there was nothing to worry about, yet the country was mobilizing. Then on Nov. 9 came Kristallnacht, the night of broken glass. Riots broke out all over Germany. Jewish-owned businesses, homes and synagogues had their windows broken. Century-old houses of worship were burning. Dad's hands shook with rage as he told us the news. "They arrested 3,000 Jewish men and put them in special camps." We were all stunned any government could do such a thing to its own people.

Wendy—Seattle
June 15, 1968

THE TIME FLEW by listening to my mum talk about her life as a child. Every picture I picked off the table gave me a new glimpse of her life in Scotland. Three cups of tea and four peanut butter toasts later, I rose to put my dishes in the sink. From the kitchen window, I could see the sky had moved from an ink black to a dark grey, and it was getting lighter all the time.

The weight of my sad heart felt lighter as I lost myself listening to Mum's stories of growing up in such a turbulent world. I couldn't stop thinking about the Jews in prewar Germany. It made me realize people can make it through some pretty rough times. I felt hope I'd weather my storms as well.

Mum came to stand next to me, and together we watched the sunrise through the kitchen window as rays of light shot through the sky. It was like looking at those black-and-white photos. Now when I picked them up, I saw my mum in beautiful technicolor. I stood there fascinated with the change light brings to the world. The landscape looked fresh, ready to begin again. Mum must have been reading my mind.

"It's a new day, Wendy. And you have no idea what God will make of it."

"Thanks for staying up all night with me." I sighed with tired resignation. My personal storm had passed, at least for the moment.

She put her hand over mine. "How about some sleep now?" Her smile was so tender. My sore heart warmed, and I felt hope.

John had been a big part of most of my days. I couldn't imagine how I'd fill the time without his constant presence.

THE DAYS that followed were full. I practiced every day for the dancing competition at the Highland Games coming in just over a month. I registered for my fall classes at junior college. It was during the spaces in between all the activities that I faced some hard realities. I'd fallen in love, yes. Now I needed to decide what was next.

I thought about Mum's stories often and realized I was learning things from them that I hadn't seen before. I found comfort in those quiet times when I could sit and listen to her talk about her past. It was late on a sunny July afternoon that I sat on the back porch with her. "Tell me more about the war. What was it like to have a genius for a father?"

Mum's parents were far from us. They lived in England after the war. Right now, they were in Australia with my grandmother's sister Jean.

Though they were far away, I always felt close to them. They sent parcels full of treats, recorded messages and always said they were proud of us, loved and missed us. My dad's parents were polar opposites. They didn't like foreigners, and that put Mum at a disadvantage before they got to know her. Although they lived only twenty miles from us, we never saw them, and I was fine with that. My sister Heather and I were that foreign woman's children, not really part of the family.

Out of respect for my father, Mum didn't say anything. I never understood why Dad didn't tell them off.

Chapter Five

Christine—Greenock, Scotland
Fall 1939

Nothing much had happened since Dad brought home those horrible gas masks. I learned to take mine everywhere I went. Everyone did. The threat of war concerned the adults but was mostly pushed aside by children.

Then on a chilly March evening, I came home from dance lessons. The kitchen was warm and filled with delightful smells. Mum set out the tea and biscuits as Dad read the paper. His face looked grim. I tried not to listen too closely; it only made me worried to think what Hitler might do next. Would he reach all the way to Scotland? I didn't want to lose another person I loved. Not one. Losing Isabelle still overwhelmed me with longing and sadness.

Instead, I tried to remember Shirley Temple's tap steps from her new movie *The Little Princess*. My feet were tapping as silently as possible under the table while I appeared to be listening to my dad read the paper. He was saying, "German troops marched into the rest of Czechoslovakia." He was angry as he finished the story, slapping the paper with the back of his hand. "And what did you think would happen when you forced the Czechs to give up all their fortified borderland?"

I knew he wasn't asking us. He was frustrated with Chamberlain for appeasing Hitler. The English prime minister wasn't popular here in Scotland. My dad, like most of the other adults in our family, felt angry at the PM's lack of backbone. Mum and I looked at each other. Da, always so reasonable, looked like he was ready to blow his bonnet. It was clear to even me that Hitler was a liar.

Dad read the last sentence: "Prime Minister Chamberlain pledged to defend Poland if Hitler attacks." Then he looked me in the eye and added, "It willna stop the bully." I didn't want to care about what could happen next. I wanted to tap dance or sew doll clothes, anything but look at the map. Da challenged me to think for myself. "See here, Chrissy." With a shrug of acceptance, I followed him to the map on our wall. So much for trying not to listen.

"Czechoslovakia is right here. It points like a spear into the heart of Germany." He grimaced before he continued. "The last war was terrible, and none of the nations wanted a strong Germany ever again. So, they struck a deal and"—his finger traced the arrow-shaped region—"annexed the land into the Czech Republic. It's an area rich in minerals, very valuable."

"So Germany wants it back for its resources?" I asked.

"Aye, but it's not only about mineral rights. The Czechs fortified this land to protect themselves from a German invasion. Now that Hitler's got it back, what do you think will happen next?"

I studied the map. "Just what you read. Germany could easily take the small bit of the country left." My impatience rose. "But why is that important to us?" I so wanted to believe all the events in Europe wouldn't change my life or hurt those I loved. My finger moved across the map from Czechoslovakia up to Scotland, and the heaviness of fear lifted from my heart. "There's a sea between us. We're nowhere near them."

He put his hand up to stroke his chin. I couldn't tell what he was thinking. "Czechoslovakia is a republic. A democracy. And isn't freedom worth fighting for?" He placed a hand on my shoulder. "God gave us freedom. It's ours, and we must protect it wherever it's threatened." He pointed to Poland. "Now that yon Hitler is invading Czechoslovakia, what do you think will happen to Poland?"

"Oh," was all I could say. My eyes traced the distance from Poland to Scotland. The North Sea and the Baltic Sea lay between Scotland and Poland. It was still far from us. Was it far enough?

As it turned out, my dad was right. The Czech president caved to German threats of a bombing raid on Prague. He opened his borders, and Hitler took the rest of the Czech Republic in one gulp.

On the morning of Sept. 1, Hitler invaded Poland. Chamberlain delivered one last ultimatum: leave Poland or face the consequences. His final note to Hitler delivered a plea for peace, accompanied by the threat that we would come to Poland's aid if he didn't retreat.

Germany didn't pull back. On Sept. 3, Great Britain and France declared war. I'd just come home from church and Mum handed me bowls to set out for our lunch. She put the kettle on, and Dad switched on the radio.

I recognized Prime Minister Chamberlain's voice. "This morning I am speaking to you from the cabinet room of 10 Downing Street." I could imagine the tall, thin, elderly Englishman. He had tried so hard to avoid war by appeasing German demands. Now he admitted his failure. "We are at war with Germany."

I sat down hard on the kitchen chair. Mum looked at Dad, her blue eyes wide. I thought of my uncles and my father. This put them all in danger. Dad's brown eyes, so like my own, were steady. They reflected strength and determination. I took what courage I could from him.

I remember that day well. At lunch we heard the news of our declaration of war, and just after dinner a German submarine torpedoed a Scottish passenger liner off the coast of Ireland. We listened to the radio all evening for updates on the fate of the thousand passengers aboard the SS Athenia. She'd left Glasgow that morning, bound for Canada, but only made it as far as the seas north of Ireland.

I shivered. Those were rough waters. Ships from all over rushed to save as many people as possible. The Athenia took a long time to sink, but early reports said over a hundred dead, many of them children. It stunned people. My hope that Scotland would escape the Germans' notice sank with the Athenia. The BBC labeled the unprovoked German attack as senseless and criminal.

By the next morning, word of the rescues started coming in. Life went back to normal. My da went to work and I to school, but just before dinner there was a great commotion in the streets. Heads poked out of doors and windows. I heard Mrs. Campbell call out to the paperboy, "Jimmy, what is it, then?"

"It's the survivors, missus. They're coming up the Clyde." With Jimmy McCoy's announcement, people forgot dinner. We all came out of our houses into the streets and stood on the hills overlooking the Clyde River. From the corner of my street, the town center was just a few miles down the hill, the docks only a short walk beyond. Grey clouds rolled in overhead with a gusty breeze whipping up the river's purplish waves. Sunbeams poked past the clouds to bounce off the water, and I squinted into the glare. We could see almost four miles across a wide stretch of the river to the town of Helensburgh on the other side.

"There," someone shouted. And we all looked as one at the slow-moving steamer motoring toward our docks.

My mum stood with the women and spoke in low tones. My

dad was with the men. Their words were few, but their expressions were frozen in deep frowns. My friend Bridgett found me in the crowd. Her hair was a mass of red curls. Her face was so pale and her blue eyes large and bright as she slipped her hand in mine.

I called her Bridie for short because it sounded happy. She was always smiling but not now. She said to me, "They went down off Tory Isle. Ye ken we were in those same waters when you came with us to Donegal."

"I remember."

Only a few years back, I had gone with Bridie and her family on a trip to Butter Hill Farm to visit her aunty, uncle, and cousins. The Irish Sea can be very rough, but my Grandma Cowan sent along a basket of fresh fruit. She told me to eat some and I'd keep my stomach settled. Thanks to Grandma, I was fine, but people all around me were throwing up over the boat railings.

I pictured those white-capped grey waves. It must have been so frightening being cast about in small lifeboats. We watched in silence as the ship docked in Greenock. Even at this distance we could see the tiny figures of the survivors being helped down the ramps and onto waiting buses.

Mrs. Campbell said, "I heard they will take the survivors on ta Glasgow." It seemed right somehow to keep vigil over their arrival. Respectful. But soon there was no more to see, and the adults turned back to their houses. Bridgett squeezed my hand before following her da.

I stood staring out at the water, feeling a foreboding that seemed to hang in the air. Mum called me in, and we ate our supper in silence listening to the BBC reports. Hitler blamed us for sinking the ship to make Germany look bad. I pounded my fist on the table, shaking the dishes. "That's just dafty."

Later the BBC said so many ships had helped with the rescue it was hard to get a count of the missing. I heard them say U.S. Ambassador Joseph Kennedy sent his son John to Glasgow to check on the American passengers. That reminded me of something Dad had read only a few days before.

"Wasn't it just the other day President Roosevelt declared the United States would remain neutral? Da, do you think this will change his mind?"

"It's hard to ken what they're thinkin'. We'll just have to wait and see." And that's what we did. We waited to see who would come to our aid.

But the Germans did not catch us unprepared. We'd seen things escalating in Europe for at least two years. Even if I hated those bug-eyed gas masks, I carried my canister with me everywhere. And life did what it always does when nothing terrible happens next; you go back to your routines. I spent time with my friends, took dancing lessons and went from sewing doll clothes to making myself new outfits. It didn't escape my notice that most of the adults were using their time to prepare.

The basement of the house next to us was very large and mostly underground. In the fall, the men on our street spent their spare time making it ready to serve as a bomb shelter. The women stocked the large room with supplies. People brought extra blankets and pillows. Water barrels sat in one corner, and even the stray bottle of whisky or two went into the storage cupboards. My dad said it was for medicinal purposes. He added his signature wink, and I was pretty sure he was teasing me.

All the while, the other adults on our street reassured us children. "This is just in case; we're not likely to need it." But I couldn't help wondering why they bothered saying such a thing. We knew a war was coming. It wasn't hard to see that everyone was waiting for what would happen next. There were bomb shelters everywhere, and people volunteered as air raid wardens or for the fire brigade as my parents did.

The other was harder to see but far more important. Dad called it being war ready. It's difficult to explain, like the hardening of your heart, steeling yourself against the likelihood of disaster. Dad would say, "Don't be afraid, Chrissy, we will get through this. Have courage." And I wondered, am I brave enough to face the hardships of war?

That winter was quiet. It didn't seem like much of a war after all. At night Dad would read about events in faraway places. All eyes turned to Poland as Hitler and Stalin invaded, gobbling up as much of the country as possible. But on the Western Front, radio and papers dubbed it the "Phony War." France tried to come to Poland's aid by mobilizing their ground forces on the German border but retreated when they realized the strength of Germany's response.

We waited to see what the PM would do to help the Polish people. He did nothing. My dad grew angry and said the PM was a yapping dog with no teeth. "If Chamberlain leads us much longer, we'll all be speaking German."

My face must have reflected the horror I felt because he quickly added, "Maybe we should send yon Hitler a sample of haggis. Then he'll think twice about ever setting foot in Scotland." He shivered and made a face. "Helen, think you could make up a care package for Hitler?"

Mum hit him with the end of her tea towel. "You said you liked my haggis." I giggled at her affronted reaction. Both Dad and I agreed there wasn't much you could do to improve the taste of a pudding made from oatmeal, suet, heart, liver, and lights—the lungs—of a sheep and steamed in a sheep's stomach bag.

He smiled and slipped an arm around her. "No, pet, I said we should save it for special occasions." Over her head he winked and added, "There aren't too many of those in a year."

Wendy—Seattle
Summer 1968

I mostly walked, not drove, when my destination was close

enough. I was on my way to the shops at Westwood Village, still thinking of Mom's story about the haggis and smiling to myself, when I had the feeling of someone's eyes on my back. I swung around to find the sidewalk behind me empty.

I knew what it was like to have someone follow you, watch your every move. Three years ago, I had a boyfriend, Fred. He was older than me and very possessive and controlling. For a time after I ended our relationship he followed me. The week after my breakup with John, Fred started calling again.

They say redheads have a reputation for stubbornness and hot tempers. That isn't me, but I have a good dose of strong will. I promised myself I would not settle for just anyone's attention to make me forget John.

At first I thought I was imagining things because of Fred's persistent interest. He called almost every day. Then there were accidental meetings in stores. But the feeling of being followed is something you never forget. And it was never stronger than when I danced at the Highland Games.

I'd been dancing in competition, and when I left the stage, a nice-looking man approached me. He had a light accent I couldn't quite place. "You, my darlin' girl, are a very pretty dancer." I looked at his name tag and recognized his official status with the Highland Games. He was handsome, for all his middle years, with auburn hair and vivid green eyes.

"Thank you. That was a nice compliment."

He reached out a hand and shook mine. "I'm Seamus, and you are?"

"Wendy."

Those deep green eyes wandered from my face to somewhere past me. He touched his badge, and his smile faltered. A shadow crossed his face. I turned to see John.

My pulse did little bounces. "Oh," was all I said.

Seamus backed away. "Goodbye for now. I'm sure I will see you again."

I smiled and nodded, aware of John's presence so close.

Composing a blank expression, I faced John, hoping he wouldn't see my heart. "You got the flyer I left." Okay, before we broke up, he'd said he wanted to see what the Highland Games were like. I blushed a little, knowing I'd given his mum a flyer in hopes I'd see him again.

He nodded toward the stranger's retreating form. "Who was that guy?"

Why would he care? But I answered, "Just a new official." Good, at least John knew I had a life without his presence. I added as nonchalantly as possible, "You said you'd like to see the games." My voice sounded flat. I didn't smile. I was trying so hard not to show how pleased I was that he came. He didn't smile either. We just stood there on the field with the wind blowing and the piper playing the *Ghillie Calum* as the next group performed the Sword Dance.

Finally, he said, "You looked great." He started again. "I mean —I was watching you dance."

"Thanks. I'm not that good, but I love dancing."

Silence.

"Can you show me around and tell me what's happening?"

"Sure. I'm dancing in competition again, but that won't be till later."

He didn't take my hand as he'd always done before. Instead, we walked side by side. I slipped into the role of tour guide as I explained tossing the caber and the other traditional games.

Even though I was proud of my Scottish heritage, this was a part of me he'd never seen. For thirty minutes we walked around the field. He seemed interested. I explained the different piping competitions and how you knew the clans by the set of their tartan kilts.

The Chieftain of the Day, Angus MacLeod, stopped to say a word of praise. I blushed.

The MacLeod was someone I'd always looked up to. Caught up

in the things I loved, it was hard to maintain indifference to John. Still, I kept my eyes from resting on his face, away from his dark brown hair and warm, milk chocolate eyes; away from his full, soft lips. The memory of his kiss was ever present on my mind. John was tall and strong and capable. I always felt protected when I was with him. *That was then, and this is now. I'm independent of all that.*

"Thanks for coming. I hope you enjoyed seeing what I've been telling you about." I said all that without making eye contact. I wanted to demand why he came if I wasn't important to him.

As I walked away, my sight clouded with the tears I held back. The pipers started playing *Devil in the Kitchen*, warming up for the Highland Fling. I made my way to stand with the next group of dancers and caught one last glimpse of John walking toward the exit. *At least I got to show him who I am.* I felt a lump in my throat, and then it was time for the Fling. I lost myself in the dance, hoping I'd lose the sadness that had settled over me.

When I finished the last step and bowed, I was feeling better. I stepped off the stage, and there was my mum. Her smile was sympathetic. "Well done." She linked her arm in mine as we walked away from the stage. "So, John came." It wasn't a question, and I guessed she'd seen us from the grandstand seating. I didn't answer but bit my lip.

"Do you want to leave now or wait for the dancing results?"

"Leave, please. I'm pretty sure I didn't place."

"Come on, luv, let's find your little sister and go to the car."

I was positive Heather was somewhere eating a scone. "Sure."

All the way out of the stadium, I couldn't shake the feeling that someone was watching us. Little hairs on the back of my neck pricked up. I scanned the crowds, but there was no sign of John. Silly that. I looked around once more, but in the end, I felt foolish.

I was glad Heather came. She chattered all the way home, leaving me with my thoughts as I drove. Mum had never learned to drive growing up during the war with no car and gas rationing. I was always the chauffeur. When I pulled up to the house, Heather clambered out of the car, calling, "Can I ride my bike?"

Before Mum could answer, Heather was walking it out of the garage. Mum smiled and waved as my little sister rode past us back down the drive.

"Tea?"

I nodded. "And peanut butter toast."

"I thought so." She put her arm around my shoulder as we walked to the house. "Did John say why he came?"

I shook my head.

"I saw you talk to someone on the field, but I was so far away I couldn't tell who it was."

"I don't know. Some official." We settled at the kitchen table. The tea whistled when it was ready, and the toast popped up from the toaster. I needed to talk but not about today. "Last time we spoke about your . . . what did you call it? Your first life? The Germans had sunk that passenger boat. What happened next?"

My mom paused, breathing in the steam from her tea. Finally, she put words to her memories.

Chapter Six

Christine—Greenock, Scotland
Early Spring 1940

I remember my mother's sad eyes as she kissed her only brother goodbye. We accompanied Grandma Cowan to the train station to send Uncle Willy off to join his unit. I loved all my aunts and uncles, but Uncle Willy was a baker. He'd made my birthday cakes for as long as I could remember, and he always wrapped a trinket or coin in foil and baked it in the cake. It was exciting to discover the wee hidden treasures. I know it was selfish of me, but I hated to see him go. I'd miss his baking almost as much as I'd miss him.

Now all my uncles were off at war. Dad tried to enlist several times, but his employer, Scotts Shipyard, blocked his paperwork. Dad was a marine engineer. He knew everything there was to know about building submarines. And his photographic memory made him an asset when a formula or a secret had to be carried without a written copy.

With Dad at home, my life stayed secure and became routine once again. Winter faded to a memory. It seemed to me, here in the foothills of the Highlands, things would be untouched. I missed my uncles, but everything else I loved about living here remained unchanged. The hills above Greenock vibrated with the intense green that comes in the spring.

I stopped paying much attention to the war until one evening when Dad picked up the paper as we sat at the dinner table eating our dessert. He read, "April 9, Hitler invaded Norway and Denmark."

As I listened, I wandered over to the map of Europe, now a permanent fixture on the kitchen wall. This was closer to us, much closer. My fingers traced the distance from Denmark to our coast. Then I looked to Norway. It was much the same. Only the North Sea to cross and the enemy could be at our eastern shores. I couldn't pretend it was too far away to affect me. I pulled my chair next to Dad as he continued.

"It all happened so quickly. In one day, German ships slipped into Norwegian ports. German troops occupied Danish cities like Copenhagen. King Christian X of Denmark, convinced that his troops couldn't defend against invasion, surrendered."

I asked, "They didn't fight? They just gave up?" That seemed so wrong. "We would never do that."

"Denmark is a tiny country. I think their king was trying to spare the lives of his people. But look ye, Chrissy, on the same day Hitler sent his navy to Norway."

I was still thinking about what it must have been like to wake up with German soldiers marching through your town. I looked toward my street, imagining the sound of marching boots. All the men in town were joining the military. It would mostly be women and children and men like my dad. It was only last week the government denied again Dad's appeal to join the military. His job put a hold on him, claiming he was vital to submarine construction. I knew it upset him, but secretly I was glad to have him with us. I always felt safe when he was near. But what if Germans marched into our town? Would Da just stand and watch? I shook my head. My dad was brave and strong; he'd never surrender.

Dad caught my attention as he read. "A pro-fascist foreign minister by the name of Quisling sent an order with command authority to Norwegian garrisons and ports to allow the Germans to land unopposed."

He looked up from his paper and uttered a word I had never heard him say before: "Espionage."

"What is that?"

"The Germans must have had quite a network of spies in Norway to manage getting the right people in authority able to open the ports and allow German occupation.

"See here." He walked me back over to the map and pointed to the sea surrounding Norway. "I know for a fact we mined these waters. The last thing we need is the enemy so close." He clenched his jaw. "No, they must have had spies in-country long before this was attempted."

I imagined the port of Greenock and thought, I don't care what happened in Norway; Scots wouldna just stand back and let the enemy in. Then I remembered the Viking dragon ship I'd seen down the coast in the village of Largs. The replica of the Viking ships that landed on that spot centuries ago commemorated a battle in 1263. A different King of Norway sent those fierce warriors to attack and even settle along these shores. They shared our history, our blood. It shocked me even more that the Nazis had tricked them into opening the door to the enemy.

Dad walked back to his chair and picked up the paper. "In what must have been a massive coordination of German naval and ground forces, Nazis took many Norwegian ports in one day, while German paratroopers landed at Stavanger, quickly capturing the airfield.

"King Haakon VII and the Norwegian government resisted. In the end they fled to London."

My eyes drifted to our windows, searching the sky, just to

make sure I was looking at puffy white clouds, not the white parachutes of German soldiers.

Dad folded the paper. "That was a bad day for one family. The kings of Norway and Denmark are brothers, ye ken?"

"One brother escaped and the other surrendered."

"Aye, Chrissy. Ye canna judge when ye don't ken the whole of it. Both brothers tried to protect their people."

My dad was like that. He challenged me to think for myself but only after seeing all sides.

I WAS on a walk with my dad the first time I saw a German aircraft fly overhead. We walked down to Gourock on a lazy Saturday afternoon. I remember Dad stopped short, listening. I listened too, and gradually I heard the hum of a plane approaching. It was very high.

Dad squinted up. I did as well, but the glare off the water made it hard to see. "Too small and far up to be anything but reconnaissance."

"What? What is it? I can't see anything."

"That's a German plane." He pointed to a dark spot moving very high over the River Clyde.

"German?" I panicked.

"Steady, luv. We've been seeing them for the last week. They're not here to bomb us, just have a look see." He didn't seem worried, so I took a deep breath, trying not to show my fear.

"What are they looking for?" My heart beat faster as I thought about the shipyard where he worked.

"Oh, I think they like the scenery. It's lovely this time of year."

I smiled despite my fear. After that we saw similar German aircraft occasionally, but nothing terrible happened, so the war seemed far away.

We went to school, did our shopping, and attended Sunday

services. My church was Mount Pleasant Presbyterian Kirk. Like our home, it sat on a hill above Greenock. Just over the rise was an open field and a water retention pond. I'd often walk up there after church and look to the south. On the next hill sat the cemetery where they'd buried my little sister Isabelle. It was a peaceful-looking place with a road that wound up into the trees. Not scary or grotesque. I wouldn't want that for her. She was such a sweet little sister. The pastor said she was with the Lord. But I knew her tiny wee frame slept there with so many others.

I think she heard me when I whispered, "Hi, Isabelle. It's Chrissy. I love you, and I miss you so much." Maybe the part of her that stayed in the ground didn't hear, but I was sure God would pass on my message. He'd say, "Isabelle, Chrissy says hi." And she would smile with those cute little dimples.

With Isabelle gone, I felt it my duty to make it up to my parents. I tried extra hard to please them. And spending time alone with them became even more important to me.

On sunny Saturday afternoons, Dad and I would walk five miles to the Cloch Lighthouse. We'd get an ice cream and talk then walk back home. He was interested in everything. It seemed to me there wasn't anything my dad didn't know. Those times made me stretch myself. I didn't want to disappoint him.

We began to see ships from all over Europe come into port and foreign military with odd-looking uniforms and insignias. For the most part we made foreign servicemen welcome, extending Highland hospitality wherever we could. Even with all the unfamiliar faces, Greenock always felt safe.

Most of our young men were enlisting, so they asked the women to keep the town running and take jobs. Mum worked at the experimental torpedo factory just off Eldon Street. It occupied ten acres on the waterfront, but it wasn't just a factory. The employees formed a social club. They sponsored all kinds of sports and had social events. With the onset of the war, it became a secret facility, but since Mum and Aunty Agnus worked there, it wasn't much of a secret in our family. I supposed it must have been dangerous, but that wasn't something we ever discussed, so I didn't give it much thought. Everyone was doing their part in the war effort. I was proud of Mum's service and looked for ways I could help her.

Today, I'd gone into town to have lunch with her. Instead of the usual early closing for half the day on Wednesday, her employer gave everyone an extra-long lunch. We planned to shop a bit before Mum went back to work.

After our shopping, we had our tea at the little Italian café on Market Street. I studied her. "Are you all right? You look so tired."

Mum played with her trifle pudding, not taking a bite. "I'm okay." She hesitated then shrugged. "Well, perhaps a bit tired."

"Is the work hard?"

She shook her head. "Not really. I . . . life is so uncertain now." The enormity of what she was saying struck me. Admitting her worries. It wasn't something I could remember her doing before. Not even when Isabelle died. Mum kept her grief and her worries to herself. I was speechless.

A faint smile touched her lips. "Never you mind." She reached across the table and patted my hand. "It's going to be fine. You'll see. Now let's finish our tea. I need to get back to work."

Her words stayed with me as I carried our shopping back up the hill to my house on Dempster Street. I could have taken the bus, but I wanted to walk these streets and think about what she'd said.

Dad says there's a psychological preparation that comes with war. Even with our mental conditioning, sometimes fear would wiggle its way into my thoughts. I was sure that was my mum's problem. Dad was such a forceful personality I felt like he held both Mum and I together with sheer willpower. But now that I thought about it, why wouldn't we be a target with the torpedo factory, the Admiralty and Scotts Shipyard?

It gave me a little shiver to think both my parents worked in such important places. I was afraid for not only them but also for the town itself. Greenock was primarily a seaport. The great River Clyde was wide and deep and flowed past us, opening to the many islands of our coast and finally to the Atlantic.

There was nowhere like Greenock. We could look across the Clyde to other little towns like Dunoon and Helensburgh. And off in the distance we could see the mist-covered mountains, reminding us we are part of the Highlands. It was breathtaking and strategic.

Norse raids and clan uprisings filled our past. The lives of ordinary men and women who accomplished extraordinary tasks packed our history books—like Flora MacDonald, who dressed Bonnie Prince Charlie in her maid's clothes. They rowed to safety on the Isle of Skye, right past the English who hunted him.

Scots were always fighting against impossible odds and powerful enemies. Though we weren't often victorious, we always survived. That's what the Highlands meant to me. Strength and courage. It's what I hoped I had inside me.

Wendy—Seattle
August 1968

OUR NEWSPAPERS REPORTED on every aspect of the war in Vietnam. Demonstrations, casualties, and battles filled the evening news on every channel. I started hearing that those friends from school drafted after graduation were already bound for boot camp and soon to be shipped to Vietnam. The Tet Offensive had started in January and was still going strong. I knew John would probably volunteer, and I couldn't stop worrying. I hated not knowing. So, after a few days, I broke my rule of not hanging onto him, swallowed my pride and called his house.

He answered with a curt hello, and I froze. Then I stammered, "I heard they drafted Dennis. And I, well, I thought . . ." What

47

was I going to say? *I'm worried about you.* I couldn't pretend indifference if he was going into danger.

"Not just Dennis. Jim and a bunch of the guys are already in boot camp." His voice echoed my worry.

"Not you?" I tried to keep the hope out of my tone. After all, he broke up with me. Why should it matter? Only it mattered very much.

"They classified me as 4F." He sounded flat with disappointment. "My hearing. I failed the tests."

"Good." I shouldn't have said that. Overwhelming relief washed over me, and I bit my lip to keep from smiling like a loon, but I could imagine how terrible he felt. "Sorry, I know you would serve if you could. That's just who you are." Time to hang up before I lost the rest of my pride. The silence dragged on. I was getting uncomfortable.

"Thanks." It was little more than a whisper. But it broke my heart to hear his pain spoken in that one word. Silence again. I couldn't think of anything else to say.

I gathered what pride I had left. "Well, bye." I hung the phone up with a clatter in my haste. Mum was coming through the room with folded tea towels.

"Everything okay, luv?"

"John's 4F." I couldn't hide my smile.

Mum asked, "Peanut butter toast or chocolate?"

I always ate peanut butter toast in a crisis, but this was good news. "Chocolate, definitely chocolate." I thought for a minute. "Your war was so different from the Vietnam war, wasn't it? I mean, people weren't protesting."

"Well, maybe not so different at first." She found me a chocolate chip cookie. "I think the difference was that Hitler wanted to take over our country, our homes. He threatened our allies, defeating them one by one."

Chapter Seven

Christine—Greenock, Scotland
May 10, 1940

The papers said lethargy was spreading across Britain. I asked my dad what that meant.

"Well, Chrissy, I think it means people are none so worried about the war. They haena lost anyone yet and dinna feel they will."

"But all my uncles are in the war. Most everyone I know has family serving. How can they feel like that?" I thought about the citizens of Poland, Denmark, and Norway. "And what about the folk who've already lost everything?"

"Oh, aye, and yer right, but when yer neighbor's hoose burns doon it's sad, but it has not touched you. You can feel sorry for him, but yer not sae upset as if the flames spread to yer own roof."

I thought about that. I was thankful Greenock had gone untouched, but it was hard to ignore the fact that the war was going to change things. On Friday, May 10, Prime Minister Chamberlain resigned and declared Winston Churchill prime minister and minister of defense. The news spread across the land. Everyone stopped what they were doing to listen to the BBC.

I was in old Professor MacBain's seventh-level history class. We had just finished an exam on the battle at Culloden. On one side was Prince Charles and the Jacobite Highlanders, full of spirit but cold, hungry, and fighting with swords and axes. King George and a well-equipped English army fought on the other side. Listening to the discussion of that battle, you could hear that resentment toward the English was still very much part of the Highlander's attitude. As Professor MacBain collected our papers, he was saying, "Charles lost the war for Scotland because he was a poor leader."

The door burst open, and Miss MacIntyre came in to whisper in MacBain's ear. The woman's face was pale. I always thought Professor MacBain was an old man with his wispy grey hair; scruffy, short beard and slightly bent posture, but he had an amiable smile and great sense of humor. His face grew somber, and I knew something was wrong. MacBain thanked Miss MacIntyre as she left the room. He slid our tests onto his desk and stood motionless looking at us all. Taking a deep breath, he cleared his throat.

"We've had news that Prime Minister Chamberlain has resigned." Everyone began talking at once, something you just didn't do in MacBain's class. But he wasn't angry. He put his hands up to shush us. "There's a difference between deserting your armies on the field of battle, like Charles did at Culloden, and realizing you are not the leader your country needs. If Prince Charles had been the right leader for our country, they'd be wearing kilts in London." Then more to himself than to us, "No, we can thank Chamberlain for caring more about his country than his career."

It was something we'd talked about at length in his class: how leadership can make a country strong or bring about its fall. MacBain explained, "If Chamberlain recommended that Churchill take his place as prime minister, that's something we can count on." He chuckled. "The two statesmen are opposites. Chamberlain is mild-mannered and Churchill a bit of a bulldog."

He had the attention of twenty twelve- and thirteen-year-olds. I think we all realized history was happening right now and thank God not repeating itself. MacBain said, "If Chamberlain isn't the forceful leader we need, he is leaving us in capable hands. I think he knows the nation needs Churchill's tenacious spirit."

It was a good thing, too. That same day Hitler invaded Holland and Belgium.

As the days passed, I noticed the mood among most people had changed again. After the initial declaration of war, everyone was getting ready to fight. Then last winter nothing much happened. The papers dubbed it the "Phony War," and people became complacent again.

This time we all went about our business, but everyone tuned their radios to the BBC. There was a genuine sense of apprehension. People were eager to catch the latest news, and it wasn't good. I felt shaken.

Two of my uncles hadn't written for a few weeks. We feared they were being sent to fortify the French borders. In those dark days in May, we never strayed far from the news. We waited for mention of their units. Both Willy and Tommy were in the thick of the fighting. Our papers and radio were full of accounts of bravery as the British Expeditionary Force, the BEF, fought alongside French, Belgium and Dutch forces to hold back the massive German attack that started on May 10 as the enemy marched into the Netherlands, Luxembourg, and Belgium. The BEF fought bravely, but the fierce German onslaught pushed it back.

Professor MacBain gave us a lecture on the importance of history. Of course, he would think that; wasn't he a history professor? The students thought he was old enough to have witnessed a great deal of it himself. But I loved history. I perked up when old MacBain used his pointer to show us the border between Germany and France on the large map in his classroom.

His room was supercharged with energetic discussions of troop movements and strategies. And for the first time, I saw a youthful energy in MacBain that challenged each of us to see how history contributed to current events. He was saying, "The French depend heavily on their Maginot Line, a massive fortification built after the Great War as France's best hope to keep the Germans from ever invading again." His pointer moved to show us how far this fortification extended.

"Things didn't go as planned. The Germans attacked over the flatlands of the Netherlands, Luxembourg, and Belgium." His pointer swooped up to show the German movement over those countries then down to south of the Maginot Line.

"Then the unthinkable happened. More German units made it through the hilly Ardennes Forest."

There was an intense look of interest on every face. Not something I usually saw in MacBain's class.

My teacher explained, "French strategists were under the assumption that the hilly terrain of the Ardennes Forest would deter any invasion. The land is very inhospitable. Few people even live there. France was wrong."

He wasn't saying something we didn't already know. It was all over the news. But we listened like people who couldn't take their eyes away from a horrific accident.

"A large force of German troops came through the forest to the south and completely avoided the Maginot defenses. The Germans rushed north to catch the BEF and Allied forces in a trap with no place to go but the sea as the Germans closed in on all sides by land. And that's where it stands now." I thought of my two uncles, Willy and Tommy, fighting with their divisions, cornered in Dunkirk, and realized I was wringing my hands. I stopped and grabbed my skirt to keep them steady. Instead, I looked out the wall of windows, but the day was grey and depressing.

MacBain finished with a question from Robert Cameron. "Sir, my dad's in the BEF. He might be trapped on the French beach right now. What will our men do?" The large lad looked like he might cry, and my heart went out to him. He quickly wiped his sleeve over his face. All eyes swiveled to the professor.

The old teacher stroked his short beard. "Well, Robert, I don't know, but I know everyone is working very hard to get them out of harm's way."

The radio was full of tales of bravery as entire units held their positions, allowing as many of the BEF to escape as possible. I wrung my hands with worry for all four of my uncles. Were Willy and Tommy the only uncles serving in France? How many of them would make it out alive?

May 19, 1940

ON SUNDAY, I joined my parents in the front room, Mum and I on the settee and Dad in his overstuffed chair. The radio played music as we listened like the rest of the country, waiting for a message from our new PM. We were desperate for any shred of hope. I remember the music was silent for a few seconds before Churchill began his speech. His words were slow and measured but even more powerful, delivered with the strength of courage.

"I speak to you for the first time as prime minister in a solemn hour for the life of our country, of our empire, of our allies, and, above all, of the cause of freedom."

The silence between his pauses crackled with static. Then his words rang out. "A tremendous battle is raging in France and Flanders."

We all leaned forward as he described what was happening. "The Germans, by a remarkable combination of air bombing and heavily armored tanks, have broken through the French defenses north of the Maginot Line. Columns of their armored vehicles are ravaging the open country, which for the first day or two was without defenders."

I could imagine Uncle Willy and Uncle Tommy amid the battle raging in the towns and villages of France. My stomach clenched with anxiety, thinking about where my uncles Jack and Davie might be. My attention shot back to the radio as Churchill said, "It would be foolish, however, to disguise the gravity of the hour."

The news coming out of France concentrated on the lives being saved, not those sacrificed to make the rescue possible. In his first speech as prime minister, Churchill seemed to reach down into his heart and delivered the hope we needed. That I needed. His words were delivered with such unwavering confidence I believed him.

"Having received His Majesty's commission, I have formed an administration of men and women of every party and of almost every point of view. We have differed and quarreled in the past, but now one bond unites us all—to wage war until victory is won and never to surrender ourselves to servitude and shame; whatever the cost and the agony may be, this is one of the most awe-striking periods in the long history of France and Britain."

He believed in us as a people and in the men fighting in France. Churchill believed in our strength, in our courage, and he refused to surrender even in the face of overwhelming odds.

"Behind us—behind the armies and fleets of Britain and France—gathers a group of shattered states and bludgeoned races: the Czechs, the Poles, the Norwegians, the Danes, the Dutch, the Belgians, upon all of whom the long night of barbarism will descend, unbroken even by a star of hope, unless we conquer, as conquer we must, as conquer we shall."

I looked at my parents as they listened with me, their faces stern with resolve as Churchill ended in what sounded like a prayer. I realized if those who could help lacked the courage to step forward, my uncles might not survive. Even children had to find the courage to believe in victory, because defeat meant death for so many.

Churchill said, "Today is Trinity Sunday. Centuries ago, words were written to be a call and a spur to the faithful servants of Truth and Justice: 'Arm yourselves, and be ye men of valor, and be in readiness for the conflict; for it is better for us to perish in battle than to look upon the outrage of our nation and our altar. As the will of God is in Heaven, even so let it be.'"

In the week that followed, I heard Churchill sent extra fighter planes to France and flew to Paris to assess the situation for himself. He bolstered the French to fight on and assigned the 51st Highland Regiment and the Royal Scots to fight alongside French troops.

I learned that Uncle Davie was with the 51st Highland Regiment and Uncle Jack was in the Seaforth Highlanders. We'd been following the retreat of Uncle Tommy in the Queen's Own Cameron Highlanders and Uncle Willy with the Argyll and Sutherland Highlanders, populated by lads from all over the Highlands and the coastal islands. It turned out every one of my uncles fought for their lives and the future of the free world.

The Scots regiments held the Germans back, giving the BEF time to retreat. Men and machines raced out of harm's way until all reached the beaches of the French resort town of Dunkirk on the French shores of the English Channel. They were cut off from any escape route except for the sea. When the Germans offered terms of surrender, Churchill said, "We will never give up, never surrender."

The next time I was at school, Robert sat at his desk red-faced, his mouth drawn into a thin line and his arms folded across his chest. When MacBain started talking about the events leading up to Dunkirk, Robert was sullen and silent. I kept glancing back at the laddie. Finally, MacBain stopped talking. He stood for a moment regarding Robert with the kindly look of a grandfather.

"Robert, have ye heard anything from yer father?"

"I've heard that Churchill is using the Royal Highlanders to cover the BEF while they retreat." There was silence in the room. I stole a glance at Robert. His face was stiff, like it would crack at any moment. I couldn't think how I'd feel if I knew for sure my dad was captured or killed. I realized my world would end. Then I thought of my uncles. They might be stranded on the beach at Dunkirk.

MacBain moved next to Robert's desk and put his hand on the lad's shoulder. "Those regiments are saving countless lives. Ye dinna ken, do ye, if he'll make it out or not? Have hope, laddie." He patted Robert then turned to look at the class. "How many of ye have family serving in France?"

Gradually hands went up all around the room. I raised my hand too. Robert looked up, and his eyes traveled to the faces of those who had their hands raised. A girl sniffed. The room was so quiet. MacBain said, "See, Robert. We're all in this together. Some of us will lose people we love. Some will make it through." He sighed then shut his eyes. "Lord," he prayed, "protect these brave men, fathers and sons."

A boy at the front of the room said, "Brothers."

I heard myself say, "Uncles."

"Aye, Father, protect all those brave laddies." After a long moment MacBain looked up. "Do ye ken why the Highland regiments are given such fierce tasks? We Scots are bonnie fighters. You're likely to find a Highland regiment on the front lines of every battle. And did you ever think on the pipers who pipe the men into battle, armed with only an excellent set of lungs? He doesna carry a gun, but he battles all the same."

Donald spoke out. "My uncle's a braw piper with the Seaforth Highlanders."

MacBain smiled. "The Germans call our lads 'the ladies from Hell.'"

There was tittering laughter around the room. MacBain held up his hands to shush us, but he was chuckling too. "It's because they fear us." The room hushed. We all looked at each other with puzzled expressions. MacBain shook his head. "Nay then, a man who would march into battle with only a set of bagpipes in his hands, it's something to strike fear into the hearts of the enemy. And they say in the morning mist the pipes echo off the trees so they dinna ken where we are coming from." A smile settled onto his wizened features. Old MacBain faced Robert. "We'll pray for your da, son, but you can be proud of his courage. It's certain he's saving lives."

Somehow, we all felt comforted. I was never prouder to be a Scot, but I worried that at least one of my uncles would be among the men stranded on the French beach at Dunkirk.

Wendy—Seattle
Summer 1968

KMART WAS HIRING, and I was looking for a summer job before community college started in the fall. The manager hired me on the spot, saying, "The last girl quit a couple days ago."

"What department?" I rocked onto my toes and felt my heart lift at my prospects.

"Pets."

I loved pets.

On my first day they introduced me to Patzy, an older employee. Her grey curls and kind, grandmotherly face made me welcome as she showed me around. "I'm so glad you're here." She smiled and patted my hand. "Since the last girl quit, I've had to help in pets." Scrunching her nose, she added, "Not my favorite department."

Patzy explained my duties and the care of fish, birds, and turtles. I stopped as we came to a large fish tank. Dark water filled only a quarter of the aquarium, and I froze. The water wriggled and moved. "What's in that one?"

"Baby alligators." I felt my stomach do a flip but told myself I'd get used to all the pets.

Patzy rushed her words. "I'll show you once. You'll want to get your pet carrier ready first." She pulled a box from under the counter and set it next to the large tank. I tried not to look at the wiggling, snapping reptiles, but the smell reminded me of a swamp with fish and rotting weeds.

"Use these heavy gloves." Patzy slipped her hands into an enormous pair of gauntlet gloves and reached into the tank. She waited till the water settled. "It helps if you pick out your gator before you try to catch it. They're just babies so they can't really hurt you." I looked at their open mouths with dagger-shaped teeth about a half-inch long.

She seized one in a quick motion and pulled it out. It was slightly larger than her hand. "Then you turn it over and rub its stomach before it can—" Her gator twisted its body, trying to get hold of something to bite.

Patzy stroked the reptile's belly with her gloved fingers, and the wee beasty settled right down. She plopped it in the box and slammed on the lid. "Get a rubber band on the box right away." She grabbed one from the pile on the counter next to the workstation.

"The thing is you want to make sure the lid is tight. The last girl didn't listen to me, and one got away. We had a terrible time tracking it down." Patzy winked. "Fast little things. A customer's child found it and tried to pick it up. There was blood everywhere." The gator started throwing itself against the sides of the shoebox.

She opened the box and slid the gator back in the water. Violent squirming and teeth snapping ensued. *Lordy, I'm not sure I love pets this much.*

"Wait, you want me to do what? I don't know about this." My

voice sounded shrill. Patzy didn't seem to notice. She was taking off her gloves and handing them to me with a look of pure relief.

"You'll be fine. Just be careful." My mouth dropped open. "And be careful of the big ones. People bring them back after they bite one of their kids or the cat. We must take them 'cause it's a liability. But the little buggers grow fast. The bigger ones bite harder, and they're much faster." She winked at me again and walked away.

I looked around the department, checking under the counters, trying to calm myself. No loose gators to nip at my toes. No one's going to want an alligator, I reasoned. I'll be fine. But I found I couldn't turn my back on the alligator tank, imagining their wee beady eyes watching me.

Half an hour later the store intercom kicked on, and the manager's voice announced, "A Kmart blue light special in the pet department on tanks. And twenty percent off any pet purchase."

I said aloud, "You have got to be kidding!"

It's amazing what you can do if you put your mind to it. I sold three baby alligators that afternoon, successfully plopping them into their boxes with no blood or loss of digits. The store manager was pleased. Patzy dubbed me the Alligator Girl.

Mum had my tea ready when I came home. It appalled her when I told her about my first day. She shook her head. "You are a lot braver than me. I could never put my hands into a tank full of alligators." She grimaced.

"Mum, I'd rather face alligators than Germans." Rubbing the back of my neck, I admitted, "I heard they have jobs on campus. Maybe I'll work at Kmart till school starts."

"Sounds sensible. I know I'd feel better if you weren't risking your fingers on the job."

"Could you finish telling me about Dunkirk? How did your uncles make it out of France?"

Chapter Eight

Christine—Greenock, Scotland
Thursday, May 23, 1940

Oddly enough, it was not from the BBC or even my dad that I learned most of what was happening in Dunkirk. It was from Professor MacBain's seventh-level history class. Since his exchanges with Robert, he'd been keeping us abreast of what was taking place with the BEF.

His classroom was full of maps of Europe and larger ones of France. On one wall we had a large hand-drawing of the coast of England showing the area around Dover, the English Channel, and Dunkirk on the coast of France. I was quite proud of the map itself since I did the final drawing.

He taught us about military movements, generals, and leadership. He explained how politics and preserving the lives of the many must be weighed against the movement of men and materials across France.

He said, "The German Panzers are nipping at the heels of our lads. The 51st Royal Scots under French command are fighting valiantly to protect the BEF and the French army while a division of Panzer tanks under the command of German general Rommel presses its advantage." MacBain likened the battle back to the conflict at Culloden. Marching across the room to the map of the 1746 battle, he pointed to the overpowering force of King George's armies. "If there'd been a way to withdraw from the field of battle to fight another day, we might have a Stuart on the throne."

Robert piped up. "Then we could leave the defense of Dunkirk to the English." There was general agreement among the boys sitting next to him.

But MacBain held up a finger. "Maybe not. Besides, there's an English division fighting with the 51st." Now the old professor stood with his hands on his hips, looking at the map. These silences were more and more common with our teacher. It was as if he saw it all unfolding in his mind.

"If you had the impossible task of saving as many men as possible so your country would still have a fighting force, a chance to survive, who would you send to hold back the enemy?" He looked from face to face and whispered once more, "Who would you send?"

It was Robert who answered, and for the first time, pride, not anger, was written on his face. "I'd send my bonniest fighters."

"Aye, that you would."

May 27, 1940

WHEN WE CAME into our classroom on Monday morning, MacBain was setting up a radio. We looked at each other, echoing the silent question: What was he doing now? He bade us all take our seats and bent over the radio, turning the knobs. As the clock ticked the hour, static cleared, and we heard the familiar voice of the BBC news commentator.

"Ladies and gentlemen, today we are witnessing a miracle on

the beaches of the French vacation seaport of Dunkirk. Yesterday the call went out across the southern coast of England for seaworthy craft and every person skilled in navigation to join in the rescue of the surviving BEF surrounded by the enemy on the French beach. Ferry boats, tourist paddleboats, yachts and fishing boats crossed the channel next to Royal Navy vessels. Doctors, fishermen, tour guides, and teachers volunteered in the massive efforts to save as many men as possible. Yesterday this unlikely armada set sail from Dover."

As the situation grew increasingly desperate, our Highland regiments held back the Germans, making the rescue of BEF troops possible. Fear grew as mothers and fathers worried command would leave their lads in France. In the shops, old men said angry words about Churchill's decision to keep the Highlanders fighting German forces while others made their escape.

For the next week, I couldn't wait to get to MacBain's class. We discussed any update on Dunkirk, any report, even a newsreel at the movie theatre. We talked about the history we'd already learned and how it related to what was happening. While our military escaped, we followed the BEF progress and became unified as MacBain's Regiment.

MacBain announced, "Our lads are under constant fire, braving German bombs and constantly dodging machine-gun bullets."

We drew another detailed map of the village of Dunkirk, its beaches, piers, and canals. It also included the villages nearby as the 51st Highland Regiment and the Royal Scots raced with the French army toward the Channel.

MacBain described the scene for us. "It's a seaside town, ye ken. Two long piers jut out into the water, making a way for vacationers to disembark where the waters are deep enough for a boat of some size to dock. But it's not a port per se." He showed the position of the piers and the breakwaters on our map. "The Germans have destroyed the eastern pier, leaving only this one. It's badly damaged along with the breakwaters that jut into the English Channel." His pointer moved about the map.

Freddy said, "My uncle told me the lads lined up along that pier waiting their turn to get on a boat. All the while the bloody German planes were shooting at them and dropping bombs."

Someone else said, "My da says Dunkirk itself is in flames from the bombing. They say the ships coming from Dover steer toward the flames and smoke."

Bridgett added, "The men have to swim to boats offshore."

Comments were coming faster than MacBain could call on raised hands, but he didn't seem to mind. Della said, "The BBC has a man at Dunkirk. I heard him say how brave, even orderly, our lads were. Those men in the water and on the beaches have no cover, nowhere to hide from bullets. They're watching as the RAF flies dogfights with the Germans."

I marveled at MacBain's patience. He didn't shut off the discussion. There was no admonishment to soften the violence taking place. I suppose you couldn't live in Britain and not pick up the gory details of the beaches at Dunkirk. Like my dad, MacBain gave us the respect of capable, thoughtful intellects, allowing us to wonder things out loud that we were surely thinking.

MacBain painted an indelible word picture of the battle far beyond the press releases. "At the last minute, for some unknown reason, Hitler himself recalled his tanks to guard the Dunkirk canals."

When our teacher spoke again, it sounded like he was thinking aloud. "Some think Hitler feared an Allied counterattack." He shrugged. "We may never know, but whatever the reason, without the threat of the German tanks bearing down, it gave the men a chance to escape."

Even with all the discussion of Dunkirk in the classroom, I

hunted for every scrap of information I could find. As soon as Dad came home from work, he tuned our radio to the BBC. We listened together to an account of one pilot shot down in the English Channel. An overfull motorboat picked him up and brought him back to Dover. On arriving home, he hitched a ride to the nearest airbase. When the reporter stopped to ask him what he was doing, the pilot simply said, "I have to get on another plane and get back to Dunkirk."

Our papers were full of stories like that and of pictures of all the tiny boats that joined the flotilla of rescue ships. Ordinary men risked everything to pull our lads from the hands of the enemy. The stuff of epic movies was reality, and it made me proud.

Dad said, "With hearts so strong, we've got a fighting chance of winning this war." I just nodded and bit my lip. I was proud of my country, but a small part of me wondered if my dad was right. Could we win the war? This was a crushing defeat.

It was terrible not knowing the fate of family. A gloom hung over us all, stealing our energy while we waited for word. After nine days of worrying over the fate of my uncles, we were finishing breakfast when a knock sounded at our front door. Unspoken concern passed between my parents, but no one moved. I knew what they were thinking. It was an odd time for someone to visit unless it was the postman or a telegram messenger. Would it be good news or bad?

I rushed to the door and flung it open. Jimmy, the lad who delivered papers and the odd telegram, was standing there. His ear-to-ear grin lifted the weight off my heart. I knew he read the messages, and this one was the good news we'd been hoping for. On impulse I gave him a hug and whispered, "Thank ye."

Dad was behind me before I got the door closed. When I gave him the cable, he held it for a minute.

Mum came in from the kitchen, her deep blue eyes watery, but she took a breath and waited. Dad unfolded the message. "It's from yer brother Will." His face lit with delight as he read aloud, "I am unhurt and in England. STOP. Tell Mum. STOP."

We threw our arms around each other in a fierce hug.

Gradually, every one of my uncles sent letters or telegrams. We laughed and cried and read their letters repeatedly. They were all alive.

June 7, 1940

GRADUALLY MOST OF our class got good news though sadly not all of us. Eleven days after our lads were stranded on the beaches at Dunkirk, we were all filing into MacBain's classroom. The Dunkirk evacuation was over, but the energy in the classroom continued to grow. Our professor was sitting and shuffling through papers on his desk. He didn't greet us with the same warm enthusiasm that had carried us through the crisis.

Robert burst through the door yelling, "He's alive." Every eye flew to his jubilant face. "Professor, it's just what you said."

MacBain looked at him with a vacant stare.

"You told me to have hope." Robert reached out to shake MacBain's hand, but the professor didn't seem to notice. "Well, you were right. My father's alive. They rescued him. We heard from him last night." He halted. "Professor? What's wrong?"

MacBain rose, a half-smile on his sad features. He patted Robert's shoulder and walked out of the room. We all looked at each other. Freddy picked up the telegram sitting on MacBain's desk. We gathered round him. He skimmed it and said, "Here then, did ye ken MacBain had a son in the 51st? This says his son is missing in action." Freddy handed the telegram to Robert.

Robert looked toward the door. "I reckon he knew how I felt." He bit his trembling lip.

I could see how bad he felt, and I put my hand on his arm. "He said it himself. Some of us will lose people we love, while they'll save others. But both will have done their part to save as many lives as possible."

Even I knew that Dunkirk, while a victory in spirit, was a crushing blow to the defense of France. Finally, on June 22, Paris, the city of light, was overtaken by a great darkness of oppression. The newsreels were full of film clips as Hitler entered Paris.

Britain stood alone. But Churchill rallied the people. He was defiant. He said things like, "Victory at all costs." And we grabbed hold of those sayings and believed we could be victorious. We had to be. Gradually, those men who'd escaped capture in Europe made their way to us. They formed units like the Free French under Charles de Gaulle or the No. 303 Polish Fighter Squadron. The stories they told were the stuff of nightmares. We had to be victorious or suffer the same fate.

Wendy—Seattle
1968

I'd been staring out the window, thinking how I would feel if John were on the beach at Dunkirk. "How did you keep your sanity not knowing for days if your uncles were alive?"

"You keep busy," Mum said, "pray a lot and, well, you go on."

"I know I'm not strong enough."

Mum patted my shoulder. "Yes, you are. You just don't know it yet." Her smile faded. "I hope you never have to find out."

Three days later, I was helping her wash the dinner dishes. I'd been thinking about what she said about having to move past your fears. What was it she said? Just go on. There isn't another choice. I realized I'd been doing that. Maybe I was stronger than I thought. But that didn't make me feel better. Guess stronger doesn't always mean happier. A thought hit me, and I asked Mum, "Did the war come to your town? Were you ever in the fighting?"

Chapter Nine

Christine—Greenock, Scotland
Spring 1941

By the time I was thirteen, the war was in full swing. Our little town was charged with energy. Everyone was helping in the war effort. I looked for volunteer work. A lassie of thirteen was no longer considered a child.

My dad, the oldest of five, was just a few months older than me when his father died and he became the man of the house. To provide an income for his family, he had to leave early entrance to the university behind, instead finding work as an apprentice marine engineer at Scotts Shipbuilders. He raised his three brothers and felt angry because he wasn't out there fighting with them. His employer made a case with the government that they considered Dad vital to the war effort and irreplaceable on the job. He filed appeals, but so far they had all been unsuccessful. Scotts won their cause to keep Dad at work.

Sometimes it made his fuse a bit short. He expected your best efforts, and he wasn't someone you wanted to disappoint. We knew he helped design and build submarines. He also took them out on time trials before releasing them to the navy, but much of what he did was secret even to us. Mostly, my dad was strict but fair. He wasn't a large man at five-foot-six, but he was a force to be reckoned with, and I felt safe when he was near.

Not that my mum wasn't cut of the same stuff. At four-feet-ten-inches tall, she was a bundle of energy, stern, no nonsense. That my da was the love of her life was easy to see. They would always manage if they had each other. There were times I felt quite on the outside, separate from them. I knew they loved me and the entire family, but they drew their strength from each other.

Sometimes my parents listened to Lord Haw Haw on the radio. Broadcast from the Reich Ministry of Public Enlightenment and Propaganda, his purpose was to demoralize the Allied population. The cultured English voice taunted us, threatening German domination.

His critics tagged him Lord Haw Haw as a disparagement to lessen his impact. Still, our government checked his facts and found him reliable. Even though he was distasteful, we could often catch a small piece about the action on the front. With all four of my uncles away at war, we were eager for any tidbits of information. And our troops listened to him because he also reported official British military casualties.

One night in early April, the familiar aristocratic voice said, "Welcome to Germany Calling. Germany calling Greenock, Scotland. Don't think we don't see you. Ha, ha. We're coming for you soon. You won't know the time or day, but we will flatten your little town. You hide your submarines, but we know where they are. We'll destroy Scotts Shipbuilding." I put my hand over my mouth, my eyes wide with fear. My dad switched off the radio.

"You know he's only trying to frighten you, eh, Chrissy?"

"But you work for Scotts." My voice quivered.

"An' didn't our submarine nets catch a big German sub just last month? We're no afraid of them." He shook his head ruefully.

After Lord Haw Haw's taunting, the Germans, or Jerries as we called them, flew over us more often, dropping a few bombs and then disappearing from our night skies.

The first time they dropped a bomb in Greenock, I was sitting with my drawing pencils in the hills above Grandma's on a sunny spring afternoon. I heard the plane coming. It sounded like an angry wasp, the vibrating hum growing louder by the minute. This time it wasn't a tiny dot in the afternoon sky. It flew in low enough for me to see the German insignia painted on its side. Instinctively, I flattened into the coarse Scotch broom. Peeking over the rock I'd been sitting on, I saw the plane sweep low toward Scotts.

My hand flew to my mouth. "Dad," I screamed. Then I realized it was Sunday, and he was safe at home. The plane dropped a big, black sausage-looking thing. With a giant splash and an even bigger explosion, the German bomb missed the shipyard entirely and landed in the middle of the river.

I jumped up, rage taking hold of me. How dare the Germans bomb my home. "You missed! You stupid Jerry." Then, thinking there might be more planes overhead, I crouched back into the shrubs. The pilot banked right and disappeared into the clouds to the north. I waited for a long while before I picked up my drawing paper and sketch pad.

Dad said the German pilots were unloading the last of their ordinance before flying home from bombing raids in England.

By the middle of April, German planes came almost every night, still not more than a plane or two. Our new warning sirens would go off between eleven and twelve. After a long day at work, people's nerves frayed. We'd just get to sleep when the Jerries would set off the alarms, but they only flew over us and disappeared to the north. By the third night, we were all cross. My dad was exhausted. None of us felt like waking. Da said, "Helen, no, you and Chrissy get to the shelter." He rolled over.

"But, Dad, you can't stay here," I said from the bedroom door.

He moaned. "I'll die if I can't sleep. Leave me be."

"Suit yourself then, Jim." Mum pressed her mouth into a thin line. I thought I wouldn't want to be Dad in the morning. If my dad was a force to be reckoned with, my mum was just the person to do it. She could be a spitfire when her temper was up.

We had just made it down the stairs and into the shelter under the house next door when the building rocked from an explosion. My ears felt like they would burst, and my nose burned. "That was somewhere close," I whispered. Within two minutes the shelter door flew open, and my dad jumped in. The door banged shut behind him. My mum didn't say a word. She was out of her seat and threw her arms around him. I could only dimly see Da's face, but his eyes looked overlarge. He gave me a nod and a weak smile.

Wendy—Seattle
August 1968

I grew up being picked on and bullied. With my flaming red hair, I stood out in a crowd, something I didn't enjoy. Even in high school, a boy in the third hall hung out by the door waiting to trip me.

It made me self-conscious. That all changed while I was going steady with John. I relaxed because people respected him or maybe even feared him.

He had a reputation as a tough guy. I overheard little things, but I never saw them. In school we both took a lot of flak for our relationship. He told me once the vice-principle called him into his office and had a stern talk about leaving me alone.

My home economics teacher threatened to fail me, even if it was my senior year, if I didn't break off with John. But we stayed together all year. In the end, they got their way. The weight of being from two different worlds finally ended us.

My family rarely had extra money at home. Now that I was

working, I decided to bring home milkshakes, hamburgers, and fries for dinner. Heather would love it.

As I pulled into Herfy's parking lot, I came close to changing my mind. The place was packed. The long, low building had four windows in front of a covered porch. Only one window was open with a line that was at least six people deep. What's worse, I recognized them from school.

I parked and came to stand at the end of the line. That's when it happened. As I stepped into queue, the kid ahead of me whispered "Mutton's girl" to the guy in front of him. I heard it repeated several times. It was like the Red Sea parting. Every patron stood aside, ushering me to the front. I flushed deeply but walked past everyone, ordered my burgers, and left.

On the drive home, I wondered how John came by his reputation. Were they all afraid of him? But he wasn't a hoodlum. After spending a school year going steady, I saw his concern for the underdog, how he always kept his word, how he opened doors, rushed to carry packages. I had to stop before I got teary. But my inner voice whispered one last thought: He's not afraid of anyone.

A big fat tear rolled down my cheek, and I wiped it away. If God planned to strengthen me by trials, I hoped he did it soon. Right now, I was miserable. I wanted John to be miserable too.

Heather and Mum were pleased, and while we ate our burgers, I told them about the "Red Sea" parting at Herfy's. "I hope this isn't a problem at college."

Heather giggled. "I'll make you a little sign for your back. 'NOT Mutton's Girl.'"

When she left to play with her friends, Mum and I had a cup of tea together and she continued her story.

Chapter Ten

Christine—Greenock, Scotland
May 6, 1941

By late April, our nightly raids had stopped for a week, and we all fell into the routine of ordinary living. Six months earlier, Grandma Cowan had fallen, hit her head and suffered a minor stroke. Her recovery was slow and moving her left leg was hard. I could see how frustrated she was at her symptoms, and my heart went out to her. She was not the type to accept her disabilities, but even Grandma had to admit she needed help.

Since her daughters shared her care, on the first of May it was our turn for her to come live with us. I loved her so; I was that happy to have her company. At night she let me braid her long white hair. It smelled like wildflowers on a spring day. We shared the same bed, but neither of us complained. Even with her speech slightly slurred, we'd talk at night before falling asleep. She told the best stories about my grandfather's adventures at sea.

Grandma spoke one night about the time Grandfather sent home a Quaker parrot. "Och, he was a beauty, and he knew it too." Almost a foot tall, the bird had soft green feathers and a white breast. It came across the ocean in the company of some very rough-spoken sailors. By the time the bird got to Grandma, it had picked up quite a salty vocabulary. Soon after it arrived, her minister came to call. The man loved parrots and remarked on what a pretty one she had. That's when it told the minister what it thought of his opinion.

Grandma chuckled. "I couldna get the bird to stop even wi' his cover on. I gave that ball of feathers fair warning, but he was hav'n none of it. Reverend Hamilton was red in the face, and my wee lassies stood wi' their hands over their ears. So, I pulled off the cover, picked up the cage, bird and all, and put him in the sink. I told him, 'A guid dousing is what ye need to clean up yer dirty mouth.' I pumped the water over his head till I soaked him through his feathers to his wee birdie hide."

"Did ye get rid of the wee fiend, then?"

"Nae need for that. All I had to do was point to the sink, and he'd clamp his beak shut tight. He wasna a bad sort, just a bletherer, like to hear his own voice, ye ken."

I giggled at Grandma's battle with the bird. Mum had told me the story too, but I loved hearing it. In Mum's version, all four sisters were secretly rooting for the parrot, the minister not being one of their favorite people.

Grandma was only with us a few days when the Jerries started sending their planes to fly over our town again. The air-raid sirens would sound, and people on our block would crowd into the shelter below the house next door. It wasn't far. But Grandma had to go down our stairs to the street and down the stairs to the basement next door. She didn't move so well after her stroke, so it was my job to help her get out of the bed we shared. Every night, I'd get her into the shelter. Then the "All Clear" would sound without the Germans dropping a single bomb. Everyone grumbled it was the Jerries' way of tormenting us. My mouth went dry with worry when I heard my dad tell Mum it was more likely reconnaissance. Were the Germans scouting out likely targets for a future bombing raid?

We started going to bed in our street clothes. You'd think I wouldn't sleep, but these late-night alarms were making us all overtired. On the sixth of May, the sirens went off just after midnight. Grandma refused to get out of bed. "No, Chrissy. You just leave me. What's the point? I'll only get down there to turn around and come back upstairs." She rolled over.

My mother heard her from my bedroom door. Her voice was stern. "I'm not going through this again. Get up, Mom. We need to get to the shelter." She moved past me and gently turned Grandma over. "Come along now." Even as she spoke those words, we heard the first bombs drop. It sounded far off, but Grandma sat up and looked at my mum. I never saw fear on their faces, just the grim determination to survive.

That night we grabbed our coats and made it to the shelter in record time. It was already full of our neighbors, but we squeezed in. All of us except my mother and father. They volunteered with the fire brigade. I watched them leave, wondering if I'd ever see them again. My world was walking away. Then I smiled as my dad slipped his hand over Mum's. He would take care of her. I felt sure she'd be safe. Tonight, they fought fires together.

It would have been torture wondering what was happening out there except for Mr. Munn, the air-raid warden in our neighborhood. It was his job to make sure we all observed blackout rules. Even a little light could give the Germans somewhere to target. Mr. Munn, like his wife, must have been as old as my grandma, but he was spry and took his job seriously. Tonight, he came to check on us regularly. I think he just wanted to see his family, because I saw him give a smile and a wink to his wife on each visit.

We could hear explosions and gunfire. We listened to sounds of battle, but it was Mr. Munn who told us what was happening.

He was a natural-born storyteller, and he painted a picture of what was happening above us with strokes I'll never forget.

"The first wave of bombs was incendiary. The Jerries are setting Greenock ablaze. They may not hit what they want, but the fires destroy everything around their impact. The fires are all over toon." His face grew red with anger as he spit out, "Then the fighter pilots come in low and kill the people working to put out the fires."

I blurted out, "Have you seen my mum and dad?"

"Ye hae brave parents and no mistake. Aye, lassie, I've seen them. They're all right for now." I snuggled into Grandma as we listened, my earlier confidence now gone. Even over the roar of aircraft engines, we could hear the rattle of the machine guns and the pings as their bullets peppered our street.

I looked at Grandma through watery eyes, and she smoothed back my hair. "I ken they're aright, luv." She looked directly into my eyes. "You believe me, Chrissy. We'll get through this. I promise ye."

I nodded, but my thoughts wandered off to what was happening outside. Much of Greenock was stone and brick, but enough wood and burnable materials were still used in construction to feed a fire. Our houses were often connected to each other with little or no space between them, and the fires spread quickly. I knew my parents were fighting to save as many homes as possible. If not checked, one incendiary bomb could destroy an entire neighborhood. I wasn't worried about losing my house or even our whole street. All I could think was, "Please, God, keep my mum and dad alive."

In the shelter, my chest vibrated with the impact of the bombs, even from those dropped far off. With every quake, dust from the house above would cover us. One ear-deafening roar made us all jump. The two electric lights hanging from the ceiling swung violently. The house above rocked. Mr. Munn's grandchildren cried out in fear, and the lights went out, plunging us into total darkness.

Mr. Campbell called out, "We're all right. We've just lost electric power. I'll get some candles, and we'll have a bit of light. Stay calm." I heard a series of yelps and knew he must have stepped on people as he made his way to the storage cupboard. But when he lit the candles, everyone settled. That little bit of light brought us all so much comfort.

Grandma and I sat in a corner near the outside door. It wasn't cold. In fact, it was hot in the crowd of bodies. This basement could probably hold fifty people comfortably, but now one-hundred men, women and children filled every space. The concussive explosions happening above transfixed us. I couldn't stop worrying about my parents. Grandma took off her coat, and I used it to cushion her straight-backed chair. Then I folded my own coat and sat on the uneven bricks that covered the floor. We waited for the sounds of war to stop. Thunderous booms and rattling bullets felt like they were right here with us in the shelter. I held my hands together so they wouldn't shake. I began to panic as the smell of smoke grew stronger.

Most of our shelter was underground. Only a few small windows were spread out along the back wall and those were high up, close to the ceiling. Mr. Campbell opened them behind their blackout curtains for a bit more ventilation until the room filled with smoke. People began coughing so he had to shut them. The shelter had vents to the house above, but it surprised me how quickly the air grew stale. In books I'd read that fear has a smell. Now I knew for sure the truth in those words. It does smell, and it's not pleasant.

A hush fell over us all as the house-shaking explosions moved away from our street for a moment. An hour later, we all jumped when someone pounded on the door and screamed to be let in. The door was unlocked, but I was closest, so I opened it. A young woman with a baby wrapped in a warm blanket stumbled into the shelter and collapsed at my feet. Mr. Campbell helped her stand and guided her to his empty seat. The baby's face was purple with wailing, and his mother's face was white as porcelain. She looked as if she'd drop her child, so Grandma said, "Gi' me the babe." The wee thing settled quickly in Grandma's arms.

His mother was still sobbing. "I was at the rail station seeing my husband back to his unit when they hit. I just kept running. Fire everywhere." Big tears washed down her face. "They're shooting at anything that moves. I thought we would die. Then a man found us and sent me here."

Old Mrs. Munn wrapped an arm around her and folded her into a motherly embrace. "You and yer bairn are safe the now."

"Do you think my man made it away?"

Mrs. Munn just patted her back. We could offer little comfort. None of us had been outside the shelter since the Germans started bombing.

I wanted to put my hands over my ears and scream, "Aren't they ever going to stop?" But I didn't. It would only worry Grandma even more. As the time wore on, I dozed on and off, my head resting on Grandma's soft lap. At dawn the bombing slowed, but we could still hear explosions.

Mr. Munn came back to check on us early in the morning on the seventh. He was hard to recognize. Ashes covered him from head to foot. But his face lit up when he saw his family. His wee grandchildren were asleep, but Mrs. Munn's eyes shone at the sight of her husband. Her voice was soft so as not to wake those sleeping, but I heard her ask, "Yer all right then, Geordie? Can we all go home now?"

His expression grew tender, but he shook his head sadly and said, "Not yet, luv, it's still dangerous topside. The word is stay put." I could see there was more he wasn't telling us. Then he added, "Ye can git up the stairs to use their facilities in the hoose above. Otherwise, stay ye doon here." Then he left.

We had food, water and one small water closet for all of us to use. It was pure relief for the women with small children to sneak upstairs to the house above as needed. People took turns going up. I expect it felt good to get some fresh air and move around a bit.

I wouldn't leave Grandma, and the stairs would have been too hard for her to manage after sitting so long, so I helped her get up to use the toilet on the other side of the room. It was good for her to move, at least as best as she could. I could see it was painful.

Some women began passing out biscuits, but no one seemed all that hungry. Even the small children were subdued, their eyes large in the dim light. I listened for the all-clear, but it didn't come.

We'd been in the shelter just over twenty-four hours when the sounds of war began to fade, giving us hope this would all be over soon. At 12:15 a.m. on May 8, the warning sirens sounded, and then the onslaught began again. In the wee hours of the morning, the door to the shelter banged open. Light from the flames on our street above flooded into our shelter. My father stood there. The fires had singed his hair into spikes. Fierce eyes stood out against his blackened face. He had hold of my mother's arm. Mum's clothing was ripped and covered with soot. Her hands were dirty, with angry red welts showing on her fingers. She was barely recognizable except for the look of anger on her face. Her lips pressed together, and her eyes glowed with indignation.

Da pushed her through the door and yelled over the noise of battle. "Keep her here. Don't let her back out." Then he was gone.

I moved out of the way. Mum crumpled to the floor next to Grandma, her face buried in her mother's lap.

I looked around the room at the able-bodied men still in the shelter. I wanted to scream at them for not helping, wanted to shake them all. Instead, I went stiff with rage. "That's my dad out there. What's wrong with you?"

No one said a word.

"I know you're all afraid. I am too. If I thought I could get past

my mum and Grandma, I'd be out there helping him right now."
They wouldn't meet my gaze. Many turned their backs. Mr.
Campbell rose to leave, but his wife grasped his hand and shook
her head. He sat back. I did too, wiggling my way into the small,
clear spot between my mum and the door. I put my hands over my
face and prayed. Please, God, let Da live through this, please.

In the dark hours before daybreak, my dad came back. Mum
threw her arms around him. Tears made tracks down her cheeks.
"Thank God," was all she whispered. He patted her back and
nodded as though he would fall over if she leaned on him. His
clothes were black. His face was like the bark of a burnt tree
trunk. Mr. Campbell rose and guided him to an empty place by
the wall. No one said anything. Most of the people were sleeping.
Mrs. Campbell brought him blankets and a pillow. Da was asleep
within minutes. I finally slept too, my world once again restored,
my family safe for now.

It was dawn when the all-clear sounded. We were the first out
of the shelter, because we were one of the last to enter. We'd been
in the shelter for over forty hours. Grandma was stiff, and both
Mum and I helped her stand. When we reached the street, we all
stopped to look around. Thank God, our house was still standing,
but down the hill the whole town was on fire, leaving the air thick
with the acrid smell of ash. I could hear the others coming up
from the shelter coughing.

Then Mrs. Munn wept. She said, "It's gone. My home is nae
more." The Jerries had bombed the tenements at the other end of
the street.

Another neighbor put an arm around her, saying, "There now,
and it's a blessing ye have a family who still live." She nodded
toward the daughter-in-law and two small bairns. "Come to my
house, and we'll sort things out. I'll send a lad to find yer man.
He'll ken what ta do next."

Wisps of conversations were happening all around, but I
couldn't take my eyes off the sky. Dark clouds rolled and boiled

above me. An eerie half-light greyed out everything, even the trees. After two days of sitting in the shelter, movement was painful for Grandma, so we stood there a moment to let her rest. We were both looking.

The light intensified as the first rays of the sun crept over the hills from the east. Dad and Mum were helping some others, but Grandma and I stood watching our dark world brighten. She straightened. "Look, Chrissy." She pointed to the cemetery where they had buried my little sister Isabelle.

Dark clouds blanketed the sky above the burial ground. A breeze off the river moved the ash-filled air coming up from the town. The clouds parted, and the rays of light from the rising sun broke through. I drew in my breath as clouds opened in the familiar shape of a cross. The sky beyond was fiery red, orange, and yellow with the sunrise. We stared at the fiery cross in the sky. Grandma turned to me. "That's hallowed ground. See there." Her face held its own kind of inner light. "In the Highlands, the chiefs would call the clan to gather for battle with a fiery cross."

"But, Grandma, the battle is over."

"Nae for the Lord. He is our chieftain, and his battle against evil is never over. He's calling us to join him."

As I stood in the wreckage of my town, staring at the fiery cross, peace washed over me. I believed God was reminding me he was my chieftain too. Her words changed me. I thought I heard a soft whisper in my ear. "You're not alone." And I felt sure He'd help me do whatever I needed to do.

Wendy—Seattle
1968

"Your Grandma Cowan sounds wonderful."

Mum smiled sadly. "She was. Her words that night stayed with me. When things are hard, I remember them. And I feel Grandma Cowan standing with me. And God, of course."

I saw the aloneness in her eyes. She didn't have her parents near, no uncles or aunts. No cousins. And Dad drove a Greyhound bus, so he lived away from home for weeks at a time. No, all she had was me and my sister. I reached for her hand and gave it a squeeze.

"I loved that you stood up and spoke your mind to the men in the shelter." I thought for a moment. "I'm not sure I would have."

She looked me in the eye. "Yes, you would. If it came down to keeping your family safe, you would."

"Maybe." I realized something I'd never put together before. "No wonder you hate fireworks."

Mum nodded. "Not all the time, but sometimes I hear the rattle of machine guns, and the smoke reminds me of the fires. I know it's just fireworks, but for a minute I'm right back in that shelter."

"I had no idea what you went through." I thought about our talk on how different the Vietnam War was from her war. "You're right. Our war isn't like yours. Not for us anyway."

Life hadn't changed for the average American. Despite all the protests, most people didn't suffer. I thought of John's friends. At least most people didn't suffer if the ones they loved were still safe at home.

THE NEXT WEEK I went out to Highline Community College to buy my books. I felt excited for a fresh start. I planned to major in Art, maybe get a teaching degree. While I was there, I applied for a job doing clerical support in the humanities building. Hopefully, I'd be able to give notice to Kmart and say goodbye to the wee beasties.

I finished my registration, bought my books, and came home. I was lucky to go to junior college. A combination of scholarships and grants made it possible for me to enroll. I never thought of my family as poor, but our pantry was bare. Mom was so great at being able to make healthy, tasty meals out of next to nothing. She sewed all our clothes, and she kept us from feeling like we were missing what other kids took for granted, like vacations, movies, or eating out.

My first day of classes ended early. Afterward, I wandered through the extensive library on campus. A familiar-looking lady stopped me. "You're a Highland dancer, right?"

I stammered yes, and she smiled at my shock.

"My son's piped for you in the past."

Her smile was so genuine I instantly felt a kinship with her.

"Nann MacDonald. My son Davy is the piper. I'm a librarian here. Taking classes this fall?"

"Yup."

"There's someone else here from the Highland Games Association. Oh, there he is." She caught the eye of a man setting down a load of books. "He's new here too. Volunteering in the library." She was motioning for him to join us.

I turned around and came face-to-face with the man I'd met at the Highland Games. He was nice looking for someone who must be as old as my father. His auburn hair and green eyes were striking. He took my hand. "Ah, Wendy, isn't it? I told you I'd be seeing you again."

"Seamus?"

"You remember me then." Seamus had a smile that lit up his face. Then he added with a slight reproof, "I rather thought you were more interested in that young man of yours."

I was sure he must be teasing me but wondered why he'd care about the love life of an eighteen-year-old girl. "He's not my young man. Not anymore."

Nann touched my arm. "I must go, but I'm sure you'll be dropping into the library for studies. Come find me for a visit." I watched her hurry off to her office, leaving me to this stranger.

I took a deep breath, wondering if I should excuse myself, but Seamus spoke before I could.

"I'd like to buy you a cup of tea if you have time."

There was something about him, an easygoing magnetism, that made my mind up to accept his offer. We walked to the cafeteria and talked over cups of steaming hot tea. He was charming and funny, and I found myself at ease with him. Despite feeling a bit awkward at his interest, I liked him.

He gestured to my hair. "Easy to see you have Scottish blood. Your coloring gives that away. Are your parents from there?"

"That would be just my mum."

"Oh, and is that where you get your red hair?"

"Actually, hers is blue-black."

"I love that shade of hair. My mother had that. And your father?"

"Canadian. She married him after the war."

His questions, like peeling an onion, touched layer after layer of my life until I said, "I'm sorry. I must go. Promised I'd be back by three." I rose and stuck out my hand. "Thanks for the tea. I enjoyed talking with you."

He shook my hand. "You almost sound surprised." His tone was teasing. Then he added with sincerity, "I enjoyed our talk too."

I left Seamus standing there and hurried up the stairs to the campus-level exit. Something prickled at the back of my neck. I glanced back down the stairs. Seamus stood looking at me with a thoughtful expression. He shoved his hands in his pockets and rocked on his toes, whistling a slow tune I couldn't place, but it sounded sad. When our eyes met, his expression went from contemplative to open and friendly. I drew in my breath at the immediate transformation. He smiled and waved.

On my drive home, I wondered what he'd been thinking. Why would he be interested in me? I'm ordinary. But Mum's life was quite the story. Her life would make good reading. I wondered if I should ask her to write it all down. But then an even better thought hit me, and I said aloud, "I'll do it. Put it all in a notebook and give it to her for her birthday or Christmas."

And I set my course.

I spent every spare minute recording everything she'd already told me. Finally, I was ready to capture the rest. But I didn't want her to know what I was doing, so I decided to write before I fell asleep at night.

The next time we had a chance to sit and talk I asked her to start where she'd left off after the Greenock Blitz. She gave me a questioning look, but I think maybe she needed to unlock her past as much as I needed to hear it.

Chapter Eleven

Christine—Greenock, Scotland
May 8, 1941

Tiredness returned to me, bringing me back to the realities of cleaning up after the bombing. My emotions were numb —put-one-foot-in-front-of-the-other numb. Everyone was quiet. People shuffled off to their homes—if they still had one. We moved in a kind of trance, thankfully too tired to think.

Our house was still mostly intact. The Germans blew out our two front windows, but almost everything else looked undisturbed. Grandma napped. But I helped Mum pick up the shattered window glass. I kept glancing out at my street. The row of houses on our side of the street was still there. But across the street some were missing like Mrs. Munn's tenements. Machine-gun bullets pitted the cobblestones and, in the center of our street, just beyond our steps, blast-blackened stones surrounded a hole large enough to swallow a car. A whole car.

I remembered that one ear-deafening explosion when the house above our shelter shook so hard it scared us all. I felt quivery inside. What if that bomb had hit us instead of empty cobblestones? Better not to think.

Down the street, the large tenement lay in smoldering rubble. I wondered what would happen to old Mr. and Mrs. Munn and their son's family. Their large-eyed grandsons, only four and five years old, had sat so quietly for a good forty hours. Now they had no home, all their things gone. From somewhere inside a voice reminded me, *They're all still alive.*

Grandma lay on my bed, snoring softly. My eyes kept straying to the bullet holes on the wall above her.

"That's right, Chrissy," Mum said. "I could have lost you and my mother as well." One large tear rolled down her cheek. She brushed it away with the back of her hand, leaving a black smear across her face. The first thing we wanted when we came home was a wash-up, but the water had gone off, so everyone looked a sight.

Without meaning to, I grinned. "Mum, your face is sae black."

A faint smile answered me. She stood to get the rubbish bin. "We need to get the glass all up. Yer Dad's gone off to find some wood to cover these windows."

I rose to look through the open frame. That's when I noticed the empty shell casing embedded outside in the stone wall below my windowsill. It wasn't large, the size of a coconut. I drew a breath sharply.

Mum heard me and crossed the room. At the sight of the bomb, she grabbed my sleeve to pull me back.

After my first surprise, I'd noticed how odd it looked, like a silver eggshell after the bird had hatched. "It's empty. Only a shell. Like it flew here and stuck in the wall."

My mother was practical to a fault. She peered over the sill and clicked her tongue. "That's all right. We'll fix Herr Hitler's evil plans."

She disappeared, and when she came back, she had a small pot filled with dirt and a tiny white rose. We call them fairy roses. She slipped the pot into the shell casing, and it fit perfectly.

"Thinks he's got us down, does he? I think not." Mum brushed her hands together in satisfaction, and we moved to the window in the sitting room. Funny how that steadied me.

My mum was strict, but she was brave and defiant. I wanted to be brave and defiant with her. I remembered from Professor MacBain's class that a white rose cockade, a badge worn by the Highlanders, was a symbol of Scottish resistance. Those wee roses grew wild all over the Highlands, and if you pinned one to your cap, others would know on which side your loyalties lay. It seemed just as fitting now.

By midday the news went out. We were told to evacuate the women, children, and elderly. Like our street, much of our town was without gas or water. The men were given time to make sure their families were situated and then return. It would take every man in town to get the water and gas back on. Thank God, my other grandma was safe, visiting friends on Skye.

I overheard Dad talking with Mum. His voice cracked with emotion as he said, "Not to mention the job of digging bodies out of the rubble. And there's nae way of knowing how many we'll find." It made me shudder to realize how awful that would be. Not something I'd let myself consider, not now, not ever.

I was helping my mum gather up a few things—a change of clothes, socks, and underwear—when Dad said, "Mind, Helen, only what we can all carry. The trains will be crowded."

"But, Dad, where are we going?"

He winked. "The important thing is to get to the rail station and find out our options. Not to worry." He paused. "Think on this as an adventure."

I looked at him for a minute. He couldn't be serious. I felt my heart sink. "I want ta stay with you."

Mum came alongside and shook her head slightly, warning me not to say more. I pressed my lips together to keep from crying.

Her eyes were watery too. We didn't want to be separated, but we had no choice. I realized it must cost him dearly to keep his emotions under control.

I took a deep breath. "Aye, Da. An adventure." And I was rewarded with a tender smile from my bone-weary father.

In the end we left with only the clothes on our backs and small shopping bags containing one change of clothing. I looked around my room before I left to see if I needed to take anything else. My tap shoes poked their toes out from under my bed. Dancing—I didn't think I'd feel like dancing ever again. But the shoes called back, "You'll need us to forget your troubles." I scooped them up and shoved them in my bag.

The train station was mostly downhill from our house. Fortunately, the train and rails were still intact. But we had to navigate through streets covered with debris from the blitz. It was slow going with Grandma. At the end of our block, we came upon my dancing teacher Mrs. Robertson and her two girls.

Mum and my dancing teacher were good friends, and Mrs. Robertson asked if we'd want to come with them, saying, "My sister lives in the tiny village of Kirkcowan. It's far to the south in the lowlands." Mrs. Robertson was sure they would offer us all shelter. "There's nothing but small villages and towns for miles around. It's not important enough for the Germans to bother with."

Dad nodded with relief. "That sounds like it will do well."

At the beginning of the war, our government had confiscated Dad's car for the war effort, so walking was our only option. As we passed Wellington Street, Aunty Jean joined us with her wee son Jackie. Last we'd heard, Uncle Jimmy was fighting somewhere in Africa. Jackie bounced over the stones, showing no sign of the horror we'd come through.

I wondered if we looked like gypsies and wished we had a horse and caravan to travel in. I glanced up the hill as a car moved slowly, skirting bomb craters but still bumping over the rubble scattered everywhere. Maybe walking was better.

As the car neared our group, it pulled to a stop. A man and woman sat in the front seat and two small children in the back. My dad waved. He seemed to recognize the driver and approached the car to speak with him. Dad glanced back at us all several times.

Relief lightened the lines on his face as he came back. "They've offered Grandma a ride to the station." We were all so grateful. Walking was hard for her. She looked grey and tired.

Mum said, "Chrissy, you go with Grandma. See that she gets a place to sit and wait for us." So I rode with Grandma, crammed into the back of the car with two sleepy-looking children. Grandma closed her eyes as soon as she settled and fell sound asleep within seconds.

I wish I could have done the same, but I couldn't take my eyes away from the view through the window. We passed the big Saint Laurence's Church on Dellingburn. It was only a shell, the roof and all the stained glass gone. Only the stone walls remained. Through the empty arch for the door, I caught a glimpse of smoldering rubble where pews had once waited for worshippers.

The man said to his wife, "Men, women, and children ran for the bomb shelter in the basement." He cleared his throat before he added, "Took a direct hit. All gone. Not one survived."

His wife stifled a sob. I had to blink away tears, unable to stop watching the devastation of my hometown. The Germans did this to us, I thought. They killed our friends and neighbors.

But you and your family are safe.

Yes. I looked at my Grandma Cowan. In sleep I could see how very old and worn she was, and my heart ached at the thought I might have lost her.

We had to go around a large hole at the foot of William Street. The man said, "I was in the command center last night on the north side of Dalrymple. The power was out early on, and we had to send boys on their bicycles or motorbikes to deliver messages for the different fire brigades. Mind, they were only boys, and they rode through all the bombs and bullets." He glanced back at his own small son asleep next to Grandma.

"A tremendous explosion rocked the building we were in, and we all went rushing out to see what happened. We saw that enormous crater." His voice shook as he finished. "At the bottom was Tim's son's motorcycle." He ran his hand over his face. "Not even a body—only the mangled frame of the motorbike. We all stood there, and I swear there wasn't a man with dry eyes. But we couldn't slow down."

The man chuckled. It seemed so out of place. I looked up sharply, but he added, "Later we heard that the boy, bruised and shaken, climbed out of the hole and ran the rest of the way to deliver his message."

He shook his head at the memory. "Wi' sons like that we will survive this." His cheeks were wet with tears. His wife reached out and put her hand on his arm. I looked away from them, not wanting to intrude.

Out the window, my town rolled slowly by. Everywhere there were charred remnants of last night's consuming fires, buildings I'd been in hundreds of times now only identifiable by one wall left standing or a half-burned sign lying in a pile of stones.

Mum and Dad had been out in all this. I drew in my breath and clamped my hand over my mouth at the realization. I'd known what they'd been doing but to see with my own eyes— tears blurred my vision for the rest of the trip to the railway station.

As we pulled to a stop, I quickly wiped my face and gently shook Grandma. Her gaze was unfocused at first. I watched her remember the horror of the last few days. I wanted to throw my arms around her and cry, but the woman opened her door to wake her sleeping children. The man pulled back his seat and offered Grandma help. "We're here. Let me gi' ye a hand."

I said, "Thank you. I don't even know your name."

"Why, and I know your name, lassie. It's Christina Finlay."

"How do—"

"I work with your da at Scotts. He's a braw man, your da, brave as they come."

We thanked him and made our way into the building. I looked around the crowded station for a place to sit. Three teenage boys were lined up on a bench near the door. I approached them. "Please, can you move? My grandmother needs a seat."

They couldn't have been much older than me. They chuckled as some joke passed between them, but they didn't answer.

"I asked you to move for my grandmother." I looked over my shoulder to where she stood leaning heavily on her cane.

"Och, go find another bench. This one's taken."

My fists curled. *I'd like to smack you in the mouth, but I won't.* I put my face inches from his and hissed, "You move now unless you'd like your friends ta see you being beaten by a lassie." I drew back. "Look at her. She's near to exhaustion." I kept my eyes on the big lad's face. *I swear my first punch will break your nose.*

There was a lengthy silence as he took my measure. He turned to his friends. "Come on then, lads."

I smiled sweetly. "Thank ye." I turned to guide Grandma to the empty bench. We sat there staring into nothing, seeing nothing and, thank God, feeling little until I spotted Mum and Da coming toward us. I jumped up, feeling so much lighter at the sight of my parents. "They're here, Grandma."

She looked up. "That's all right then, Chrissy. We're all together the now."

All but little Isabelle. She wasn't here to see this. And how much harder would it have been to lose her now?

I shook off the thought and ran to meet them.

Wendy—Seattle
1968

"Mum, would you really have hit him?" It was hard to picture her punching someone. I watched her think about it, and her face transformed into fierce determination. "You would have, wouldn't you?"

"Maybe, but it doesn't matter as long as I convinced the lad."

"Guess that's true." There was a side to my mother I'd never suspected.

Later that night, I chuckled as I wrote all I was learning about her. My smile faded as I realized it was the trial of the Blitz that changed her. Now that determination to do whatever she needed to protect those she loved was at her core.

I didn't want to go through a bombing to gain strength. Maybe that's why I was so comfortable with John. He was strong and unafraid, taking the pressure off me to stand up for myself as long as he was there. But he wasn't there, not now. And I couldn't be the woman my mother was no matter how hard I tried.

Then there was the fact that second sight runs in our family. I'd seen and heard stories about Mum's second sight. Without thinking, I put my hands up to rub my shoulders as if a chill had passed through my bedroom. That was one part of her I'd rather not experience myself. I didn't talk about it much. The few times I did people looked at me like I was crazy. The other reaction was even more disturbing. Extreme interest. Questions. No, she could keep that part of her personality. It wasn't for me.

Chapter Twelve

Christine—Greenock, Scotland
May 8, 1941

The train station filled with more people by the minute. It reminded me of the newsreels I'd seen at the movies, brief clips of families fleeing from German invasion. We were like those people, red-eyed and tired. Children held onto their mothers and were subdued and quiet, except for a few like my five-year-old cousin Jackie. His wild, curly brown hair framed mischievous eyes. He bounced around his mum.

Glancing at the bench where I'd left Grandma, I slipped my hand in Mum's, giving her a little squeeze. Her eyes followed mine. Grandma was asleep where she sat, her chin resting on her ample bosom. We shared a brief smile.

An hour later we were all settled in a train headed south to the borderlands. In the past we'd taken the train into Glasgow or Edinburgh for shopping, but this time I didn't know where we were going or how long we'd be away from home. I leaned my cheek on the cool glass of the coach car's window, watching as we traveled past towns down the coast from us.

The rocky Scottish coastline slipped by. White, foamy waves crashed against rugged rust-colored rocks. Beyond them, the greenish-grey sea stretched to the horizon. Many people got off at Largs and Ayr, and I wondered how safe they would be.

How far do we have to go to hide from German attention?

Our train sped inland, past small villages and glens then back to the sea. This far south the coastline was empty, and I thought about MacBain's history lessons. These shores must have looked the same when we fought English invasions. No, I corrected myself. Those rocks saw the Vikings pull their dragon ships up on the sand. Then I remembered. We lost both those wars. "Oh," I said aloud and swallowed hard to keep from crying.

Mum touched my arm. Her own face was bleak, but she must have read my thoughts. "Try not ta think, Chrissy, there's a lass. Close your eyes and sleep a bit if ye can." I didn't think it was possible, but I drifted off. Thank God, I didn't dream.

It was three hours later that we disembarked at a small station in the middle of nowhere, just a covered bench, a deserted building and rolling pasturelands dotted with sheep.

Mum looked around. "This can't be right." But the conductor assured us the connector train would be along shortly.

Mrs. Robertson promised Mum, "It's always the same. I've been this way many times en route to my sister's in Kirkcowan." So, we all got off and waited on the empty platform.

My dancing teacher was right. Within thirty minutes, a small engine chugged into view. We boarded the only passenger car. The old man who came around to take our tickets recognized Mrs. Robertson and her girls with a pleasant greeting. It trailed off as he regarded their distress. Her little daughters sat on either side of their mum, faces buried in the folds of her coat. Mrs. Robertson's arms gathered both girls close. She nodded slightly. It seemed to surprise the little man that the rest of us weren't traveling on to Newton-Stewart but stopping at Kirkcowan. I could see he wanted to ask us questions, but he didn't.

It must have been only forty minutes later when the train slowed and the conductor called out our stop. Mum and Dad, me, Grandma Cowan, Aunty Jean and her wee lad Jackie, Mrs. Robertson and her two girls could hardly keep our eyes open by the time the train rolled to a stop. All of us looked rumpled.

The stationmaster stopped short when he saw Mrs. Robertson and her girls. "Welcome ye back, Mrs. Robertson. It's good ta see ye again." His friendly smile faded to bewilderment as his gaze drifted to the rest of us. My dancing teacher looked like she would cry if she said a single word.

Dad stepped forward and extended his hand. "The name's James Finlay, sir, and you are?"

The little man pulled himself up straight and took my father's hand in a hearty shake. "Tam McGowen, sir, the stationmaster here for the railways."

"Thank ye, Mr. McGowen."

"Tam will be good enough."

Da smiled. "Thank you for that as well. We're from Greenock on the Clyde side. Do you know the place?"

"Aye, I do. Looks to me you've had a bit of trouble."

"The German's hit us on the sixth and kept up through the seventh. They hit us with incendiary bombs first."

"God preserve us."

"When we came to put out the fires, they sent in their machine gunners to fly in low and strafe our people." Da ran his hand through his thick brown hair, and it stood up on end, making him look even more a refugee.

The stationmaster spit on the floor. "Dirty Jerries," he said with genuine anger in his words.

"The town's a mess. We've no gas, no water, and there's rubble and bodies buried under it still to be dug up." Dad looked back at all of us; the look of anguish on his face nearly broke my heart. "The call's gone out. Get yer women and bairns to safety and haste ye back to repair the damage. Dolly Robertson has a sister here, so here we are."

I watched the emotions play across the stationmaster's face as my dad described what we'd been through. Mr. McGowen was in his middle years like my father. His kind eyes darted from Da to rest on each of us. I saw sympathy at first then outrage at the Germans. He looked away and cleared his throat.

"Willy," he shouted. A lad of about my age appeared from the small station office. "Get on your bicycle and ride down to the postmaster. Tell Mr. Scott to bring his lorry and come here as quick as possible."

He stopped the boy before the lad could turn away. "Then go to every house in the village and ask who would have an extra bed or settee for our friends. I ken you were listening, so you tell them what you heard, aye?"

The boy's eyes met mine, and there was a kind of awe in them. I suppose it's as close as he'd come to the war down here. It made me feel envious but oddly proud too.

Mr. Tam turned to my mum. "Would you ladies like to come into my office? I'll heat some water and get ye some soap and towels. I expect you'd like to freshen up a bit."

"Thank ye, sir. You must be a married man to think of that."

"Aye, missus, and three daughters as well."

He led the way to his cozy office and brought in a box of unclaimed clothing that people had left on the train. "I expect you might need some sweaters and coats. Evening looks to be chilly." I wiggled into a sweater and hugged myself. I hadn't realized how cold I was.

By the time we were presentable, the postmaster was there with his truck. We all piled into the bed except for Grandma, who sat in the cab with Mr. Scott. The first stop was at Dolly Robertson's sister.

Word had already spread through the village. Her sister was waiting on her doorstep. Tears streaked her cheeks when she caught sight of my dancing teacher and her girls. The next stop found a place for Aunty Jean with wee Jackie. Jean looked back at my mom.

"Go ahead, Jeannie. I'll take guid care of our mam." Aunty Jean nodded. She looked as if she could sleep standing up if wee Jackie would let her. He was quite a handful. I found it amazing he still had enough energy to bounce around his mum.

Then it was our turn. Mr. Scott drove us all to his own house. Before we left, Dad asked the stationmaster about the next train back to Greenock. It wasn't till morning so Da took the settee. Grandma, Mom, and I crowded into a tiny downstairs bedroom. Mum and Grandma Cowan slept in a small bed, and I slept on the floor cocooned in a pile of quilts. I could hear snoring from the bed within a few minutes, but I lay trying not to cry. I began to pray but stopped. No words were big enough to say thank you for saving the lives of the people I loved.

Then I remembered Grandma saying. "He's our Chieftain. And He's calling us to battle." I steeled my heart and whispered, "I want to be ready when you need me." I closed my eyes and felt sleep take me away.

Wendy—Seattle
September 1968

I'D BEEN WORKING on my English lit when my mum came into my room. She looked at the books spread across my bed. "Why don't you take a break? Take a walk over to Westwood Village Cleaners and pick up your sweater."

When I hesitated, she added, "Come on, it'll do you good."

She was right. I did feel much better taking a break from my studies. Our house stood as a boundary between rural South King County and the Seattle city limits. We sat on a quarter-acre lot with trees behind us and commerce to one side. The Roxbury

Bowling Alley parking lot was our next-door neighbor. Across the street from that was a newly built Larry's Market and the Marketime drug store, but on the other side it was all older houses on large lots.

I walked past the businesses and crossed the main avenue. Now I was in the city of Seattle. The dry cleaner was only a quarter-of-a-mile north on the other side of a small city park. I followed the gravel path, wandering in and out of landscaping and sparsely planted trees. There were grassy glades and playground equipment full of squealing children. My mind drifted to my classes and the new job I'd started in the humanities admin building.

It's funny how one small thing can rob you of your peace. Halfway through the park, I felt an odd prickling at the nape of my neck. The park was full of people, but no one was looking my way.

After picking up the sweater, I bought a pop and sat on a bench enjoying the warm sun. The third time I glanced over my shoulder, it dawned on me that I was feeling that same odd tingling on my neck. I remembered I'd felt it last at the Highland Games and years ago when Fred followed me after we broke up.

Fred had been home from college all summer. God, I hoped he wasn't up to his old ways. I went home through one of the neighborhoods bordering the park, trying to look casual as I glanced around.

Was I being foolish? I wasn't sure, but I was a lot happier when I climbed my front steps.

The phone rang as I entered my front door. A familiar voice said, "Hello?"

"Fred?" I knew it. He must be up to his old tricks.

"Yup. I was wondering if—"

"Why are you following me?"

"What? I'm not."

"I don't believe you." Heat flooded through me.

"I didn't call to talk to you." He sounded truly insulted. "Can I speak with your mom?"

"No."

"Come on. I need to talk to her."

"Why?"

"It's not about you."

"Well, if you want to speak to her, you'll have to go through me."

I heard him sigh. "Look, I'm headed back to college, and I'll be taking a psych class this fall." He sounded almost condescending, like talking to a child. "The syllabus says I'll need to interview someone who has experienced the paranormal." He paused. "You know, sixth sense."

I was silent.

"I remembered one of your mom's stories and, well, thought I could use an interview with her as extra credit." That approach didn't sit right with my temper. I wasn't a child falling for one of his schemes.

I hung up, adding to myself, "Not on your life, buddy. Never again."

I found Mom hanging laundry on the line in the backyard.

"I heard the phone ring," she said. "You sounded angry."

"You could hear that all the way out here? It was Fred. He said he wants to interview you about your second sight for a psych class that touches on the paranormal."

She gave me a wry, sideways look. I remembered her warning me not to talk about the Sight. Some people are obsessed with the supernatural. And some look at you like you just grew a set of horns.

She put the last clothespin on Dad's shirt. "If Fred were following you again, I could see why you're angry, but if you really think that, why not tell him?"

I rubbed my shoulders, feeling frustrated and a little embarrassed that I had told him but then refused to listen to what he said. "I get this prickly feeling on the back of my neck." I reached up, touching just where that feeling came. "It's creepy. And fear— fear makes me angry."

"Come on." She left her empty basket on the grass and sat on the back steps, patting the place at her side. I sank down next to her. "I don't know that I think he'd follow you. Maybe I'll give him a call and find out."

"No, Mum." *That would be embarrassing.*

"But you need to find out for sure before you accuse him of something he didn't do."

Not what I wanted to hear. "I thought you'd be as mad as I am."

When she looked me in the eye, her gaze was intense. "I'm not saying I wouldn't be mad that someone might be following you." Mum paused and pressed her lips together as if trying to think what she wanted to say.

Interrupting her before she could get started, I asked, "Can we talk about this later?"

Her face softened. "Sure."

"Please, can you tell me about your first life? Where were you?"

Wartime was a good place for me to hide from my own feelings. I laid my head on her shoulder and listened.

Chapter Thirteen

Christine—Southwest Scotland
May 1941

I came awake, inhaling the heavenly scent of frying sausages. Only a day since we'd heard the all-clear siren, and now I was a refugee. The newsreels in the cinema often showed long lines of families escaping advancing German troops with only the clothes on their backs and what they could carry.

Like the refugees in Europe, I'd slept in what I was wearing. I only had one change of clothes and the tap shoes in my shopping bag. Mum would probably say, "Well, at least you don't have to hunt for something to wear." I quietly folded my blankets and followed that wonderful smell. I tiptoed past my father, who was still asleep on the settee. A faded quilt was pulled up over his face, but his dark hair stuck out in all directions. I could hear the muffled sounds of snoring, and it made me smile.

Mrs. Scott, a well-padded bundle of comfort, welcomed me to her round kitchen table and plunked a plate of sausages, eggs, and baked beans in front of me. She didn't ask questions or remind me of our losses. Her attention was all on her cooking, leaving me to savor every bite in blissful silence until Mum and Grandma Cowan came to table.

Then the three of them chatted over tea like old friends. It amazed me how much better things look when your stomach is full. I was finishing when my dad walked into the kitchen, his eyes still hooded from sleep. He took a seat next to me.

A rap at the kitchen door, and Mr. Tam called out, "It's me, Effy."

"Right, Tam, come in and break your fast wi' us."

"Don't mind if I do and thank ye for your hospitality."

She chuckled. "I know for a fact yer Mary is a wonderful cook. So, this must be yer second breakfast."

Mr. Scott came into the now crowded kitchen. He kissed his wife on the forehead and said to Mr. Tam, "At least leave me somethin' ta eat, ye wee gnome."

Mr. Tam winked, his mouth already full of sausages.

I counted three large mouthfuls before the skinny little stationmaster told us he'd managed to get permission for us all to stay at Kirkchrist Farmhouse.

Mr. Tam said with pride, "My father was the overseer when the old laird was alive. Now the young one lives in Edinburgh, but he has me look after the place, see to any repairs and such. The big house has ner been let out, but the farmhouse has seen several tenants over the years. I got a telegram off last night." He held a cable in his hand, waving it as proof. "This morn he sent his reply."

"Thank ye, Tam." My dad looked so grateful.

He assured my da, "Have nae worries. We'll see your family settled there this very day."

I knew Da would leave this morning. We were all safe, but he was going back to Greenock. It wasn't fair. How could they make him return? But as I watched him over my steaming cup of tea, I knew he'd go back even if they did not order him. That's who he was.

He was ready to leave. I could see it in his eyes. He finished his tea and thanked our hostess for her hospitality. Then he rose to follow Mr. Tam.

Mum looked as worried as I felt, but she smiled as she crossed the room to say her goodbyes. Then it was my turn. I went to him, trying to hold back tears. But he surprised me with a fierce hug.

I was afraid, afraid the Germans would come back and bomb Greenock again. I held him tight, but he pulled my hands off his shoulders and held them for a minute.

He didn't wipe my tears or even scold me for crying. He just said, "Chrissy, you must be strong for yer mum and grandma."

He stared at me hard like he wanted to make sure I would do what he said. But I couldn't speak. I knew my voice would quiver if I tried, so I nodded. For an instant he gave me such a tender smile. Then he went out the door.

I stood staring at the closed door, willing this to be a bad dream. I jumped a little when Mum slipped her arm around me and gave me a sideways squeeze. "Don't think of all that might happen to him." I stared into my mum's face. Her blue eyes were red-rimmed. "Ye must think of all we've come through and believe he'll be safe now as well."

I straightened my back and gave Mum's hand a pat. "I know," was all I could say with a steady voice.

Right after our lunch, Mr. Scott took us to the farmhouse in his truck. Grandma sat up front in the cab. Mum and I sat on the empty bed. I felt my spirits lift as the fresh air whipped through my hair. I could see Mum wasn't as thrilled to have such a grand view of the countryside, bumping along in the back of a truck.

Kirkcowan was an ancient-looking place with only one street. The little grey stone houses butted right up next to each other, their doorsteps on the edge of the walkway.

Like home, the street was all uneven cobblestones. Flower boxes were already blooming with color, and several of the doors stood open as if ready to welcome any passerby. A wee girl sat on her step and waved at us with a shy smile. I waved back and shared my first genuine smile in days.

The land here wasn't as flat as I'd imagined the lowlands to be. There were low, rolling grassy hills dotted with sheep. And on the top of one hill stood a circle of forest with a stony dyke surrounding it. Those low stone fences were made from the rocks picked out of the pastures. I'd seen the same thing as we'd traveled down on the train. Is that a special place? I wondered. Like a fairy circle? I'd ask someone as soon as I could.

We must have driven at least a mile out of the village. It was all farms and pasturelands. The road we turned on was a narrow lane. Brambles thrived on each side of the hard-packed dirt road, and tall trees arched their branches to make a beautiful green canopy over the truck. The sun peeped through the leaves to dance on my face. It's so beautiful, I thought. Maybe staying here won't be so bad. Then we turned off the road and jolted down a rough drive.

From the cab of the truck, I heard Mr. Scott say to Grandma, "The big house is doon the next drive. There's nae one there the now and nae likely to be. The owner doesna come much."

"You said they rented the farmhouse?" Grandma asked.

"Aye, mam. It's another matter. The last family to live at the farm were some years ago, and they moved to Glasgow ta work in a factory."

I could hear the disdain in Mr. Scott's voice. But when I looked through the back window of the cab, he was smiling again as he said, "So both the manor and the farmhouse have been empty for some time."

I craned my neck to see if I could glimpse the manor house, but there was a thick copse of trees surrounding it. I could only see the top of the roof with all its chimney stacks.

The truck bounced over the rutted drive, and I settled myself so I wouldn't fall. Stony fences surrounded green fields. Mr. Scott was saying, "The owner lets the land out to surrounding farms for grazing. Mostly sheep but some cattle as well."

His old truck gave one last shiver as we pulled into the dooryard where the drive ended in a wide turnabout in front of the farmhouse door. I wrinkled my nose at the smell of manure drifting in from the fields. It wasn't at all like the well-kept village cottages, no flower boxes here. It had a feeling of abandonment. The farmhouse was a long, low whitish stone building that hadn't seen a coat of paint for some time. Green shutters hung askew, but at least all the windows were in place and the door stood stout against the elements.

I can't say why, but I liked the place straight off. I think this first sight of where we would stay turned my heart from the horrors of the air raid shelter and the Blitz to what adventures I might have ahead. I jumped down and gave Mum a hand as Mr. Scott helped Grandma out.

I think Mum caught my growing excitement. "Och and isn't it lovely?" she said to Mr. Scott.

He'd already stepped forward and opened the door. He nodded for us to come inside. "There's no key. No need for one, aye? But there's a good stout bolt if you'd feel safer at night. I ken things are different in the big city."

I put my hand over my mouth to stifle a giggle. Greenock isna a big city. Mum shot me a sharp look that said to mind my manners.

As I stepped through the door of Kirkchrist Farmhouse, I felt welcomed. Like the house needed people to take care of it.

Cobwebs hung from the rafters. It was very basic, one large room with a big fireplace on one side, and at that end stood what must have passed for a kitchen—an old woodstove, a counter with a large sink fitted with an ancient-looking cast-iron pump handle. Not so different from Grandma's sink. I looked her direction and smiled. Mr. Scott sounded apologetic as he said, "There's no electric or gas here."

But Grandma broke in, "Just the way I like it. Candles or lamps are cozier."

He smiled in relief. "I know the chimney has a good draw, and there's wood in the shed out back for the cooker." Walking toward the kitchen sink, he gave the handle several good pumps and water poured out. "You'll find no water finer than ours in all of Wigtownshire."

He led us down a short hall to show us three good-sized bedrooms and one tiny room. "Room for all of you and your sister and her wee bairn." Opening the back door at the end of the short hall, he gave us a peek at the yard behind the house, adding with a sheepish smile, "You'll find the necessary back here."

I peeked out the back and saw an outhouse about thirty feet from the door. Oh my goodness, I thought. How am I to get up in the cold, dark night to find the loo across the yard? I felt a little dismay at our new circumstances. But Mr. Scott was walking back to the main room, and we all followed. He was silent for a moment, regarding the dust motes floating in the air. For the first time, I saw this kind man look doubtful. "It will take a guid cleaning and no mistake, but it'll be large enough for all of you."

My mum smiled as if it were a suite at the Royal Hotel. "It will do very nicely. I thank you for yer help." She looked around her as if just realizing. "Do you think I might borrow a broom and dust-pan, and maybe some rags and a—"

Noise coming from outside stopped her mid-sentence. I ran to the still-open door. A group of people was coming down the drive. I could see they carried brooms and mops, buckets, and baskets. My throat clogged with gratitude. "Come see," was all I could say.

"Hello, the house," called a man I'd never seen. He carried a basket with peat for the fire. "This is my wife Jenny, and I be Rob."

My mum's smile broadened. "Welcome. Come in all of you and thank you." And they did. With them came mops and brooms, curtains, and food. Tam McGowen drove an old truck piled with odds and ends of furniture.

As soon as he stopped, people began unloading it. Mr. McGowen carried in two straight-back chairs and set them in front of Mum. "I promised yer man we'd see ye well settled, and that we will."

Mum put her hand over her mouth, and I thought she might start crying. Her big blue eyes swam in tears, but she nodded her thanks and said, "God bless you, Mr. McGowen."

He said nothing back, but he patted her shoulder as he turned to get more chairs.

Someone settled Grandma Cowan into a comfortable rocker and handed her a wee thermos of tea. Grandma looked a bit confused at all the activity, but I could tell she was enjoying herself by the smile that never left her face.

People came and shook Mum's hands, introducing themselves. They laughed and talked and set to work.

I turned around in that big empty room as it filled with people. Life filled every corner. All the smiling faces floated past me. Several ladies patted my back in friendship. Someone stuck a scone in my hand then went off to clean the small kitchen and fill the cupboards with plates and food stores. It was all too much to take in.

The room became one large blur, and I realized my dismay had vanished. I didn't feel so much like one of those refugees in the newsreels at the cinema. We were welcome here.

A girl of about my age with wild, curly blonde hair approached me. I focused on what she was saying.

"Hello, A'm Moddy. A'm ta help you get settled. But I ken we'll be friends." Her smile was infectious. She reached for my hand and pulled me along. "Let's find yer bedroom, and we'll work there first."

She led me past all the open doors to the small room at the back. "There now, this room looks like a good place, aye?"

I nodded, and Moddy stuck a broom in my hand. "You sweep the floor, and I'll go find a dustpan." We worked like that until I felt at home in my new room, and I put aside the shock of what we'd come through. I was just Chrissy again.

Fascinated because our lives were so different, we talked nonstop. She brought curtains, and we hung them on my window. I threw up the sash and looked out at an empty field. Past the trees, I could see the roof and attic floor of the main house. "Mr. Tam said no one lives there?"

"What, in Kirkchrist? No one the now. They don't come there much, at any rate. It's haunted ye ken."

"Why?" I pulled back as if her words had hit me. "Is this place haunted too?"

"Not this place." She shook her head at the thought. "Only self-respecting farmers ever lived here. I know some stories about the big house, but not all of them. Way back, there was a monastery right on the spot. When the borderlands turned to the Presbyterians, and the English throne wasna Catholic, lairds sent night reivers driving out those still Popish." I know I looked puzzled because she added, "Raiders, ye ken? Bands of men burnt the place ta the ground, wi' the monks and their dogs still inside."

"That's horrible."

"Oh, aye. My da says you can sometimes hear their dogs howl when the mist lies on the fields like smoke from a fire." She laughed.

"Oh, you were only teasing me." Relief washed over me, but it vanished an instant later.

"Nae then, I was laughin' at how big yer eyes were."

"So the dogs haunt it?"

"Not the house. But what I said is true enough. In the house, a wee lass walks the halls crying."

"Who is she?"

"No one knows. And I expect no one ever will."

I leaned out the window again. "Is it named Kirkchrist for the monks?"

"Nae, the laird who built it had the name carved above the door, along with, 'As for me and my house, we will serve God.' It canna be an evil ghost with that above the door."

I smiled at her reasoning and felt sorry for the little girl who walked the empty halls of the big house. "No, not an evil ghost."

Wendy —Seattle
September 1968

I could picture the low ground fog covering the farmlands of Kirkcowan. It must have been an eerie sight. I turned to Mum. "Did you ever hear the hounds baying?"

She smiled at my reaction. "Spooky, right? I never heard the hounds, but I saw the little girl in action."

As much as I wanted to hear about my mum's life, I knew I'd never be as brave as she was. Still, I was fascinated. "Go on, tell me."

Mum sighed. "There's so much to say about Kirkcowan." She looked out across the backyard to the trees beyond our land, but I thought she was seeing Kirkchrist. Her voice had a dreamy quality. "That summer changed my life."

Chapter Fourteen

Christine—Kirkcowan, Scotland
1941

They say Highland hospitality has no equal, but the lowland people of Kirkcowan welcomed us into their small community as family. That deserted old farmhouse now stood full of homey touches. The villagers provided everything we needed.

The greatest gift was mine. Moddy's friendship was a breath of fresh air. She gave me back my childhood for a time. She didn't leave that first day until she'd settled my wee room.

Saturday morning, she rapped on our door. When I opened it, Moddy stood there holding two chickens upside down by their feet and thrust the flopping feathered bodies toward me. I stepped back and called for my mum to come. Moddy was undaunted. "Di ye no keep hens in the city?"

I shook my head doubtfully.

Mum put a hand on my shoulder and said, "Oh my."

Moddy's grin was ear to ear. "They're twa of me mither's best layers." When we said nothing, she added, "I spied an empty coop out back."

She looked from my face to my mum's, and her smile broadened with delight. "Fresh eggs every morning, ye ken? And there's nothin' to it. Chickens are gay easy to care for."

Relief washed over me, and she laughed again. "Ye didn't think I meant you to eat them?" She shook her head. "My mum would be fair fit ta be tied if ye ate her birds."

I laughed with her. This was so far from what we were used to at home everything—even chickens—turned into an adventure.

Sunday night, Moddy asked me if I was still at school in Greenock. I answered doubtfully. "My school is just doon the street, so I ken for sure it's still there." I hesitated. "Or at least it was there when I left." I could hear a tremble in my words. "It's called Highlanders Academy, and it's a bonnie big place."

"I expect yer like us," she said. "We still have our term till late June."

I nodded, thinking we might not be back in Greenock till long past that.

Moddy said, "Right then, you'll come wi' me and finish your year at the village school." Before she left for the day, Moddy had it all arranged.

On Monday morning, she was at my door ready to walk me to the one-room village schoolhouse. It wasn't as old as the Highlanders Academy, but it had lots of windows and held all Kirkcowan's twenty children.

We walked to the village together every morning for class. Those were the best times. Moddy had a sort of inner light. She was always smiling. I don't think I'd ever known anyone who laughed as much. And she was game for any new adventure. I thought I'd miss my friends at home, but I didn't think about anything sad when she was around.

Miss Third was our teacher. She taught everyone, all of us together at once, first year through graduation. She'd even sent several of her students to university. She didn't seem very old either, well, at least younger than Aunty Jean, who was my mum's youngest sister. Miss Third wore her plain brown hair pulled back in a severe bun at the nape of her neck. She looked strict, but that was only at first. She wasn't at all like the profs at the Highlanders Academy. She made me feel special, and she made learning so much fun we forgot about our different ages and abilities. She engaged us all.

I knew she'd been told everything about us refugees, but she never asked. Miss Third treated me as if I'd been one of her students since I was a wee village bairn. She took an interest in me but only asked about the things I liked to do. Soon she was incorporating drawing, sewing, and putting wee plays into her lessons.

Miss Third said that people called Kirkcowan "the village that time forgot." A fanciful thought, but I can well see how it got its nickname. It was so isolated from the world outside. I knew the war went on. Da came down on the train most weekends and with him came the reality we'd left. News of what was happening reminded me that this rest from the world was only temporary, and I should treasure every minute.

Moddy had a big brother not but a year or two older. Eddie was so handsome with his blond hair, blue eyes, and dimples but very shy. My heart ached for their family. I knew he'd be leaving in a few years to go to war. There were other lads of an age in the village. Soon enough, the war would be a reality to them all. It saddened me, so I tried not to think on it.

Instead of worrying what the future held, I concentrated on what I could do now. Moddy became my cohort as I organized little shows and musicals for the villagers. Thanks to her, there wasn't an old sheet or extra bit of fabric left in Kirkcowan. We begged the village women for any scrap of fabric as we worked together to make costumes for our productions.

Miss Third gave us the idea of raising money to help with the war effort. Soon Moddy and I spent all our time working on scripts that would incorporate even the smallest village bairn.

Together we wrote stories about fairies and how they interfered with the lives of the farmers. Then we decided where to add songs and dances to our scripts.

Moddy assured me, "Fairies love a guid dance. My mum says you can hear them sing when the wind moves through the trees."

We set up a wee stage in the grass field next to the school. The entire village came to see us perform. Kirkcowan had a reputation for having musical talent, and we often had instrumental accompaniments from musically gifted villagers.

We set out a large jar marked donations to help build Spitfires for the Royal Air Force, or RAF. People in small places like Kirkcowan didn't have a lot of money, but they were very generous. A military commander visiting family in the village saw one of our productions. He asked me afterward if we would be a part of a troop show. Mum said he probably wasn't serious, but it made me glow at the thought of his compliment. Still, in Kirkcowan, the village that time forgot, the war seemed distant.

Then one afternoon the war came crashing in again. Mum came home from the market with news. A group of orphans was coming to stay at the big house, Kirkchrist.

She volunteered us to get the house ready. I'd told Mum about the little girl said to haunt the house, and she proclaimed it ridiculous. She insisted I come help.

It was my first time inside Kirkchrist, and my imagination was full of what it must have looked like long ago. To me it was a magical place. I know it sounds silly, but even with the tales of the lassie who walked the halls crying on some nights, I loved the time I spent there. In my mind's eye I could see how it must have been long years ago when it was new and hosted parties.

Tall ceilings gave every room the feeling of grandness. The main salon was clearly intended for parties and dancing. To one side, a long dining room with a giant table waited to be filled with dinner guests.

They had covered the furnishings with sheets to protect them from dust. We went from room to room gathering up the sheets for washing. Under them sat leather chairs and tapestry settees. Mum stuffed a small flask of oil and soft cloth into my hands, nodding toward the ornately carved woodwork. I polished everything till it gleamed.

The main staircase had a beautiful wooden banister leading up to the second floor. And there were narrow stairs back by the kitchen, I expect for the servants to use.

At the foot of the back stairs I paused, looking up into the shadows on the second-floor landing. I suddenly felt a presence. Something in me reached out to the ghost of the wee lass. I could feel her sadness but not just that. She was curious and mischievous too.

It was silly, fanciful, not something I'd ever admit, especially not to Mum. But I whispered into the space above, "I ken yer there, but I'm not afraid." And it was true. I wasn't afraid of her. If you could feel a smile, I think I did just then. And I knew there was peace between us.

Mum and I had started with the main floor and by the end of the week the church sent ahead two young nuns to ready the old house for the children. I hadn't been in the company of Holy Sisters before. Their black gowns and headdresses made them look austere, but that was only at first. These ladies were friendly and hardworking.

One evening after we'd worked all day, we were sitting around the table in the large manse kitchen. I looked up, nodding toward the brass bells around the top of the kitchen walls. "What are all those bells for?"

One of the nuns said, "At one time the upstairs guests used those bells to call downstairs to the servants." She pointed to the faded labels denoting which room was ringing. "The lady of the house would pull a cord, and her maid would come."

The nuns were chatting, and I heard one say there were nearly thirty children coming to this house. The younger, Sister Marie

Jean, said, "Most of them lost their parents in the war. Some were lucky enough to make it out of occupied countries. All of them suffered great loss at the hands of the Nazis."

Mum asked, "Are they all Catholic then?"

"Some are Polish Catholic, aye, but many are Jewish. And there are many who lost their families in the London Blitz."

"Och," I said. "That's sae sad."

A single bell rang. Mum gave me a pointed look. I knew she was thinking of my story about the ghostly lass. She turned to the ladies. "Mice, I expect. All old houses have them."

Another bell rang from a wall across the room. Well, even that could be mice. But I thought it was fair odd. They must have too, because they stopped talking, and a look passed between the women. Mum said, "Perhaps we should get some traps before the children come." The ladies both agreed and went back to chatting.

For one breathtaking minute, all the bells rang at once. We sat there looking at each other, our eyes round in surprise. Sister Marie Jean crossed herself. The bells stopped as suddenly as they'd begun. "Should we get a cat as well?" she said.

Mum assured them she'd ask in the village. Then she gave me one of those looks that says, "I know what you're thinking, but don't you dare say a word." I didn't. After all, the wee lass had been alone for a long time. I didn't think she'd bother those sad children much.

Later I heard she stole underwear. The nuns said they were always missing underclothing. They were quite cross about it and had their suspicions it might be one or another of the children. I like to think the lass was playing, making a bit of mischief.

Wendy—Seattle
1968

We were still sitting on the back steps. I was picturing my

mother's memories in my mind's eye. "It must have been really frightening when all the bells rang at once."

She smiled. "It was but even more so when they all stopped ringing abruptly." A soft wind came up and blew black curls across her eyes.

"I'll bet you weren't that frightened. You never seem really worried about the second sight stuff that's happened over the years."

She laughed. "I learned early on I'd drive myself crazy if I worried about the Sight."

Ever since we'd moved into this house, things had happened. We'd get up in the night and find the rocking chair rocking away on its own. Sometimes the pole lamp was on next to the chair like a ghost had sat down to read. But that's not all. I thought for a minute and asked, "Didn't you want to know why the little girl ghost walked and cried?"

I expected her answer.

"No, if God wants you to know why unexplained things happen, He'll tell you." That was something she'd often said to me over the years.

I thought about all the hype about the sixth sense and ESP. Articles and TV shows explored the paranormal. "That's not the way people look at it here."

She patted my hand. "I know, luv."

"Kirkcowan sounds like another world."

Something about that summer still made her look sad, and she said, "Sometimes the war had a way of dropping in on you."

I cocked my head to look at her. "What do you mean?"

Christine—Kirkcowan, Scotland
End of Summer 1941

WHEN DA CAME DOWN for the weekend, he'd catch us up on all the news. I knew he glossed over the details and gave us as few facts as possible.

He described how our new prime minister Winston Churchill was as defiant and bold as ever. Churchill started making a hand sign, spreading his two fingers into a vee and saying, "V for victory." It took off like wildfire. We needed Churchill's words like, "Victory at all costs." He rallied the country to fight on. His brave defiance carried us through some very bleak news.

After the fall of France the year before, Great Britain stood against the full force of the German war machine. Only Hitler's preoccupation with Russia gave us hope. Hitler told his generals: "We have only to kick in the front door and the whole rotten Russian edifice will come tumbling down." But the Russians were fierce fighters. Hitler slowed his air strikes against us while his attention was on his eastern front.

Without the constant barrage of world news, we savored simple pleasures. We all settled into our new life at Kirkchrist Farmhouse. Grandma was getting stronger in the country air. And with the constant fear of being bombed lifted, my mum looked years younger.

The time Da spent restoring Greenock after the Blitz took its toll on him. He still looked tired when he arrived, but as the weekend progressed, he relaxed. And we all slept well. What a luxury that was. On one of his trips down, he brought my bicycle. I jumped on and rode down the long drive with a whoop as the wind rushed through my hair. Now Moddy and I could ride our bicycles all about the countryside.

Summer wore on. The brambles near the road took off. They sported small juicy berries. One afternoon my mum handed me a bowl. "Go ye doon to the road and pick us some berries for a pie."

"Pie? Is Da coming?"

Her face glowed with pleasure. "He'll be here on the late train."

I was peddling down the drive with a bowl in my basket in no time at all. The brambles grew thick along the country road bordering our fields. I set my bicycle down and began picking. It was a warm, late summer afternoon. My aunt and wee Jackie were in the village shopping. Mum and Grandma were alone at the farmhouse. My thoughts drifted to the way Moddy's older brother smiled at me.

The trees on either side of the road formed a green canopy, allowing the sun to peek through. I looked away from berry gathering when movement from above caught my eyes. But instead of a bird or a wee furry beast, something white and puffy like a big cloud floated past the sun. I stepped into a clear spot, squinting into the sky to get a better look.

My heart pounded. Thoughts swirled around my head as I remembered Da reading about the German paratroopers who took over parts of Norway. The bowl slid from my fingers, spilling berries around my feet.

White parachutes dotted the sky. Men were landing in the open fields. My legs wobbled, and I tried to catch my breath. Lord Haw Haw was always threatening an invasion. Could this be it?

A pair of legs plunged through the trees on the edge of the road. I covered my mouth to keep from screaming as a soldier crashed through the leafy canopy and landed hard. He was facing away from me, not over six feet up the road.

I heard his breath explode with the impact, but he rolled to his feet and slid his rifle off his shoulder and stood it against a tree. A swastika armband announced his nationality.

Oh God, he's German, what should I do? Then I realized. *He doesn't know I'm here.* The soldier began gathering his chute with a frenzy of motion.

I melted into the bushes, brambles scratching my skin. Mum

and Grandma Cowan were up at the house. And what about the nuns and all those children? I looked toward Kirkchrist Farm and back at the man.

How could I protect them? A whisper floated through my thoughts, and I was sure I heard the words, "You're not alone." I argued I was alone here on this country road facing down the enemy. But I felt the pressure of a hand on my back. Frozen with fear, I turned my head slowly, but no one was there. The hand didn't leave me. So, I gathered my courage and looked for something to stop the German before he hurt my family.

His rifle stood only three feet from me. With two large steps, I reached out to grab his gun. *How do I shoot?* I recalled the self-defense classes at the Y. They said trust your training. The gun swung into my arms, my thumb releasing the safety to shoot. I lifted the bolt and slid it back. The noise announced my intention.

He spun, reaching for his weapon but grabbing at empty air. I stepped back a foot to see that he was as frightened as I. His face was drained of color and clearly panicked.

So, this is what a German looks like. He's not even a man, only a scared lad, not a monster. But I'm the one who stands between him and my family.

I pushed the bolt forward and pulled it down, bringing the round into the chamber. He threw up his hands but didn't lunge or grab for the gun. My finger was on the trigger. *Lord, can I end his life before he takes what's dear to me?*

"Blimey, stop. I'm not a German." His eyes were so large the white showed all around the pupils. "Awright geeezzaa! I'm on yaaahr side. I'm English. Name's Herbert Brown." He put his hands up higher. "It's a trainin' exercise, see. Ye can't blow me brains out before I even make it ta the front."

"How do I know you're not German?" My voice sounded shaky.

"Blimey, luv, do I sound German? I'm from Cheapside. I've never been farther north than York in my life afore now."

He looked like he might cry. My face was wet, and I realized I was crying too. I ordered myself to calm down and think. *No, he doesn't sound German, but is he using an accent to fool me?* I had to be sure. I steadied my voice. "Tell me something a German wouldn't know."

He looked confused and finally said, "I can buy a stick of Edinburgh rock candy for a ha'penny back home, and it melts in yer mouth. A fair treat."

Well, true enough and not something a German might know. I lowered the gun a bit.

"We're playing war games is all. They said this was empty country. CoooEee. If this is what yer like in the north, I'd pity the bloke who lands here."

I started shaking.

"Peas and carrots if you'd take your finger off the trigger. My mum will kill me if I get shot before I go to war."

"My mum and grandma are at the house." It felt as if my legs wouldn't hold me up, but I believed him and lowered the gun, flipping on the safety just in front of the trigger, thankful again for the class at the Y.

He sank to his knees. "Would you mind not telling my commander what happened? I'd get a right bit of razzing about this."

I nodded and stepped forward to hand him back his gun, hesitating only a moment before letting it go. He stood and put a hand on my shoulder.

"You're a brave one. I'll give ye that. I pity the Jerries if they're daft enough to come this far north."

When we both had calmed down, he helped me gather up my berries. I blushed at his compliment, but I wasn't brave at all, only thankful that I hadn't killed the lad. I wondered, *If God is my chieftain, would He have given me courage to pull the trigger if needed? And did He give me the wisdom not to kill an innocent lad?* I relaxed as I remembered the hand on my back, and I realized I didn't have to find strength in myself alone.

Wendy—Seattle
1968

I shook my head in utter disbelief. "You went through so much. Did you ever tell anyone about the paratrooper?"

"No, never. I promised him I wouldn't. My mum would have had a heart attack if she'd known I faced down what I thought was a German paratrooper."

I wondered how she'd kept that promise all these years. And if she could do that, what other secrets had she kept? "And you never tell me to stop whining? I haven't gone through anything like you."

"This is a different time, a different country."

A cool breeze brushed past us, and I felt goosebumps rise on my bare arm. A crow cawed at us from the little woods behind our property. Mum put an arm around me and pulled me into another sideways hug. "No, your heartache is real. If you'd had a crush on John, you would have been over it long before now." Love and understanding radiated from her. "I know that."

I managed a smile. But the hairs on the back of my neck pricked up. I put a hand on her arm. "Ever feel like someone's watching you?"

"You do now?"

I nodded. We both looked toward the bowling alley parking lot next to our house. It was empty. Nothing moved through the trees behind us. She looked back at me.

"This is how you were feeling before?" I nodded again. "And you never thought it was John?"

"No, not his style and besides, he broke up with me." I didn't want to say that it gave me a bad feeling. I don't have the Sight. I never wanted the Sight. But I couldn't ignore my feeling. "No, this is unsettling. I don't know, maybe even evil."

She rose. "Let's go inside." I was expecting her to tell me I was imagining things. Instead, she locked the back door behind us, odd for this time of day. As the deadbolt clicked into place, my stomach jumped. She did believe me.

We walked down the hall to the living room, and she asked, "You figured it was Freddy?"

"He did it once before. Remember, after we broke up?"

She sounded skeptical. "He may have been an overly dramatic teenage boy, but he was never evil. And that was two years ago. Plus, he's been away at college."

"Oh." I caught her meaning. He was older, had a life, and had stopped trying to contact me. "I suppose it wouldn't be likely, would it?" I swallowed hard, remembering how I had accused him. "Maybe I owe him an apology."

"Maybe."

"So, you think I'm imagining things?"

"I didn't say that, but it likely isn't Fred's fault."

She took my hand and sat me down on the couch. "The first time I had a brush with the Sight, I thought I was going crazy."

"Was it after the Blitz?" A weight rested on my chest. Was she trying to tell me that feeling, that knowing I was being watched, might be second sight?

She looked nowhere, seeing a time long past. "It was while we were in Kirkcowan."

"Oh, that poor paratrooper."

"I know. In hindsight it was kind of funny. It wouldn't have been if I'd shot him."

I gave her another double take. "You would have shot him, really?"

"I think I would have, but what was more important, so did he."

"A lot happened to you in Kirkcowan. Start from there. I don't want to miss anything."

Chapter Fifteen

Christine—Kirkcowan, Scotland
August 1941

Scotland had new high- and low-level radar. Now we could spot planes above one-hundred feet. When the German planes learned how effective a tool this was, they took to flying very low, almost buzzing the treetops. The Jerries came in over the lowlands where they weren't as likely to fly into a mountain.

Our civil defense posted lookouts at high places across the country. The military often used ancient stone towers built hundreds of years ago. These same old towers were once used to spot enemies approaching on horseback, on foot or even by sea.

In strategic locations, the government constructed modern bunkers. Anywhere high enough to give the watchers a commanding view of the sky would do. They equipped the lookouts with phones when possible or radio equipment when not. The government trained those too old to join the military or teens too young to enlist to watch the skies for German aircraft. Sometimes our watchers were more reliable than the new radar equipment. They weren't dependent on electronics or power, only good eyesight. The only drawback was the dark. Since this was summer, we had the gloamin'—a soft light over the land, often later than midnight—increasing their effectiveness by hours of extended daylight.

Moddy and I planned to ride our bicycles up to the local watchtower where her brother Eddie was on lookout duty. I was thirteen, and he'd turned fifteen. I suppose I was only his little sister's friend, but I lived for Eddie's smiles. Mum gave me special permission to stay out late, and she packed us all a fine picnic basket that I carried on my handlebars.

We rode past farms with only the light of the moon to guide us. I was expecting a mountain, but the lookout was a high spot in the landscape, easily climbed even with our bicycles. We left the country dirt road and pushed our bicycles across a farmer's field and up a steep incline to the rise of the highest hill. An old stone tower stood at the summit. It looked like a stand-alone turret on a castle but not nearly as big. Brambles covered much of the watchtower. Underneath, the stones looked grey and as jagged as the rocks in the field we'd crossed.

I stopped at a doorless opening and peered up. This watchtower wasn't large, not a place to house armed men, but it was snug against the wind and weather, built for one man to stand guard as an early warning to the surrounding villages and farms against attack from border reivers and now from German aircraft.

My gaze wandered up the old stone walls. "This is like a place I used to visit as a child."

Moddy seemed pleased that I appreciated the old tower. "It's nae sae big, but it gi's ye a guid peek about the countryside."

The floor of this small keep was hard-packed dirt over broken flagstones. It must have been a place the sheep liked to visit in winter. At least all their leavings were old. Still, it smelled like a stable. I wrinkled my nose.

Moddy gave me a quick glance. "It's nae so bad up on the battlements."

It was circular inside and out, about eight feet across. We leaned our bicycles against the old walls, and I looked about. Stone steps curled around the walls, ending twenty feet above our heads. They were narrow and crumbly looking in places, but Moddy jogged up them without care. She stopped halfway and beckoned me to follow.

I squinted past her to where the steps led to an opening above, a hole in the battlement roof. The stone walls were thick, and even on this warm summer evening it was chilly inside.

Moddy bellowed, "Eddie! Eddie, we're here."

A voice called from above. "An if ye were any louder the Jerries will hear as they fly over."

Moddy giggled.

She waited while I started up the old steps. They were so solid beneath my feet I forgot about the drop to the floor below. Instead, I was caught up in the ancient, rugged beauty of this place. There was plenty of moonlight streaming in through the narrow slits along the walls.

I touched the old grey stone as I climbed and imagined archers shooting arrows at the attacking English through those very slits. My head was first through the opening at the top of the tower. I grabbed hold of the waist-high stone wall that circled the outer edge to steady myself as I stepped on what felt like a surprisingly sturdy wooden floor. The wind whipped my hair as I looked around the countryside below us.

This wonderful old place sent my imagination off to long-past clan wars and brave young warriors like Eddie. He was so focused on his duty; he didn't even notice when we stepped onto the battlement roof.

"Ye dolt. Ye ken I brought my friend Chrissy wi' me."

He spun around. "Aye, sure, ya wee besom, but ye didn't say it was tonight." His face was flushed. I wondered if he was mad that I'd come or embarrassed by the way Moddy spoke. I didn't have a brother, so I wasn't sure how to take their banter.

But Eddie grinned and beckoned me to his station. I tried to hide my pleasure at seeing him and only smiled back. I couldn't think of anything that wouldn't sound foolish to say.

"See here, Chrissy." He pointed to the softly lit hills. "All planes have a distinct sound. That's their motors, ye ken. Sometimes that's the first we know they're here. So, we must listen." He cocked his head this way and that, testing the air for any out-of-place sounds. It was quiet here. Even the sheep below had settled to sleep.

Eddie held up his spyglass. "My da's," he said proudly. "I've been training for two months before my birthday to spot the enemy, and my da let me use it." He put it to his eyes, scanning the sky. "I'm the first of my mates to serve up here."

"Oh, aye?" I said. "Quite an honor."

He beamed with pride, and Moddy giggled again. "But ye haven't spotted a single plane since ye started."

Eddie scowled at her. "Well, that's a guid thing, too. Unless ye mean ye want the Jerries flyin' over us. I have spotted planes. They've been all ours."

He turned toward the northeast, standing straight and tall. His attention focused on a far-off stand of trees. "Hush now, hear that? It's a plane."

I looked north too. I saw nothing, but the sound of a motor floated on the breeze toward us.

He pointed to the sky above the treetops. "Look there." A single aircraft flew low on the horizon. He followed it with his eyes for a few seconds and through the spyglass for a few more.

"It's a bloody German Heinkel." His eyes still tracked the low-flying craft as he added, "Looks like one of their He-70F2s."

Moddy rolled her eyes and whispered, "Ye ken, my lout of a brother is showing off."

Regardless of what Moddy said, I was impressed.

Eddie cranked up the radio and called in his sighting. "Aye, sir. Eddie Grant, Kirkcowan lookout. I spotted a Heinkel He-70F2, I think. Heading north toward Barrhill." He paused and rang off with, "Aye, sir, thank ye."

Afterwards he turned to us and said with a crisp nod, "Probably a reconnaissance plane. But they count, too. If we can shoot them down, they can't tell their chappies where to go, ye ken?"

I was truly interested in planes. "Tell me how you know what type it was from here."

He handed me his spyglass, and I looked toward the northeast sky as the plane grew steadily smaller.

"It has a low, sleek silhouette."

"Aye."

"And the nose juts out a bit. The pilot sits in a bubble, almost over the wing. And if he banks again, you can watch the shape of the wing; it's blunted like a flower petal."

"He's too far now." I handed Eddie back his spyglass. "I heard that reconnaissance planes can carry bombs too."

Eddie looked so much older than his fifteen years. With a tightness in my stomach, I thought, it won't be long before he's in the fighting.

He was saying, "Like as not, at least for this plane. He only has one bomb. Maybe not even that since he came this far west and south." He shook his head. "No, I think he's scouting for the Jerries, looking for guid places to bomb us. Thinks he's snuck past our defenses, but now we know where he's headed, we'll shoot him down for sure."

Moddy's voice came out of the gathering darkness. "Can we eat now?"

I was in love, at least as much as my thirteen-year-old heart could manage. It was a wonderful evening. Eddie told us about the different aircraft he'd been studying, their size and abilities. I'd always loved planes, so I was deeply interested.

Later, when we collected our bicycles to go home, Moddy said, "That was nice of you to let Eddie talk. I think it made him feel important to tell you all that rubbish."

"It's not rubbish. He may save lives doing lookout duty."

She snorted with laughter. "Oh, God, if I tell him what ye said, he'd be impossible to live wi'."

We were quiet for a bit, walking our bikes down the hill to the road. When we mounted our bikes and started peddling home, Moddy spoke again, her voice was wistful. "It's almost the end of summer. It'll be back to school soon, and I expect you'll be off ta Greenock and your Highlanders Academy. I'll miss ye, Chrissy."

"I'll miss ye, too, but we won't lose touch. We can write and—"

She chimed in, "We can spend summers together." I heard optimism creep back into her words. "Sunday there's a church picnic doone by the Bladnoch river. Would ye like ta come along?"

Fear and dread settled on me like a blanket. My heart raced, and my legs went weak. *What is wrong with me? I'm not in danger. We're safe here in Kirkcowan.* I slowed and dropped behind Moddy, wondering where this intense fear was coming from.

A voice floated to me on the wind like a chilly breeze rustling dry leaves. It whispered, "If she goes to the picnic, she won't come home."

I slowed my peddling and listened. All was quiet on this warm August night. There was no longer a breeze. No leaves rustled on trees. Only open fields bordered this part of the road.

Then it came again. This time it was the sound of a strong wind. I stopped my bicycle and squeezed my eyes closed as a voice roared in my ears. "Moddy won't come home."

She rolled on for a few feet and stopped to call back at me. "Something wrong?"

"You can't go to the picnic. You can't." Tears pricked my eyes, and I was glad for the dim light. "I have a terrible feeling about it.

Please, I know it sounds dafty, but don't go, please. You'll—" I could barely breathe. "You'll die."

I could barely see her vexed expression. I didn't know whether she thought I was being dramatic or I'd gone crazy. I didn't know either.

She hesitated then said, "You don't really think that do you?"

"I'm afraid for you."

"I'll promise to be careful, but Chrissy, I really want to go." There was a firmness in her voice.

No, no, no, my inner voice railed. I took a deep breath, trying to settle myself.

She encouraged me. "Why don't you come wi' me? Ye can keep an eye on me that way."

I didn't want to go. The fear was overpowering. I couldn't tell if I was afraid for myself or just for Moddy. I bit my lip. "Aye." I couldn't let her go alone and implored, "Think on it first. Please."

Her words came at me out of the gathering darkness, flat and cheerless. "Aye, I promise."

MY DAD WAS DOWN for a weekend visit. At dinner on Saturday night, he said, "I put new glass in your window, and you'll be happy to know your wee rose is still in place and doing well."

"You've been watering it?"

Mum looked at me and beamed with pleasure. Dad said, "Sometimes it's the wee things that encourage us the most. I have ta say it pleased me, my girls planting a rose in yon Hitler's bombshell."

I hugged my dad, and he patted my back. "That's all right, pet. I'm just happy you don't think yer auld Da's dafty."

His words brought back my dread for Moddy. I'd been able to push my anxiety away while Dad was with us. I hadn't spoken to her since our bike ride to the lookout, and tomorrow was her church picnic. My stomach clenched into a knot. I prayed. Lord, tell her not to go, please. But I knew she would go.

Sunday morning, we saw my da back to the station. Afterward, I rode my bicycle to the place on the Bladnoch river for the church picnic. It made sense. This way there might be something I could do to protect her. There must be a reason I felt so terrible. Since Da's words the night before, the dread had grown by the minute. I'd slept very little. I couldn't eat more than a bite before my stomach churned.

I must have looked like the witch in the "Wizard of Oz" flying down the road on my bicycle with a scowl on my face. I couldn't help noticing the beautiful day. Hot, not a cloud in the blue sky. I took the country road from town that led right up to a flat open space next to the river. The Bladnoch was wide and rolled quickly past the trees that lined both banks. I realized I could see the chimneys of Kirkchrist House far off on the other side of the river.

I scanned the crowd for my friend. Maybe twenty or thirty villagers laughed and visited together. Children were playing, women sat in clusters talking, and the men were on the grass field completely involved in a game of football. Everyone was having a good time. Sunlight danced through the leaves of the shade trees, and a soft breeze followed the path of the river. I saw Moddy's mum, and she waved me over to her blanket. "Chrissy, come have some lunch."

I stopped at Mrs. Grant's blanket. "Thank ye, but I was wondering where's Moddy?"

Mrs. Grant sat up straighter and looked around. "I don't know, luv. Could be she's down wi' the bairns sailing their boats in the shallows." She pointed down the shore to a place where the land formed a small inlet.

I could see Moddy's blonde curly head bobbing about as she chased children. There were whoops of laughter and lots of splashing water.

"Oh, aye. Thank ye, mam." Despite the feeling of oppression, I couldn't help but smile. You would think Moddy was six the way she was carrying on, completely lost in the joy of playing.

My eye caught sight of a lad separate from the others. He was reaching for his boat before it sailed toward deeper waters. As the wee boat moved farther out, he did as well. His hand extended, trying to catch it before the river's current swept it away.

Fear seized me, and I dropped my bike and ran in their direction. That was when Moddy glanced up and made eye contact with me. I yelled and pointed to the boy. "Moddy, look, the lad in the water."

She whirled just as the wee boy lost his balance and fell face first into the river. Moddy was closest and dove in after him.

I shrieked as I ran, "Help, help, in the water," and pointed to the place I'd last seen her.

Moddy's head surfaced. She had the lad in tow. Everyone started running to the water's edge. Women pulled the other children out of the shallows. Men were behind them, having run from the playing field. As soon as the first man arrived, he was wading into the river to grab Moddy and the boy.

I was closer now, running along the bank, trying to keep my eyes on Moddy. Her face was a study in concentrated effort. She was an excellent swimmer. She told me she'd won medals in swimming races. Every muscle in her arms showed the strain as she fought what looked like a strong current to get back to the bank.

Then they disappeared and surfaced much further downstream. The current carried Moddy away, still clutching the boy to her, doing her best to keep his head above water. People ran down the riverbank, shouting encouragement. A man jumped in and was swimming to catch up with them.

Again, Moddy struggled toward the bank. This time other men waded deep enough to reach them. I saw her brother Eddie there in the water. He grabbed for the lad's outstretched hand and caught hold, pulling the child in. All eyes were on the boy. He was white as a sheet and not even crying, but he was breathing. People were whooping and clapping, smiles of relief on every face.

I looked back at Moddy to call out, "You did it, Moddy." But she was gone. The man swimming toward them was reaching out to grasp hold of Moddy when she slipped below the surface.

The swimmer looked panicked, turning in circles, his head swiveling to scan the surface. He dove under the water and surfaced several times. Eddie lunged back into the river, but an old man held fast to his arm. "Nae, then. Go to yer mam. She'll need ye the now. Robby's a braw swimmer. He'll find her."

Eddie shook off the old man's grip and plunged into the river. Other men jumped back in to help find Moddy. The current was swift and carried them past the trees and out of our view.

I went to stand with Moddy's mum. She looked at me with tearful eyes. "I canna swim a stroke. But both my bairns are bonnie swimmers."

I leaned into her with a gentle hug. "I never learned ta swim either."

A woman came up to us. "She's probably on shore further downstream. I'm sure it's all right."

But I knew it wasn't. I held onto Mrs. Grant and bit the inside of my cheek to keep from crying.

The men came back to us with Moddy in their arms. Blood covered her blond curls and plastered them to her white face. A gash ran across the side of her head. She was limp. Lifeless. All that energy, all that laughter was gone forever. I heard women whisper to her mum what a brave lass she'd been.

The mother of the wee lad came and put her arms around Moddy's mum and cried her thank you. I heard the woman whisper, "I'm so sorry."

The man holding Moddy walked forward. Mrs. Grant stood there stunned. She was as white as Moddy. A statue. Then she said, "Gi' me my bairn. Gi' me my bairn." He put Moddy in her mam's arms, and they just seemed to sink to the ground together. She rocked Moddy and cried.

I had to turn away. I couldn't bear to watch all that pain and loss. It was my fault. If I hadn't yelled for Moddy to grab the lad, she'd be alive now.

Why, God, why? Why would you tell me ahead? It only made it worse. If I hadn't been so worried, I might have stayed home. I picked up my bicycle and rode toward our farmhouse. Tears rolled down my cheeks. I couldn't sort out my thoughts, and the weight of guilt I carried was overwhelming.

Then the whisper came: "If she hadn't gone after the boy, he would be dead tonight."

I railed against the voice. Moddy was important too. Why did she have to die?

I'd only known her a short time, but in those few months we'd become so close. I wanted to shake my fist at God. Did He have to take everyone I cared about?

I rolled into the dooryard of Kirkchrist Farmhouse. Grandma Cowan was home alone, napping in the rocker by the hearth. She looked up at me when I came through the door and opened her arms. Refuge, safety. I crossed the room to where she sat and put my head in her lap.

"Chrissy?"

It all came pouring out. Not the part about the whispers. I couldn't bring myself to tell anyone that. "I called out to Moddy ta grab for the lad. She did"—I hiccupped and gulped back a sob—"and I never her saw her again till they pulled her out. She saved the boy, Grandma, but she lost her life doing it. It's my fault. I yelled and she—"

"Shh, Chrissy. Ye ken she would ha saved that lad if ye were there or not." Grandma smoothed hair off my face and handed me her handkerchief. "That's who she was, luv. That's who she was."

I struggled to understand why it happened, running through it again and again in my mind. What good was it to know something ahead of time if there was nothing you could do to stop it? I didn't understand. I didn't tell Grandma or my mum or anyone about the whispers or the overwhelming feeling of dread. Who would believe me? Moddy hadn't.

Wendy—Seattle
September 1968

WE'D BEEN SITTING on the couch talking all afternoon. Now the room was full of golden light. The perfect end-of-summer afternoon. Lost in Mum's story, I jumped when she cleared her throat.

Her lips trembled, and my heart ached for her. Even now, all these years later, her eyes shimmered with tears over her friend. I put my hand on hers. She looked back at me from the past, slowly refocusing on the present. That was the thing about my mum, she shared her thoughts and feelings with me like a close friend.

"People should know there's more to life than they think," she said. "And that it's possible for God to invade our lives in a supernatural way." I wondered if she was talking about Fred's interview.

"Are you talking about the Sight or what people call ESP or the things we see on TV like *The Twilight Zone?*"

She thought for a minute. "Yes and no. If we don't show people that God is supernatural, then they'll go on thinking that some people have powers." Her face transformed from its former grief to a lopsided smile. "You should call Fred back and tell him I'll do his interview." She patted the back of my hand. "And maybe apologize?"

I rose and hesitated, thinking how much grief she went

through talking about her friend. "You don't have to tell him about Moddy."

"I won't. Anyway, Moddy was only the beginning of my brushes with the Sight."

Before I called him, I had one frightening thought. Could the feelings of being watched be my first experience with the Sight? I hoped not.

Chapter Sixteen

Christine—Kirkcowan, Scotland
September 1941

It didn't seem right to have a goodbye party, not with the entire village in mourning over Moddy's death. Mum asked Mr. Tam what would be best. We wanted to thank everyone who'd lent us furniture and brought food.

He said, "Och, it isn't necessary, but if ye've a mind to, you and the young lass might visit about a bit ta say yer thank-yous. I'll make sure everyone gets back their things."

My mum protested, but Mr. Tam held up his hand to stay her worries. "It'll be nae trouble at all."

We'd been saving rationing coupons to buy sugar with this time in mind. Together we made a dozen pots of bramble jam. Then we set off to visit each person in the village and surrounding farms.

Everyone was as sad to see us go as we were to say goodbye. And everyone spoke about losing Moddy to the Bladnoch river. I bit the inside of my mouth so often to keep from crying that I had a growing sore in my inner cheek.

Mum saved the last stop for Moddy's house. I picked a bouquet and brought the pillow cover we'd been embroidering as a surprise for our mums. Moddy hadn't finished, but I'd spent the last few days stitching it together.

Their farm was close to Eddie's lookout post. Had it really been only three weeks since we'd climbed those steps to watch for enemy planes with him? Three weeks since I heard the whispered warning. Since the night that changed everything for me.

We walked past fields of sheep. I saw Moddy's da out with his black-and-white sheepdog moving his flock to a different pasture. Mum waved, but he didn't see us, all his concentration on one stubborn, unmoving ewe.

Their house was a small, whitewashed stone building. Green shutters and a bright green door made the cottage cheery. Behind the house was a large ancient-looking byre. I remembered talking with Moddy on the sweet-smelling straw. Now I stood at her doorstep with my mum. She rapped lightly, and I shrank back.

Eddie opened their door. I kept my eyes on my hands, avoiding his face. I thought how they all must blame me for Moddy's drowning, probably because I blamed myself. I hadn't wanted to come here, but I had to do this one last thing for Moddy.

It wasn't like that, though. Eddie ushered us into their wee house. Mrs. Grant came right up to me and threw her arms around me.

"And there's my girl Chrissy. Ye were so dear to Moddy." The small woman's eyes were red and swollen. She looked as if she'd aged years since I'd seen her last when they laid my friend to rest in the small Kirkcowan cemetery. She drew back and patted my cheek. "Ye must come and see me sometime again. When you're with me, it's like having my girl back for a bit. She loved ye so much." Mrs. Grant gave me another fierce hug.

I left the Grants in a much better state of mind. They didn't hate me or blame me for what happened even if her death was partly my fault. Of course, they didn't know about the whispers.

No one did. I carried the burden of wondering what else I could have done to save Moddy from drowning.

Greenock was finally restored; the power and water were back on, and jobs were ready for workers to return. Mum decided the two of us would be the last to leave Kirkcowan. She wanted the farmhouse in pristine condition. Over the next week, my dancing teacher and her girls returned to Greenock. On Tuesday, Grandma Cowan, Aunty Jean, and wee Jackie took the train home. Da came down to help them and brought most of our personal things back with him. The country air had been healing for Grandma. Walking was much easier for her. That was good since it was Aunty Jean's turn to care for her mum. I think Grandma was looking forward to helping with wee Jackie.

We swept and cleaned that old farmhouse. Not that anyone was coming to live there, but at least we left it in better condition than we'd found it. On Friday morning, we walked to the train station carrying only what we could easily manage. Funny, that's how we came to this place. A melancholy sense of loss settled over me.

Moddy and I had ridden our bicycles down these same roads. As we came to the main street, villagers waved their goodbyes, calling out best wishes. My dancing teacher's sister hurried from her house with a bag of sandwiches. It touched my heart to see how much they'd made us welcome.

In the village train station, I stood looking at Mr. Tam's wee office, the passenger waiting platform and the empty track. Hard to believe that only five months ago we'd all arrived with almost nothing, still covered in the soot from the Blitz, homeless and afraid like refugees. We were leaving with a wealth of wonderful memories. Friendships. Mum went to talk to Mr. Tam, but I stood embracing every detail with my eyes.

What was it Da said before we left Greenock? Oh, aye. "Think on it as an adventure." I remember rolling my eyes. But it had been an adventure.

A lone tear rolled down my cheek. I turned away from the track, not wanting to leave this dear place behind but not wanting to stay here any longer without Moddy. There was Eddie standing a few feet behind me, his hands in his pockets as he watched me. Then he moved toward me slowly.

"I've come ta say goodbye but not forever, aye?" He searched my face. Then he reached out and gave me a hug, holding me tight while he spoke.

"I ken ye blame yerself."

"What?"

"It's in yer eyes, lass." He sounded so much older than his fifteen years. "But dinna do such a thing. Ye saved that wee lad as much as my sister. If you hadn't been there ta see him fall in, Moddy couldn't have lived with herself, knowing she was so close and didn't save him. It would have changed her forever."

I looked up into those sparkling blue eyes, so like his sister's. And for a minute he smiled, and it was Moddy there smiling at me.

I smiled back, and Eddie waved as he walked away.

The train came chugging in and steam filled the waiting platform. Mr. Tam ushered us into the connector. He gave my mum a warm handshake and hugged me, whispering in my ear. "That wee lad ye saved wi' our Moddy, he's my sister's only bairn. I always meant ta thank ye for calling the alarm."

That would have been terrible to lose your only child. Moddy had given her life to save him, and I had given my friend.

As we took our place on the train, I leaned my head against the cool window and watched the village disappear. The further I got from Kirkcowan, the more I felt it was all a dream and now I was slowly waking. Eddie's words had lifted a weight from my heart. And Mr. Tam had reminded me of the life saved on that terrible day. I relaxed as if I'd put down a heavy load and slept most of the way to Greenock.

My dad was there to meet our train. As a treat, he'd hired an automobile to take us all home. As soon as I walked through my front door, my world righted. I was back, and all my things were here. That sense of belonging was so comforting.

I threw open the sash to my bedroom window and beamed at my wee white fairy rose. It had grown over the summer and now was more the size of a tiny bush, sprouting a bouquet of white rosebuds. I leaned out the window. Further down the street, Mr. and Mrs. Munn's tenements lay in rubble. My happiness faded at the memory of her words the morning of the all clear: "My ain hame is gone." And I wondered where the Munns were now.

Kirkcowan had changed me. I found that I could look on my war-torn town without reliving the horrors of the Blitz. I went down to Kirkcowan a frightened child and came home settled and older.

Bridie, my Irish friend, called "You're back!" from across the street. She nearly fell off her bicycle with excitement. I was down the stairs and out the door in a flash. Maybe there was still a child inside.

In the next few weeks, I plunged back into my schoolwork, and my life filled with activities. I don't know how the mayor of Greenock found out about our shows in Kirkcowan, but early in October he asked if I'd come dance in a show at the town hall. It set a pattern that followed me throughout the war.

I'd always loved the old town hall building. Its tall spire was visible from all over town. But it was the large hall and stage that thrilled me. Instead of plain old Chrissy, I became Ginger Rogers or Ann Miller on that stage. I worked on my costumes and sat through countless screenings of American movies, memorizing new tap steps.

At first, I was only an opening act for the well-known performers, but I didn't mind if my tap steps made their way across that stage. Before the winter was over, I was one of the principal attractions. My mum warned me not to let all the attention go to my head. "People are probably only being kind," she'd say. Her lack of enthusiasm kept a lid on my excitement and helped me focus on the purpose for my dancing. The ticket sales raised money toward building Spitfires. I had a twice-removed cousin who helped develop the Spitfire Rolls-Royce engine, lovingly called the Merlin.

I was proud of my distant connection to Reginald Mitchell. I had a passion for aircraft, and these sleek little planes outmaneuvered the German Messerschmitt BF-109. They flew faster and higher than anything in the air. Their eight wing-mounted machine guns were a wicked weapon against the enemy. I dreamed of flying, but they didn't allow female pilots.

I wondered what it would be like to sail through the sky in those fast little planes. I spent my last year in school drawing them in aerial dogfights, fearing that was as close as I'd ever get to flying one. My artwork decorated the halls of the Highlanders Academy. A flight instructor visited our school and saw them. He asked to speak with me.

"Miss Finlay, these are really quite good."

A blush crept up my cheeks. "Thank you, sir."

"But your angles are a little off, and this pilot wouldn't be able to pull out of his turn." He looked me in the eye. "That pilot would crash for sure."

"Och, aye? I'm sorry, sir." I felt terrible for my imaginary pilot.

He smiled at me, seeing my reaction. "If I spent some time with you describing maneuvers used in aerial combat, do you think you could draw them?"

My grin was so wide it made my cheeks hurt. "Aye, sure, I'd like that very much."

"Could you do them bigger? I'd get the paper. And I like how you drew them with pencil and added the paint here and there to show the fire when we blow those bleedin' Jerries out of our skies."

I laughed despite his influential position. "Aye, sir, I can do that. But can I ask why you want the drawings?"

"For training. I have nothing like this to show the lads clearly what I'm describing."

I reached out a hand to shake his. "Thank ye, thank ye. I'll do my best."

THAT WINTER the war raged on. With the advance of Japanese forces against the Americans and British interests in the Far East, World War II covered the whole globe with violence. In January, Japanese forces attacked Burma and began their reign of terror. Closer to home, Hitler was busy fighting the Russians. Thank goodness, here in Greenock the skies were clear of bombers.

I was almost fifteen when I finished my school term at the Highlanders Academy. The solid three-story brick building had been my school since Isabelle and I were wee lasses. I guess I felt melancholy about leaving.

There was a brief ceremony, and the principal awarded me a medal for academic excellence. My mum and da were there, looking so proud. Afterward we had a small reception, and they wandered off to talk with other parents. The school served refreshments, and I sat around talking with all my friends.

Moira scrunched down in her seat. "Oh, Lord. Professor Magillicuty is coming this way."

I turned to look, and sure enough, the one professor who struck the most fear in our hearts was marching toward our table. I say marching because that's how he moved, like he was on the parade grounds in front of the big brass. I don't think he'd ever left the military, at least not in his heart. He was still a tough Sergeant Major, exacting, demanding, and able to bring even the strongest lad near tears with the flick of his very sharp tongue and occasionally the strap. All my classmates ducked their heads, hoping he'd pass on by.

Robert said, "Don't look at him. It'll just draw him to us if he smells fear."

"What can the old tyrant do now?" Della sounded defiant. "We've graduated. We're not in his army anymore." Brave words but I glanced up and Della had her shoulders hunched and her eyes down.

Even in the crowded room, I could hear the click of his heels on the tiled floors. He stopped at our table and bellowed, "Finlay."

All eyes flicked to me. I stood slowly. "Sir, yes, sir." It sounds silly to say that now, but that was how we were used to addressing him. His weathered, stern face transformed into a warm smile.

"I just wanted to thank you."

"You're welcome, sir, but for what?"

"All these years you were the only one"—his eyes darted around the table— "who ever greeted me with a smile. Every time I entered the class, you'd look my way and give me that welcoming smile. I just wanted to thank you and say how much that meant to me."

"Oh," was all I could answer before Magillicuty turned and walked out of the room.

My friends all looked aghast.

"Well, I told my da how much he scared me, and he told me a trick." I sank into my seat as relief washed over me.

Della asked, "What trick?"

"Da said, 'When the old duffer comes through the classroom door, imagine a bucket of water falls on his head.' I did, and it made me smile to think of him soaking wet."

Robert chuckled. "I wish I'd known that trick years ago. I almost wet myself every time he called my name."

We all laughed and talked about what we'd do after graduation. All the boys were enlisting as soon as they could, and so were some girls. I couldn't bear the thought of leaving home. I needed to be where I could help my parents and grandmothers.

I wrinkled my nose. "Those military uniforms are terrible. Just to be fair, I asked if I could redesign their outfits. I was told no, so I decided it wasn't for me." It made them laugh, but it also kept me from talking about the fear that if I left I'd never see Greenock again.

One boy said, "We know what you'll do, Chrissy."

That caught me off guard. "What? What do you mean?"

His smile was full of admiration. "With your test scores, you're bound for university." Everyone looked at me.

"No," I said. "I'm going to volunteer as many places as I can right here in Greenock." The conversation went on, but I didn't hear a word. I'd thrown down the gauntlet. I knew Dad wanted me to attend Glasgow University and become a marine engineer. It wasn't what I wanted. I wasn't the engineer type, and I didn't want to be left out of helping with the war effort. But I'd never stood up to my father before. It promised to be an epic moment.

Wendy—Seattle
End of Summer 1968

John's green Studebaker sat in our driveway. I could see him sitting inside. Sitting, not getting out and coming up the stairs to the front door. Was he deciding if this was a big mistake? I waited to see if he'd leave, but he didn't.

Ten minutes passed before he looked up and saw me watching.

Enough of this. I walked down the stairs and met him halfway. As quickly as my irritation flared, it morphed into longing for the way things were. And what do you say when your heart hurts so bad you just want to be held?

Luckily, I didn't say that. I only said, "Hey." But he wasn't looking at me.

Instead, all his focus was on his shoes. "The weather's great. Thought I might go to Tom's place on Lake Sammamish Saturday."

The sun was in my eyes. I squinted up into his face. "Oh." If he was going to ask me to come, I wasn't making it easier. Maybe they're right about redheads. We are stubborn, even when we know it goes against everything we want. I smiled at the thought.

He smiled back, ending the awkwardness between us. We started chatting about his apprenticeship at South Gate Ford. I knew he'd been taking night classes all year to be accepted into the program. Now he was working for the company and getting a real paycheck. He started saving to buy a Kawasaki motorcycle.

I told him about applying for a new job doing clerical work for the humanities professors on campus. And how I was thinking of trying out for the fall play. Not so much on stage but maybe helping with costuming. It was small talk. But a clever man once said that "Small talk often leads to big talk." Important talk. And I was willing to wait.

I rode with John to Lake Sammamish on Saturday. It was a nice day together. Nothing too romantic. Coming through the front door that evening, Mom asked, "So, how was your day?"

I shrugged. "He sang along with his eight-track tape deck all the way out and back."

"That must have been nice. He has a wonderful voice."

I nodded. "He sang every wild biker song. The only time he stopped singing was when he played *Never My Love* by The Association." I plopped down on the couch. "I really don't know what to expect next. Is he trying to tell me to forget about us? He's going to live the wild life. But why ask me out?" I shook my head in frustration.

"Sounds like he was avoiding anything . . ."

She seemed to search for a word, so I helped her. "Anything important, anything real, lasting. Anything like why he broke up with me." I blew out all the breath in my lungs. "Life after high school isn't what I thought it'd be."

She smiled. "I remember going through quite a few trials after graduation."

Chapter Seventeen

Christine—Greenock, Scotland
Summer 1942

As I walked home with my parents from graduation, I gathered my courage to tell them that university wasn't for me.

Da asked, "What was that sour old professor saying to you?"

I guessed he must mean Professor Magillicuty. "He wanted to thank me."

"Aye? For what?"

"For always welcoming him with a smile when he came into class." I told him how I'd put his advice to work, and we were all laughing by the time we got home. Mum went to put the teakettle on. I hung back, weakening at the thought of talking to Da. An inner argument insisted now wasn't a good time.

A faint whisper entered my thoughts. "You can do this now."

I squared my shoulders and stopped my dad before he'd taken off his coat. I wasn't a schoolgirl any longer. I needed to be the master of my fate. Now was the time to broach the subject before he bundled me off to the university in Glasgow or Edinburgh.

I took a deep breath. "Da, I need to talk to you."

He turned to me, his face still glowing with pride. I hated to disappoint him, but I had to tell him before I lost my nerve.

"I know you want me to follow in your footsteps. University was your dream." His eyes were direct, but so were mine. "If your da hadn't died, you would have gone. But you still became a marine engineer.

"I don't want to be an engineer or anything else I might get from going to university. My life is here. I want to help where I can, do what I can do." Silence. No expression. Was he waiting to blow his bonnet or thinking about what I'd said?

Finally, he reached one hand out and gave my shoulder a small squeeze. "You're a bonnie lass, and I couldn't be prouder of you." He walked away, leaving me to stare after him.

I was relieved beyond all measure, but he'd laid a burden on my shoulders. I would have to bear the weight of his trust. At fifteen, I joined the workforce to support the war, help with expenses at home and do what I could to volunteer.

I think we all wanted to keep close what family we had in Greenock. It was hard enough to be separated from my uncles who were off to war.

Sometimes we didn't get word from my uncles. Usually, they were pretty good about writing letters and even posting me small trinkets from the places the military sent them—a bracelet from Egypt or a fancy scarf from Italy. But when we hit one of those times they didn't check in, it was truly frightening.

Uncle Tommy hadn't written for some time. Grandma Finlay's sharp sense of humor muted; worry and restlessness settled on her. I could see Da was anxious as well. One afternoon, I took Grandma to the movies. During the newsreel they did a short piece about the curriers who rode their motorcycles through many dangers, even crossing behind enemy lines to keep the different commands connected. The camera panned out to show the muddy fields and stony dykes of European farmland. In the forest, off in the background, you could see the turrets and guns of German tanks.

The camera swiveled back to Allied forces hunkered behind the rock fences and in the ditches between pasturelands. There was a distant boom and puff of smoke from the trees. A cloud of dirt erupted halfway across the field.

In the silence that followed, the newsreel picked up the high-pitched sound of a single motor. Out of the falling debris sped one lone motorcycle racing across the open space. Machine guns rattled from the other side, spattering more clumps of grass and mud, but the rider swerved this way and that. German bullets stopped as the wild-looking currier accelerated out of range. He jumped a trench, sliding to a stop, throwing mud everywhere.

The motorbike fell as the rider hopped off and put a packet in the commander's hand. The currier pulled off his muddy goggles, leaving two clean circles around an otherwise mud-splattered face.

And there was my Uncle Tommy. The camera caught his unmistakable impish smile. Giving the Allied commander a salute, he lifted the motorbike, jumped on its back and took off through the mud, disappearing over a ridge.

Grandma Finlay stood up and yelled, "That's my wee laddie, my Tommy." The whole theatre erupted in applause. She collapsed into her chair weeping with relief. Uncle Tommy was still alive. I patted her back and leaned over to whisper comfort in her ear.

Later, a theatre attendant offered to run the newsreel again at the end of the screening, and Grandma had another look at her son.

Those kinds of difficulties were a part of our lives. We couldn't escape missing the people we loved. Mum always said worry was best fought by keeping busy. And I did my best to fill my days and evenings with activity.

The Canadians needed a holding base for naval personnel

being transferred to other ships, a resting place for their battle-weary and a hospital for their injured. Since many Canadian ships came into Greenock for repairs or for safe anchorage, the Canadians looked around for a facility large enough to meet their needs.

Ravenscraig Castle fit the bill perfectly. In the past, the castle housed mental patients and served as a workhouse. Currently, the Smithson's Institute used it as a hospital of sorts, but it was always Ravenscraig to the locals.

The Canadians had a habit of naming their holding facilities and naval hospitals after Naval vessels. Here, they renamed Ravenscraig Castle HMCS NIOBE after the first large ship in the Canadian navy. They decommissioned that ship after the First World War.

Ravenscraig was a long, sprawling castle built of the rusty-red stones so prevalent in this part of the Western Highlands. Its many turrets poked up above the surrounding stand of trees. The castle sat at the wooded base of the same hills I roamed as a child.

There were small lochs in the foothills above Ravenscraig and fields full of grazing sheep. So even as close as it was to the town, it felt secluded. Though we always thought of it as a small castle, they had built Ravenscraig in the last century as a home for some very wealthy mental patients.

Now wounded filled the wards of the part of Ravenscraig used as a Canadian naval hospital. I organized little shows to entertain the patients and brought in my dancing teacher's girls or her younger students to dance a Highland reel for them. Sometimes I put on a record and the sound of my tap shoes echoed through the wards. These were mostly young men, and they loved the Glenn Miller band as much as I did. The doctor said we were the best medicine he had.

After graduation, all my school friends were finding their way in the adult world. We really weren't that old, most of us a little more than sixteen, but you had to grow up fast during war.

My friend Della McConnell and I had attended the Highlanders Academy. As a child, she'd had a hard time. Her father drank and her mother worked hard to keep a roof over their heads. She had six brothers and sisters. As the oldest, they expected Della to care for the younger ones. She was a pretty child, but I noticed that some profs and other children scorned her because the family was so poor. It gave Della a hard edge to her personality, but once you got past that she had a good heart. I liked her.

She turned into a beautiful young woman. And it was her looks that gave her the power to move beyond her earlier shunning. I watched how the lads looked at her and how she used that to her advantage. I couldn't blame her, but it worried me sometimes.

I wasn't like that. I still felt alone inside. Oh, I had my flirtations, but really I was too busy to think much about the opposite sex except as dance partners. One afternoon, Della asked me to come with her and visit her new boyfriend at the hospital. Afterward, we stood down by Inverkip Road waiting for the bus to go home. There was a lot of construction noise coming from an old, deserted biscuit factory on the edge of the base property. A lad perched on a tall ladder, repairing some masonry, called out to us, waving his hand.

It was someone Della knew, and she caught hold of my hand, pulling me along.

The sun glistened off her long blond curls, and she shaded her eyes to look up at the laddie dressed in military fatigues. "What are you doing up there?" she asked with her cheekiest grin.

"What are you doin' down there?" he answered back with the same amount of cheek.

"Just visitin' a friend."

I bit my lip to keep from saying what I thought. When we'd left her boyfriend at the hospital, she'd declared her unfailing love for the young injured officer. Honestly, was there no end to her flirtatious behavior? I thought probably not. Della was finally enjoying her life.

An older woman came out of the building, and the conversation halted as the lad went back to looking industrious. The woman eyed us and then approached with a friendly expression on her face. "You ladies are local?"

She had a Canadian accent. "Aye, I'm Christina Finlay and this is my friend Della McConnell." I stuck out my hand in a very adult, businesslike manner.

"Mrs. Wagner." She shook both our hands and seemed to be sizing us up. "I think I've heard your name. Finlay? You do shows up at the hospital?"

"Nothing much, only a bit of entertainment for the lads."

"Would you like to come in and see what we're doing here?"

I looked at Della, and she shrugged. We followed Mrs. Wagner into the old building, walking around empty paint cans. Plasterboard crunched underfoot as we tried to listen. She was saying, "I've been told this was once a factory. Is that right?"

"Aye. It was a biscuit factory, but that was some years back," I answered as we walked down a long hall and into a big empty room. I thought this must have been the factory floor. There was a balcony of sorts or a catwalk about twenty feet up that circled the room. High windows lined the length of both outside walls.

Mrs. Wagner said, "This will be the base canteen. We'll be putting blackout curtains on all those." She pointed up to where I'd been staring. "There's a big kitchen back there." She was looking toward the hall we'd come through. "And we'll have a stage down there at the end. For bands and such."

"It's going to be very nice." Even as I spoke those words, I realized it was going to take a lot of work. That's when Mrs. Wagner's smile turned calculating.

"Think you'd like to help us?"

I looked at Della, but she rolled her eyes and said, "Of course she'll help you. She can't say no to a good cause."

I knew she was right. I was going to help. In fact, a bunch of us, even Della, worked hard to transform the old building into a gathering place for the off-duty Canadian servicemen. We were all so proud of our labors when the new Canadian canteen opened. Only the old catwalk reminded us how the building had started life. We transformed it into a lovely balcony with little round tables and chairs.

Mrs. Wagner's rules for serving as a hostess once the club opened were strict. Before you could volunteer in the canteen, you had to pass a background check, have a letter from your pastor about your character and one from your doctor certifying your virginity and overall health. She explained that the men based at NIOBE were young, and she didn't want them to fall in with gambling and prostitutes. The canteen would offer dancing and wholesome entertainment.

We submitted our paperwork and waited for our letters of acceptance. The post came early on a day I was volunteering at the hospital. I tore open my letter and was pleased at the official-looking Canadian document announcing I'd passed my background check and should consult with Mrs. Wagner as soon as possible. I was on my way to NIOBE to help write letters for injured servicemen, so I planned to pay her a visit as soon as I finished my shift.

I found Mrs. Wagner in her small new office at the canteen. For once she seemed aglow with her accomplishments—even if it was our hard labor that achieved her goals.

"Ah, I see you've received your letter." She extended her hand. "I'm holding a meeting on Saturday morning at ten for all my hostesses."

I shook her hand with vigor. "Della and I will be here on time."

"Oh." She withdrew her hand from mine, and I wondered at the change in her. "Sorry, your friend didn't pass the check."

I couldn't believe my ears. "But she worked hard to get this canteen ready."

"Yes, I know, but we can't have her sort working here."

"Her sort?" Heat flared through my body.

"I heard rumors. I really can't discuss this with you."

"Did ye send her a letter, then, rejecting her application?"

Mrs. Wagner held up a slip of paper as if it were as distasteful as she now felt Della to be. "I really hate sending letters like this one, but it must be done."

My hands shook with rage as I pulled my letter out of my handbag. "I've known Della all my life, and yes, she comes from poor circumstances, but she's a kind soul." I slammed my letter down on her desk. "An if she's nae guid enough for ye then I'm not either."

I glared, completely losing my natural self-restraint in the heat of anger.

The older woman looked stunned. She slipped into her stern matron persona for a moment, meeting my defiance with her own steely command. "Sorry you feel that way."

I narrowed my eyes. This was one time I wouldn't give in to authoritative blether. "I'm sorry you feel you can hurt others on rumors and snobbishness. I won't be back, and I won't hesitate to discourage anyone who'll listen to me from coming here.

"And don't bother sending yon mean-spirited letter. It's unnecessary. I'll tell her myself we weren't good enough for the Canadians." I reached for the door handle.

Really, I didn't blow my bonnet often, especially with an adult. I could feel my cheeks on fire with my barely contained anger when Mrs. Wagner stopped me. Her voice wasn't loud. "Miss Finlay—"

She began again as I glanced back. "I—perhaps I've been too hasty." She seemed to shrink a bit. Her voice softened as she leaned over her desk. "I trust your opinion, of course. If you vouch for Miss McConnell . . ." She hesitated. "Then she'll be welcome, and I hope you'll reconsider your opinion of us and come volunteer as well."

That pulled the wind out of my sails, and I almost felt bad for the way I'd spoken. Almost. Instead, I asked, "Will you send Della a letter of acceptance as well?"

"It'll be in the post today."

I relaxed in relief and extended my hand to her in a firm handshake. "You won't regret your decision, Mrs. Wagner." I hoped Della would prove me right.

Wendy—Seattle
1968

School started and so did my job in the humanities building. It had an inner courtyard, and where I worked all the windows looked onto the beautiful landscaping. I met the professors, learned how to answer the phones, transfer calls, and of course there was the exciting job of filing. Still, I couldn't complain; no baby alligators waited to bite my fingers off.

My mindless job gave me time to think. John was a mystery. We dated a bit, and then I didn't see him for a while. Were we only friends now? But he kissed me every time we were together. He held my hand, reminding me of how he was when we were in a steady relationship. I was getting frustrated. I hated to admit it —I probably needed to go on with my life and quit waiting for him to want me back.

So when a guy in my English 101 class asked me to the movies, I accepted. But before our date, he scolded me. "I'm canceling our date." He sounded hostile.

"Okay, but what's up?"

"You didn't tell me you were Mutton's girl."

"What? You've got to be kidding." Even here people knew his reputation. Even here. I was so angry. I practically spit back, "Well, if I were, I wouldn't go to the movies with you."

I was irritated with John and done with guys for the foreseeable future. I began looking for activities that interested me. There was an opening for a costume designer in the fall play. I also had a part in the cast as an extra in the village scenes. It kept me busy and my mind off John.

I started hanging out at the library. The quiet suited me. I could do homework before rehearsal, and often Seamus was there. We would talk. I told him about the play and how much I was enjoying the costuming. "I'm afraid I'll never be an actor, but I like the atmosphere."

"I'll have to come see the rehearsals. I'm quite good at acting. Maybe I could give you some pointers. When do you rehearse?" He set his stack of books back in his cart and came to sit across from me at my table.

"Mostly after school around six."

"Aren't you afraid on campus after dark?"

The lady at the check-out desk put a finger to her lips and scowled at us.

Pretty sure he'd just been shushed, I hid my smile and whispered, "Should I be?" My first thought was that he was teasing me.

He leaned closer, his voice a hoarse, anxious whisper. "The other day some people were talking about a student who was . . . you know, attacked and murdered here a couple years ago."

"You're serious? Did they catch who did it?" Seamus was very hard to read.

He shook his head. "Don't think so." His expression was intense, and he seemed to be studying my reaction.

I began to feel uncomfortable. "So, what? Am I supposed to be afraid of her ghost or her attacker?"

Seamus chuckled. "They said her ghost walks the grounds after dark. That's enough to scare me."

I'm pretty sure my answer surprised him. "You haven't lived with a mother who has second sight."

His brows shot up. "Your mum has the Sight? Knows things before they happen like?"

"Sometimes. But unexplained things seem to happen around her." The next time we talked about the war, Mum proved my point.

Chapter Eighteen

Christine—Greenock, Scotland
1943

I wanted to show my father I could make a difference right here at home. By the time I was sixteen, I was volunteering at two or three other canteens in town.

On Wednesdays, I went back to the Canadian canteen during the day to teach dancing to the young men who only sat and watched because they were too embarrassed to say they didn't know how to dance.

My love of dancing had taught me to push myself forward, but inside I felt that unexplainable aloneness. Watching those boys sit on the sidelines while their friends were enjoying all the fun touched my heart.

I also visited the wards and helped with reading or writing letters home. I felt sorry for the lads who were alone in a strange land with no family to visit them. Oh, sure, there were some very handsome fellows in those beds. Young women came and went, giving them more than enough attention. No, it was the homely boys who lay alone by the hour who drew me.

I approached the doctors with an idea. Then I got the help of my mum and dad, and we set my new venture. Each week I'd take one of the more mobile patients from the hospital for an afternoon trip to my home to sit by the fire, eat a home-cooked meal and talk. When I asked for only the lads who weren't good-looking, the chief nurse was skeptical about my motives.

"Watch which lads never have visitors," I said. "Those are the ones who need a time to feel important, you know?"

She did. Her compassionate expression mirrored my concern.

This was when I began hearing stories about HMCS NIOBE, or Ravenscraig Castle as I knew it. The boys were afraid to return to their hospital beds. At first I thought this was a ploy for a little extra sympathy. That is until one rather burly-looking young commando named Bob asked, "How old is that place?" He had a bulky bandage on his left foot, so I helped him onto the bus for the ride to my house.

When we'd settled into our seats, I said, "I'm not sure. Not that old." I thought for a minute. "Almost a hundred years. Why?"

"If I tell you, will you keep it to yourself?" He looked around at the other people on the bus.

"Aye, you can say what you like. I'll not say a word to anyone."

Bob cast a glance back over his shoulder as the bus pulled away from Ravenscraig. "We're quartered in one of the long wards, you know. About ten of us to a room. Well, we were talking at night, just joking around. A new guy came in. He wore a bathrobe ready for bed, but otherwise there wasn't anything odd about him. He leaned against the wall at the edge of our group."

Bob's eyes got glassy like he was seeing it all again. "There are always new guys coming in for a bit of rest. I remember glancing at him. I nodded, and he smiled and nodded back." Bob looked at me sharply as if deciding whether to go on. "Someone told a good one, and we were all in stitches laughing. The newcomer smiled but didn't laugh or make a sound.

"Some guys are in an awful place when they return from the

front. I think it helps if they can talk to someone who understands. I hobbled over to him. I was just a few steps away when
the stranger got an odd look on his face. Then it happened."

I waited to hear the rest of his story, but he was staring off
into space. "Bob, what? What happened?"

Bob swallowed hard. "He turned and walked right through the
wall, just melted into the bricks and disappeared." He waited,
watching my face. I waited too in case there was more.

"Oh," I finally said. "That's all?"

He snapped, "You don't think that's enough?"

"When you live in an ancient place"—I shrugged—"things
happen." He looked at me and his mouth dropped open then
clamped shut, and he turned away to look out the bus window.
We didn't talk much after that. I thought of the ghost of
Kirkchrist. I knew firsthand how unnerving a supernatural
encounter could be. One thing I'd learned from that experience
was that in the end it didn't do any good to make too much of it.

At first, the young men I brought home thought I was
romantically interested in them. I could see the hurt and disappointment on their faces when I made it clear this was friendship, not courtship. I almost stopped my plan, but soon word
got around as I checked out different patients every week. They
accepted my invitation with only the expectation of a good meal
and some great conversation. Really, all I had to do was get them
to my house. My mum was a wonderful cook, and my dad could
regale them with anecdotes about building and test-diving
submarines.

Dad took the new subs out on their shake-down cruises to
make sure they were seaworthy before handing them over to the
British navy. He'd had some hair-raising experiences. Mum and I
tried not to listen, but the young Canadian sailors loved his tales.
The one thing all the lads had in common was their fear of
returning to NIOBE.

Those young men told stories too. Most were harmless, not

scary at all, but others must have been quite terrifying, like the one told to me by Rupert.

It was a Wednesday, and I was giving him dance lessons in the empty ballroom at the Canadian Overseas Club. We'd stopped the record to a take a rest. He was a shy lad but had been opening a bit more with each lesson.

It didn't surprise me when he started telling me about something that had happened when he was standing watch on the east perimeter of the Canadian base at Ravenscraig in the dark hours of the night. A thick mist rose from the ground, looking like an eerie white cloud creeping down from the hills.

He stared at the empty dance floor in the shadowed ballroom as if he could see it all playing out before him. "I thought I saw a figure of an old man with a shepherd's crook in the mist. I said, 'Halt. Stand and identify yourself, or I'll shoot.' We didn't want to shoot any locals, but the man kept coming.

"Sheep were walking ahead of the shepherd. I could make out the man's blank expression, as if he didn't see me. I called to him again. 'You're trespassing on a restricted installation. Stand now or I'll shoot.' It's not that I was really planning on shooting him, but I couldn't let him pass." Rupert looked over his shoulder to see if anyone was listening. We were alone.

I put my hand on his arm. "You can say it. I think I've heard this before."

Again, the word incredulous would best describe his expression. He did a quick double take at my face but went on. "He was an old shepherd, and I thought his clothing strange, but what do I know? We're not in Alberta. Then it dawned on me the old guy must be hard of hearing, so I yelled, 'Halt.' But as his sheep came to me, they passed right through my body. I froze.

"I know what you're thinking, and no, I wasn't drinking anything but water." He shuddered. "Then the old man walked right through me too. I spun around and there was nothing there.

Nothing—not even the mist." Rupert looked at me, flushed pink right up to his ears.

"Believe me, you're not going crazy, any more than the half-dozen other lads who told me stories just as strange as yours." I smiled. "We know we have ghosts. We live with the old ones. We don't question who they are or why they still walk. They are what they are. That's all. Only God understands the mysteries of this life, and maybe someday he'll explain the shepherd to you."

My words caught in my throat; good advice for me as well. I still struggled about my experience with Moddy in Kirkcowan. I should stop questioning why it happened, but this advice was easier to give than to live.

Wendy—Seattle
1968

I HAD some time to kill after my morning classes, so I strolled through the campus. Summer was slipping away, leaving crisp fall air. The colors of the trees were already changing to reds and golds. I walked into the library. One side of the building was floor to ceiling windows. Even the light on this fall afternoon had a soft golden aspect.

It was so quiet. I didn't see any friends. That made me wonder if Seamus was around. We were becoming good friends. The fact that he was my own dad's age and took an interest in me filled a gap I hadn't realized was there. My dad was always gone, but I could talk to Seamus about anything. He was interesting, and I enjoyed our talks. I took the stairs to the second-floor balcony. From there I could see almost the entire lower level. I didn't see him anywhere. I was about to turn and leave when I heard someone whistling softly. The tune was slow and sad. I remembered the time Seamus had whistled a tune like that in the cafeteria. I followed the whistle till I found him putting books back on the shelves.

He stopped abruptly when I came around the aisle. "Oh, and wouldn't you be the very one I was thinking about, my darlin' girl."

"How are you?"

"Enjoying the hunt." His smile was oddly feral but changed so quickly I assumed I'd imagined it. "It's a game I play with myself."

"A game?"

"Lookin' for where a book belongs, don't ya know?"

I felt like he had some double meaning I didn't understand, but I remembered something I wanted to ask. "You asked me once what my connections are to Scotland. But you're Irish, so why are you involved with the Highland Games Association?"

"That's easy. I traveled all over Scotland during the war. Learned a lot of interesting things."

"Were you ever in Greenock?"

"Now let me think. I can't be sure. Does it have a replica of a Viking ship on the beach?"

"No, that's Largs. I wonder if you might have met my mum. Her name was Christina Finlay." I thought I saw a flash of anger. Could it be that he knew her, remembered her name? But why the anger? His face changed again quickly.

Instead of answering my question, he glanced at his wristwatch. "I'm sorry. I must run. We'll have ta talk later."

As he walked away, I thought about how cryptic he seemed today. I decided to ask Mum if she remembered him. But when I got home, the TV news was full of a story about a University of Washington coed strangled to death in her dorm room. The police had no leads.

We didn't end up talking about Seamus.

Chapter Nineteen

Christine—Greenock, Scotland
1943

The Allied forces were a ragtag mixture of European freedom fighters, the Canadians, Australians, and us Brits. We'd been fighting for two years. Before Christmas in 1941, the Japanese launched a devastating attack on the Hawaiian Islands. The Americans joined the Allies. By May 1943, the entire world was at war. Now we fought in the Pacific, and the Americans joined us in Europe. We saw the results in wounded men coming into NIOBE. Even here in my little corner of Scotland, servicemen from all over the world walked our old cobblestone streets and visited our canteens while the men of our town repaired their ships.

As civilians, we worked hard to support those who did the real fighting. I wasn't the only one volunteering and working a part-time job as well. All my friends were doing it too. My mum and Aunty Agnus worked in a secret munitions factory. The whole country mobilized to help with the war effort.

My dad made a good living; we weren't well off, but we were

comfortable, well cared for. That's not to say we didn't face rationing and wartime shortages. The government issued ration books in 1939.

Before the war, only a third of our food was homegrown. That was why the Atlantic became a focus for the Germans. Hitler hoped to demoralize the civilian population with hunger by sinking convoys of freight ships carrying our food supplies. But he didn't know what tenacious spirits we Brits possessed.

We grew what vegetables our climate would allow and learned inventive ways to stretch our resources. There was no room for waste. The government also rationed clothing and fabric. A man's wool overcoat might take eighteen rationing coupons while a new suit would take twenty-six or more. By 1943, they allotted us thirty-six ration coupons a year for clothing. Basically, one new outfit a year.

Everything in life drilled down to one question—was it important enough to spend coupons or time on? When a package arrived from Aunt Tina in Canada, the world stopped. For a few glorious hours, I was a teenage girl with new shoes and some beautiful fabric to make a new dress. In those rare moments, I completely indulged myself. If I'd seen a dress in a movie or magazine, I learned to make my version. I wouldn't copy anyone exactly because I considered myself a designer.

There were times my mother decided Dad needed a new suit or overcoat. I immediately asked for the old one. My parents objected at first, but when they saw what I made with a bit of fabric from used clothes, I'm pretty sure I impressed them. After all, it took hours to unpick the old suit and see how much usable fabric I could scavenge to make something new. I admired the tailored business styles of American film stars like Myrna Loy in the *Shadow of the Thin Man*. Sometimes I surprised even myself when my da's old suit became my new outfit inspired by one I'd seen in the movies.

Despite the war, my mum was a change-things-up kind of

person. She only went so long before she repainted a room. But it really thrilled me when she saved coupons for new drapes. No seam ripping. That was a treat.

There were no coupons on used goods and soon friends would bring me old dresses to change or their fathers' old suits to do something new with. It's not like I made any money sewing. There wasn't much money in our wartime economy. Sometimes we traded things. But I did it because I loved the challenge, second only to dancing. My chalk, scissors, needle, and thread were my weapons against the war Hitler waged on our economy. Maybe I had followed my father after all. Isn't an engineer someone who sees how things fit together to build something new? I did that with dresses.

There are only so many things you can do to distract yourself from war. But distractions were momentary, short-lived. The war was ever present in the papers, in the faces of the servicemen on our streets, in the absence of our loved ones, and even on our radios. It was hard to ignore Lord Haw Haw. Sometimes it felt like he drew us to his radio broadcasts. It was frightening when he started mentioning things about Scotland again. He wasn't the only British voice coming from German radio stations, but he spoke with specific details about Scottish towns, the names of people and the streets they lived on. It was hard to fathom, but it became increasingly clear. We had a spy in our midst.

We didn't talk openly about the growing certainty that someone we trusted was spying for the enemy, but we whispered with our friends. On one Wednesday, it had been an unusually quiet night for the church canteen at the Y in town. Toward eight, the room was empty except for the band and a few of us at the tables ringing the dance floor. The musicians gave up playing, and we all sat talking while the band finished up the leftover sandwiches.

Della looked around and whispered, "I'm that frightened to listen to the radio, but I'm scared not to."

"Oh, aye," Moira chimed in. "Did ye listen to what the stinker said about Aberdeen last week? It was like he'd walked their streets. And no a long time ago." Her grey eyes were so big. "I have an aunty who lives there, and she says some things Lord Haw Haw reported were recent changes, like armament movements made since they blitzed Aberdeen last month."

An older woman who worked in the kitchen stopped at our table. "You girls should get home afore curfew."

Della rolled her eyes and screwed her mouth up like she'd been sucking on lemons. Thank goodness her back was to the woman.

We all stood and began getting our coats. I asked, "How would they know those things?"

Moira lowered her voice even though we were almost alone in the dance hall. "My da says it's likely spies."

It was Della who scoffed. "And what would they care about us?"

I knew she was being sarcastic, but Moira shot her such a harsh glare. "You say that after the Blitz?"

"Aye, sure," I said. "Della kens we're a prime target with Scotts Shipyard and the Canadian base." I kept thinking of reasons they might bomb us again. "What about the Hall- Russell shipbuilder in Aberdeen? The Jerries might come back and hit them again." We walked up the hill toward home, talking about movies and clothes as if those common, everyday things helped push the fear out of our thoughts.

I came through my door, surprised to see my great-uncle Angus sitting with my dad by the fire. One of my great-aunts had married a constable. They were older than my parents, and he'd served on the police force in Greenock for years. He looked so official in his dark-blue uniform. I wondered if he was still on duty or if he'd stopped by for a wee chat with my dad on his way home from work.

I knew better than to eavesdrop, but when I saw the shock on my dad's face, I stopped dead in my tracks. Both men looked up at me.

Dad said, "Chrissy, come ye here. Yer Uncle Angus was tellin' me something you should know."

Uncle Angus reached out to stop my da. "Are ye sure, Jim?"

Dad winked at him. "My Chrissy's as brave as they come." A colossal overstatement, but I came to stand next to Dad's chair. He was saying, "And she volunteers all over town. If she knows, she can keep her eyes and ears open, ye ken?"

"Well, if'n yer sure." Angus looked at me squarely. "I've been tellin' yer da, we have a spy in Scotland. No just any fiend, this one's been killin' lassies."

A spy was scarier than contemplating a bombing raid from the Germans. A spy who preyed on innocent women was much worse. I shook my head. It couldn't be true. Like any other country, Scotland had her share of crime, but it wasn't usually violent. There hadn't been a murder anywhere in the Highlands or even in the borderlands in my memory.

"At first they were looking for two different blokes, but now it appears to be one man. The things Lord Haw Haw says on the radio, well, they're very specific."

I relaxed a bit. What Uncle Angus was saying was still speculation.

"And the girls." I swallowed hard. "Are they from around here?"

"Nae then, lass. So far, they've been mostly on the east coast."

I relaxed a bit more. Imagining a fiend far from my town was terrible but not nearly as threatening to my friends and family.

Uncle Angus was saying to my dad, "The latest broadcasts coming out of the Reich were very detailed about Scotland."

I interrupted. "But why would the spy and the murderer be the same person?"

Uncle's voice dropped a bit, and I had to lean closer to catch everything he said. "It's the radio. Whenever Lord Haw Haw gets very detailed about a town—enough we're sure we've had a spy in our midst—a lassie goes missing. Not many know this, but they've all been nice girls, no easy targets." His eyes wandered to my hair as he added, "All the lassies were much alike; dark hair, pretty."

My mouth was open, and I shut it, trying to hide my shock. "There's been nothing about it in the Greenock Telegraph." A feeling of dread pressed on my chest. Murders didn't happen in Scotland—in places like London but not Scotland.

"Aye, that's just the thing, and we want to keep it that way."

"What about the girls in Greenock? Don't you want to protect them?"

Both men shot me a sharp glance which infuriated me, but I knew if I wanted to hear more, I'd have to keep my mouth shut. I clamped my lips together.

Uncle's tone was patronizing. "If he knows we're on to him, we might never catch him. Chrissy, ye canna tell your friends. Not another soul." He looked a bit worried, but Dad broke in.

"Chrissy will do as ye say, no worries." His expression was one of total confidence, and it touched my heart.

I wanted to object. They were asking me to allow some fiend to prey on my friends. But I couldn't let my dad down. I asked, "What should I look for?"

Uncle Angus hesitated but Dad said, "She can be your eyes and ears with the young ladies."

It took Uncle Angus a minute. "My superiors would have me badge if they knew she was in on this, but aye, you're right."

He turned to me. "All his victims are dark-haired young lasses. Watch those girls and see who shows an interest in them. He might pose as a serviceman or as someone with a reason for not being in the fighting." His pointer finger waved in my face as if to emphasize his next words. "And above all, be careful. You know you fit the victims' descriptions. Don't say a word. Not a word."

"Aye, Uncle, I'll not say a word, to be sure." I wondered if there was some way to warn my friends without breaking my word. The fear had followed me up the hill after all.

Wendy—Seattle
1968

I swallowed the last of my tea and made a face.

Mum looked over at my cup. "Gone cold has it?" She got up and took both our teacups to the sink.

"I guess I forgot to drink. I was so caught up in your story. Did they ever catch the guy?" A knock on the front door interrupted us. "I'll get it." I opened the door to John, who was looking very uncomfortable. He shifted his weight and stuffed his hands in his pockets.

I wanted to kick him for coming by after weeks of silence—I'd just decided to go on with my life. But one look at his face and I knew something was really bothering him. I ignored better judgement and didn't tell him to get lost. Instead, I asked, "What's wrong?"

He met my eyes, and I saw his hesitation. "Can we talk?" I stepped back, beckoning him in, but he shook his head. He glanced past me. "I mean in private. Will you come for a drive?"

I turned back to grab my jacket and tell my mom I was going. He took my hand as I closed the door behind me. I felt that rush of affection I always did when he folded his large hand over mine.

His eyes lingered on our hands as if he could read my mind. "Let's drive down to the beach."

WHITE CENTER WASN'T FAR from the Sound. A couple miles from my house, a heavily wooded street curved down the hill to a deserted beach. John told me once a pump station for the local sewer district was there. We parked on the wee bit of gravel at the end of the road.

He didn't get out. And he didn't tell me what was on his mind. I started wondering why I had come with him.

Finally, I said, "Out with it. What's wrong?" He looked at me, those beautiful dark-brown eyes so intense. But his expression was unreadable.

He broke his silence with, "I think I love you."

My heart raced and skipped beats. I was frustrated with all he'd put me through yet wildly excited at hearing him say those words. I kept my eyes on my lap, afraid to meet his eyes. "What makes you say that?"

"I can't stand the idea of you seeing someone else."

I stopped myself from saying, "Don't worry. No one wants to date Mutton's girl." Instead, I waited to hear him out.

"Could we try this again? I'm asking for a second chance."

This was what I wanted all along. Why was I so hesitant? Just when I thought I might be brave enough to leave him behind, he says this. I had to know why this seemed so hard for him. I wanted someone who wanted me. If I was just comfortable, he should look for someone else.

"Will you tell me why you broke up with me?"

"Because I wasn't ready to leave my freedom behind."

I remembered him singing. "You haven't seemed like someone who wants to be tied to a girl, Mr. Born to be Wild."

His face reddened with a full-on blush of embarrassment.

"Why is it such a struggle? I don't want to be someone you're only passing time with."

"It's not like that. I've been trying to talk myself out of this, but it isn't working. We're so different. My friends said we'd never stay together." He looked out over the beach, staring at the waves rolling in.

I could barely breathe waiting for him to finish. Before he did, he reached over and took my hand, searching my eyes. "When we were apart, I kept realizing how much you made me laugh. I love our differences. I was miserable without you."

"Me too." I swallowed the lump in my throat.

His smile was slow but gradually lit his entire face. "What do you think?"

"Yes. I think yes."

Chapter Twenty

Christine—Greenock, Scotland
1943

Many Allied naval vessels put into the Clydebank shipyards for repairs or even rest. I knew part of my father's work involved repairing all kinds of ships. But if the men of Greenock helped to keep the naval vessels afloat, the women of Greenock fed their sailors and gave them what small encouragement they could.

There were canteens set up all over town, places where servicemen could come for wholesome fun. The older ladies of the churches would make cakes and sandwiches. They stocked little tables with stationery and pens in case the young men wanted to write home. Mothers and grandmothers in the churches oversaw the food, but they often asked the younger girls to help with hospitality.

Sometimes we'd listen to the lads talk, but music was the one language that touched every soul. We played records, or on social nights there might be a band and dancing. I volunteered at several of those canteens. Not because of Highland hospitality. These lads were fighting to hold back the Nazi terror from taking our country, our homes, and enslaving us. This was our way of giving them rest.

This afternoon, I was late getting home from my dance lessons at the Canadian canteen. I called out as I came through the front door, "Sorry, Mum, missed my bus and had to—"

My friend Bridie sat at my kitchen table with a cup of tea in one hand and a mouth full of one of my mum's wonderful scones. I'd almost forgotten we'd agreed to help at a church social that evening.

"Och, Bridie, sorry I'm so late." We were supposed to be at the church canteen in half an hour. I walked past her saying, "I missed my bus, had to walk home," and called to her on my way to the bedroom, "I'll change my clothes, and we can go."

"Thaazaa right. Yer mum fud me." Her mouth was full, but I got the gist of what she said. I threw on a dress and ran a brush through my hair. Even after a day teaching dance to Canadian sailors and a long walk home, it took only a minute to brush the shine into my black hair. Little blue-black highlights reflected from the lamp on my dresser. My hair fell in heavy waves halfway down my back. The picture of the Gypsy woman came to mind. I remembered wanting to look like her one day. My skin is pale and hers was sun brown, but otherwise we both have brown eyes and a heart-shaped face. Then I glanced at the clock and shrugged at the girl in the mirror. "Better hurry. Besides, no matter how it looks now, it'll all be in ringlets by the time I'm done dancing."

I was back in the kitchen in five minutes, only to find a steaming cup of tea and a plate with one scone sitting at my place.

My mum's "so don't bother arguing" voice told me, "Sit doon and have some tea and a wee bite of scone." I held my hand up to stop her, but she added. "Or don't go at all." I wondered if she'd treat me like a child for the rest of my life.

I landed my seat in the chair and prepared to eat the scone as quickly as possible. Bridie smiled at me, her mouth still full.

That's what I loved about my childhood friend. She always found a way to make me smile. She took her last bite, and my mum offered her another scone.

"No, mam, but thank ye all the same. If I eat another bite, I wouldn't be able to walk down the hill to town." A red curl slid out of its pin and bounced off her freckled nose.

"That's all right, Bridie," I teased. "I'll give ye a push, and you can roll doon the hill." We laughed. There weren't many fat people during the war, not with rationing and food shortages, and certainly not Bridgett Donoghue.

I hurried through my tea and grabbed my coat. After a quick kiss on my mum's cheek, we were out the door and walking down Mount Pleasant Street toward town.

A conglomeration of three or four churches in town sponsored the church social. St. John the Evangelist on Union Street hosted these canteens because of its large church hall and its nearness to the waterfront. I loved the place. The hall had vaulted ceilings, a good kitchen at one end and even a small gallery for the band at the other. Its many large windows, covered with heavy curtains once night fell, gave the room a golden glow during daylight hours. All the same, my true love was the dance floor and the echo of my taps off the old beams that arched overhead.

Once we arrived, they put us to work in a flurry of activity. Finally, the sandwiches were made and the kitchen settled. One lady said to the group of young women, "Can ye go out into the hall? Talk to the lads, show them where the stationery is in case they want to write letters." She pointed at us. "I don't have to tell you to dance with them, do I now?"

Bridie and I looked at each other and laughed again. No one had to talk us into dancing.

Lads from different countries and branches of the military drifted in. A small band took the stage at one end of the hall and played a Tommy Dorsey song. We were both on the dance floor within minutes.

Over the sound of the band, we heard Bridgett's father call out, "Bridgett. Bridgett, over here." Mr. Donoghue looked like he was on his way home from work. He still had his lunchpail, and his work overalls were worn and dusty. He stood at the entrance with a group of five young sailors who were scanning the room with a mixture of surprise and confusion.

Bridie shrugged her shoulders as if to say, "Who in the world are they?" I shrugged too. I didn't recognize them, but their dark-blue uniforms were wrinkled and dingy. It looked like they'd been at sea for quite a while.

We made our way past dancing couples to her father. When he saw us coming, his smile was pure relief.

"These boys are from a Russian sub. They put in for repairs. I found them wandering around looking lost. The tall one speaks a little English, the rest . . ." He shook his head. "At least they could eat and maybe relax a little. But make sure they go back to their ship before nine o'clock. Point them in the right direction."

From their bewildered expressions, I wondered how often they got leave in a foreign port. Dad had spoken once about the Russian navy. At the beginning of the war, he said Hitler was a fool to discount the Russians. It was the largest submarine fleet in the world. And a fearless group of sailors manned their subs.

So, these were the brave lads of the Russian submarine service. They looked more like lost boys.

"Right, Da, we'll see to it." Bridgett motioned for them to come in and found them a table.

I went to get a tray of sandwiches, but they only looked at me. No one took any. Then I said, "Please have some. They're great, and they're free."

The tall blond's eyes lit up, and he repeated, "Free, *besplatno*," and bowed slightly. Soon there was a cacophony of the word "free" repeated several times by each sailor.

Bridgett said, "Seems that word translates into every language."

I had to agree. My tray emptied in two minutes. With full stomachs, the lads were all smiles.

A few of the older women always stayed on to chaperone and make more sandwiches if needed. Two of the Russian lads left the table and went back to the kitchen. Through the long open serving window, I saw one of them reached out to kiss the worn hand of old Mrs. Dalrymple, saying a string of syllables that ended with *"spah-see-bah."* He repeated this with the two other ladies.

His friend led the women to some chairs. The ladies were all smiles and giggles but looked very confused until the lads rolled up their sleeves and started wiping down counters and washing dishes.

Boys are boys, but these lads were so different. When they relaxed a bit and their peacoats came off, they all wore navy-blue-and-white striped, long-sleeved sweaters under their coats. Most naval uniforms were similar, but I hadn't seen this before.

I realized those of us left at the table were just staring at each other.

Bridgett said, "My name is Bridgett." They all repeated something that sounded like an attempt at saying Bridgett. She looked at me. "Seems Bridgett is a hard word for them."

I smiled. "Can ye say Bridie?" That went better. "My name is Christina."

Their only English speaker stuck out his hand. "I am Vyacheslav. It is most pleasant to meet you, Christian. This is my friend Timofei. And that youngster is Anatoly."

He motioned to the shorter dark-haired lad. They all bore a similar bone structure—long straight nose, high cheekbones and eyes that looked a bit slanted. Nice-looking young men, especially the leader. His white-blond hair and steel-grey eyes were striking.

I gave his name a try and had as much trouble with it as they had with Bridgett. He was good natured and said, "Vy will be easier for you, I think."

Bridgett reached for Timofei's hand. "I'll call you Tim, a fine Irish name. Do Russians dance?"

Vyacheslav translated, and Tim's face lit up. They were on the dance floor in minutes. I realized Tim was not a dancer, but he sported quite a grin. Bridgett was a beautiful redhead, and I was sure he'd be bragging to his friends tonight.

Vyacheslav asked, "I would like to do the dancing with you, if you dance?" He was so shy and handsome. His eyes wandered to my hair. He said something in Russian and blushed a bit, adding, "Beautiful. Your hair."

I tried not to roll my eyes, sure it had all gone to ringlets, but said, "Why, thank you" and gave him my hand as he led me onto the floor. That night we danced with all the Russians, but the tall blond kept coming back to dance with me.

Bridgett talked away to Timofei. Mostly he smiled and nodded. I was sure he didn't understand a word of what she said, but he was enjoying her company.

I spoke with Vy. His parents were teachers, he said.

"Their English is pretty good. They taught me to speak English but not like they do in Scotland. This is an unfamiliar language, no?"

I laughed. "Different accent, but it's the same language."

The two young men came back from helping in the kitchen. One sailor rattled off a string of words. Vyacheslav said, "These are Oleg and Lyev. They would like to make dancing with you again, please." I couldn't remember the sailor's name, but his smile was comically lopsided as he led me out to the dance floor.

During a break for the band, we all came back to the table and sat around smiling. It was hard to make conversation since most of them had so little English until I said, "My father works at Scotts. He's probably working on your sub right now."

"Your father, who is please?"

"James Finlay."

Vyacheslav's face lit up. "I know this man. Very fine man." He said something to the group, and they all stood and bowed, saying "Finlay" and a string of words lost on me. Vyacheslav explained. "He is supervising repairs. Very capable man, very Russian."

I nearly laughed. I'd have to tell Da that he was very Russian.

We had an enjoyable evening with the Russian sailors. After every dance, they each bowed and kissed our hands. We were all dazzled by their manners, and several other girls came over to dance with them.

Bridgett watched the time and soon said to Vyacheslav, "It's time to go back to your sub, and we have a curfew. We'll be leaving for home." The hall was emptying, and the band had played its last song.

With a few words from my tall blond friend, we were moving down the hall toward the door. Every building had some arrangement so that when you left, you exited through a dimly lit area. Heavy blackout curtains covered even the doors. After the Blitz, we were careful not to give the Germans any targets, especially at night.

Vyacheslav and I were the last to move down the hall toward the door. When he stopped me, I wasn't afraid. This was a shy, sweet lad. I could hear the uncertainty in his voice as he asked, "A minute, Christian." He backed me toward the wall, and I was sure he'd kiss me goodbye when he said, "This will only take a minute. Hold still. Close your eyes."

That was strange, except he was a very shy young man. But instead of his lips, I felt his breath against my cheek. Uncle Angus' warning about a killer came back to me, and my heart began racing. I pulled away, but he held me tight to the wall. My eyes flew open, and his face was next to mine.

I wanted to scream, but I was suddenly so frightened I couldn't seem to get any air. I squinted my eyes closed as his large hand held my forehead, and something like cold steel slid down my cheek. I felt a tug on my hair and heard a snip, and he said, "*Spasibo*."

My eyes popped open again as Vyacheslav released me. There he stood with a long ringlet of my black hair. He looked like a small boy with a prize.

"I have never seen hair so black and shiny." He looked up hesitantly. "I hope it's all right."

I was so relieved to see the steel was a small knife he closed and dropped back into his pocket.

"When I get home, I will tell them about my perfect night with the most beautiful girl, and they will not believe." He held up my long ringlet. "I will show them."

I was still speechless when we joined his friends and pointed the way back to the shipyards. It wasn't until Bridgett and I were walking home that I described the sheer terror I'd felt in the hallway.

Bridgett laughed. "You'll always remember the day the Russians came to town." She looked at my hair. "If you'll pin it back, it won't even be noticeable."

When I got home, I walked to stand by the large map on the kitchen wall. My dad was late with his supper, and Mum was keeping him company, her knitting needles clicking away as she worked on a sweater.

My finger traced the boundaries of the Baltic Sea. Russia, Estonia, Latvia, Lithuania, Poland, Germany, Denmark, Sweden, and Finland surrounded it. I'd heard Dad say once that the Germans and Finns had underwater mines at the two pinch points: the Gulf of Finland, which led to Russian ports; and the Danish Straits, which led to the North Sea that borders Scotland's east coast. It was much closer to us than I first imagined. But how had those Russian lads made it through those submarine-killer mines?

"What are ye lookin' at, Chrissy?" Dad stood to join me.

"I met some sailors off that Russian submarine you were working on."

Dad's eyebrows shot up. "And how do you know I was working on their sub?"

"I said your name, and they recognized it. They said"—I imitated Vyacheslav's accent—"Finlay, very capable man, very Russian."

Dad chuckled. "Quite a compliment, I'd say." He told me how the Russian navy had been tasked with disrupting the convoys of precious iron ore from the mines of neutral Sweden to the war factories in Germany.

"Was that where they came from?" I pointed to the Baltic Sea.

Dad shook his head. "Oh, they're a tight-lipped group, but my guess is they were guarding convoys of munitions and war supplies bound for Russia up north."

His finger strayed to the Barents Sea north of Sweden and Finland. I shivered at the thought of Vyacheslav's and Timofei's submarine moving through the cold depths of the sea to hunt or be hunted. I reached absentmindedly for my missing curl. If it comforted him, it was a small price to pay.

Mum sounded concerned. "Chrissy, what's wrong with your hair?"

I tucked what was left of my curl behind my ear. "Nothing, Mum." I changed the subject quickly before she decided I'd need to cut my hair to match the missing piece. "They were friendly lads."

We never saw those boys again or any other Russians.

Wendy—Seattle
1968

POWDERED SUGAR and bits of cookie dough covered my hands. I was helping Mum make Russian tea cakes while she spoke. I thought about her story as I took a bit of a cookie still warm from the oven. With a full mouth, I said, "I'm not so sure I would have been such a good sport about losing a chunk of my hair."

"Guess I was so relieved that it didn't seem that important."

I thought for a minute and realized she'd never told me about meeting my father. "Did my dad come to Greenock?" She gave me a side glance. "How old were you when you met him?"

"Sixteen."

"Sixteen. So young?" I realized my tone was judgmental, so in a more teasing manner I asked, "Was it love at first sight?"

"No, I thought he was arrogant."

I sobered at the thought of myself at sixteen choosing a partner for life. "No wonder you don't lecture me about being too young."

"Yes, but you grow up fast during war." She added with a sympathetic smile, "Your dad broke up with me, too, and I didn't see him again till after the war."

"Wait, what? Why didn't you ever tell me?" I thought about how I suffered over losing John. "It might have helped." My heart felt wounded.

She dusted the flour off her hands and folded me in a hug. "I thought about it. Believe me, I did, but I didn't want to sway you." She held me away, giving me direct eye contact. "The best way to know how you really feel is to work it out. I can tell you my experiences, but then you'd have false hope." She had a smile just for me. It was full of complete love and understanding. And I knew she'd done the right thing.

"Thanks. I've been thinking of John's return, and I'm not naïve. I know it still might not work out. But I think we're both ready to try again."

"I'm always amazed your dad and I could build a life together on the foundation of our first meeting."

Chapter Twenty-One

Christine—Greenock, Scotland
July 1943

Two of my friends, Della and Moira, worked in town at Boots Chemist on Hamilton Street. When an opening came up, they put a word in for me. I was working with a bookbinder, but his business was slow. It was a good move to work at Boots. Not only did I enjoy working with my friends, but I found another good friend and mentor in an unlikely place.

Nurse Graham was a stern older woman with grizzled steel-grey hair and deep frown lines. She seemed long past the age of retirement, but that didn't slow her down at all. A registered nurse in her own right, she ran the dispensary at Boots with the high expectations of a ward nurse.

All first impressions aside, she had a heart of gold and a deep concern for everyone who came across her path. She taught me basic first aid and the names and uses for all kinds of medical supplies. I was her assistant. Sometimes that meant restocking shelves or filling orders. Mostly I did whatever she asked. I was a little intimidated by her, but I admired her as well.

Our store was nestled above the main street in a second-floor space. Wide stone stairs between a wool shop and the candy shop at street level led up to the chemist and our little dispensary on the second floor and then to a bookshop above us. Our front windows looked down on the cobblestones of Hamilton Street. It was a busy place and never more so than when a new ship would come to port for rest and repairs.

On a misty July morning, I waited for the bus to work. My attention drifted to the River Clyde. I spotted three large ships that hadn't been there yesterday. I was pretty sure they were Canadian ships. After all, the Canadians had a hospital and naval base in Greenock. Last week, we'd seen the newsreels at the cinema about a big Allied push to take Sicily, our first foothold in Europe. Canada played a major role in the Sicily offensive. They were probably back for a rest and to tend their wounded.

The Canadians were not a quarrelsome lot, but with that many sailors in town, squabbles happened. I expected it would be a busy day. Nurse Graham's small infirmary was in the back corner of the store. We filled orders for physicians and served as a walk-in clinic for minor medical matters. The rest of the store sold medicines and things one might find in any pharmacy. Della worked in cosmetics, and Moira assisted the chemist. Eventually Australians, Poles, French, Americans, and Canadians visited our little shop.

Occasionally a fight would break out in town, and the lads would sometimes need a bit of patching up before reporting for duty. Nurse Graham had a no-nonsense attitude that calmed even a wayward Yank or two.

After the heavy rain yesterday, customers were tracking muddy footprints all over the store. Nurse said, "Chrissy, get a broom and see what ye can do to clean the floors." I didn't mind doing any task, and I think that's why I often ended up with jobs the other girls would complain about.

Today I was in a get-it-done mood. After I swept the store, I started on the wide stairs from the street to our shop, glancing up the steps occasionally to check the foot traffic. But a steady stream of customers kept getting in my way. I grew tired of waiting while they passed only to sweep the same steps again and again. Finally, I decided if I put my head down and went at it, they'd walk around me.

A young man in a Canadian sailor's uniform came out of the bookstore at the top of the stairs with an open book in hand. I wasn't sweeping in the middle of the steps, so there was plenty of room to pass. My broom swept out, and he got his feet tangled. Before I knew what happened, he tumbled down the steps in front of me. I realized he hadn't been looking where he was going. I rushed to help him to his feet, that is, until he said, "What were you trying to do, kill me?" He jerked his elbow free.

I'm not usually contentious, but really, who walks down steps reading? I picked up the book he'd dropped and noticed it was on local geography. As I handed it to him, I said, "It's easier to learn about local geography if you try looking at it. Surely a big sturdy lad like you would have walked doon a few stairs in his life before."

He snatched the book from my hand as he stood. He stared at me for a moment, humphed, and strode away.

Arrogant fool. Well, nice-looking, arrogant fool. He was tall with broad shoulders and a small waist and hips. His white sailor cap sat to the side on his longish sandy-blond hair. It was a shame he wasn't born with common sense.

He stopped at the bottom step and made eye contact with me as if he'd heard my thoughts. An odd expression crossed his face before he stepped out onto Hamilton Street.

The heat rose in my cheeks, and I glanced around, wondering if anyone was watching. For once, the steps were quiet. A good time to get this job done. Even as I attacked the sweeping, I kept an eye out for another foolish Canadian. It might be a common character trait.

Things died down by five. A laddie I'd met at the Canadian hospital had said he'd like to take me out. Since he still had a limp from an injury, I figured a concert would do best. We planned to meet after work. While I waited, I looked around for something else to keep me busy until my date arrived. Still no sign of the lad, so I straightened shelves and dusted. Everyone else had left for the day. I was about to do the same, date or no date.

I pushed the shop door closed and heard a loud yelp. I jumped and flung back the door. There stood the same sailor I'd tripped on the dispensary stairs.

"What on earth are—?" I stopped myself when I saw the young man's face was a mask of agony. As he cradled his right hand, blood was already flowing over his fingers onto the floor. Of all the foolish Canadians, why did I suffer this one twice in one day?

His face was scrunched with pain, but he gasped out, "I tried to stop the door before it closed, but it felt like someone"—he gave me an accusing stare—"pushed it shut."

"Oh, sorry." I felt bad about that, but he shared half the blame.

"Didn't you see me standing there?"

I ignored his question and went into my Nurse Graham mode. "Give me yer hand a minute." He hesitated, and I added, "I just closed the door. Yer the one who stuck his fingers in the jamb." I had the odd compulsion to make a face at him, but I controlled myself. He might be cute with those deep blue eyes and his sandy hair but, God knows, he was annoying. "And, no, I didn't see you there."

He held out his hand for me to examine. It looked like two of his fingers had caught the edge of the door when I pushed it shut. Slice marks ran across the tips. "Right, come with me, and we'll get you fixed up." I found a small basin and bathed the hand. He stood without comment except for a few small squeaks when I put iodine on the cuts.

I tensed at his continued silence, expecting him to unleash a tirade of accusations on me at any minute. Well, that's all right. I had a thing or two to say to him. Why would he grab the edge of the door? Didn't they use door handles in Canada? I positioned his hand for bandaging, but when I looked up at him, his gaze was on me instead of his fingers. He had a slight smile on his full lips.

When I finished bandaging, I used my matter-of-fact Nurse Graham voice. "There you go. The cuts aren't that bad. Keep them clean and dry, and it'll heal soon enough."

His voice was soft with a slight country drawl when he said, "My name is Russell. I think we've gotten off to a poor start. Do you think you might let me take you for coffee or something?"

I answered rather curtly, "Name's Christina." I reached out to shake his hand but remembered his injury, so I gave his left hand one shake.

As I turned to leave, he held on. "I'd like to talk."

I felt guilty for all the injuries I'd inflicted on him, so I tried to sound sorry when I said, "I'm waiting for a date. We're going to a concert at the town hall. He's meeting me out front at half-past five." I slipped on my jacket.

He followed me out the door and, to my surprise, lingered while I locked up.

"If it's all right, I'll wait with you. We can talk." I must have looked skeptical because he added, "You might like me. Truce? No more blood and bodily injury?"

Really, the poor laddie had a bad day himself. "I guess it'll be all right." Once outside, a soft mist started.

"Oh," he said, "It's raining. Should we wait inside?"

"It's no rain, really. We call it a *smirr*." He raised an eyebrow, so I explained. "Ye ken, a soft mist only. It willna penetrate your clothes or even soak your hair. A quick shake and it's gone." As we waited for my date to arrive, I learned he was born in Canada in Saskatoon, Saskatchewan. And they think we have odd names for things.

I said, "My aunt lives near Montreal. She married after the last war, and she's been there ever since. Do you ken that place?"

He shook his head. "Canada's a big country, and I've never been to Quebec except to pass through on the train. I grew up on the prairie land. It's all flat. No hills or mountains."

That piqued my interest. I'd just been to a Western at the cinema. "Do you have Indians?"

"There's a Blackfeet reservation across the river in the States."

I loved Westerns, so I warmed to the topic. When he wasn't being difficult, the laddie had a remarkably boyish quality.

I must have been smiling like a loon because he said, "Gosh, you have a beautiful smile."

I looked away quickly.

"Your date isn't here, and I am. Can we go to the concert and get out of this smear?"

"*Smirr*. I guess, but I'll give him five more minutes first." Maybe my date had to work an extra shift on base. A nice enough lad, but he was only a friend, and I wasn't that disappointed. We waited, but my date didn't show, so we caught the bus to the town hall.

By the time we got there, the concert hall was nearly full. We sat in the back. I had friends performing, so I had to crane my neck to look at them. I glanced at Russell. He was staring at me. "Why are you doing that?"

He smiled slightly. "Doing what?"

"You're staring. Don't you like the concert?" I'd been so annoyed with Russell earlier, but there was something about him that drew me. I hadn't let myself feel romantic about anyone since Moddy's brother Eddie. I dated and volunteered, but there was never anything more than friendship. Guess I was afraid of another bad ending.

Russell's voice was quiet. I'd swear he was embarrassed. "I want to memorize you. Your face. Your hair. It's so long and curly. I want to remember every detail."

I gave him a hard look, but his expression was open and honest. It took me back a bit, but my walls came up. You had to be careful with so many young men far from home, from sweethearts, hoping for the comfort of someone's arms around them. That sounded a little too much like a pickup line. I glanced at my watch, hoping it was time to leave. "Oh, look at that," I said. "It's seven thirty. Don't you have curfew soon? Is it time to go back to your ship?"

He shook his head. "I'm not from the ships. I was wounded."

Well, at least I wasn't the cause of all his infirmities.

"I have shrapnel in my body. I'm well enough now, but they haven't sent me back to my ship yet. I'm temporarily stationed at NIOBE.

With a naval hospital right here in Greenock, I was used to hearing lads had been wounded. I didn't want to seem hardhearted. Still, it was time for me to leave. "Well, I must be getting home. I have a curfew, and my parents are very strict." I rose and he with me. He helped me into my jacket, and we made our way out the door.

He looked crestfallen. I heard him murmur under his breath, "So early?"

Life wasn't like the American teenagers in an Andy Hardy movie. And our dramas were not the kinds of things I'd seen at the cinemas. When you live in a war zone, you grew up fast. I'd matured beyond my sixteen years. My parents trusted me, but they kept close tabs on when I got home.

"Is there any reason I can't walk you home? We can talk some more."

I didn't really know him, but I heard myself say, "I guess it'd be all right." He walked me all the way home, asking questions and talking about his life in Canada. When he left me at my doorstep, Russell flashed me a sweet smile. I asked if he knew his way to the bus stop.

He jerked his head back as if I'd insulted him. "I have an excellent sense of direction." He sounded so prideful that I stifled a giggle as he added, "I never get lost." He took my hand and shook it, saying, "I'll see you soon." Then he set off walking toward Ann Street.

"Oh, Russell," I called out. "If you go back doon Mount Pleasant Street, you can catch the bus on the old Inverkip Road. It'll take you to the base."

He stopped. "Right. I was going to walk around a bit." He gave me a sheepish smile before he turned back on his chosen path.

Maybe Canadians were too prideful for their own good. I shook my head. As rocky as our meeting had been, I still felt attracted to him. Then again, he looked like a young John Wayne. He hadn't even tried to kiss me good night. I gave him one last glance before going inside, hoping he'd find his way.

After that, I saw Russell often for the better part of two months. He would show up at work or come to the Canadian Overseas Club when I volunteered. He didn't dance, but we'd talk whenever I was free. One sunny summer afternoon we wandered down to the Clyde. Blue waves sparkled and bounced on the river. The sky was amazing, so clear, no clouds. The wind was soft; then a sudden gust would come, and I'd have to hold down my skirts.

Sitting on the rocks by the Cloch Lighthouse, we took off our shoes and dangled our feet in the water. The day was hot. Russell rolled the dark wool of his naval uniform to his knees.

I couldn't help noticing his white calves. "Don't get much sun on those?"

He gave me a double take. His grin was infectious, but he said nothing back. I thought, this is good, peaceful. His sandy-blond hair formed little damp curls around his face. He had that young John Wayne air about him, rugged, manly—not strikingly handsome but deeply attractive. I looked away. Bad habit that, always comparing people to film stars.

I watched the sea birds dive for fish and sighed. "I could almost forget there's a war."

"I'm glad there's a war." He sounded incredulous.

My mouth fell open. "What?"

"I never would have met you if there hadn't been a war."

I was about ready to break our peace and give him a piece of my mind when he said, "Christina, you're the best thing that ever happen to me."

I closed my mouth. Not the first time I'd heard that one.

His voice was soft and heartfelt. "No, you don't understand. I mean it. It's not a line or something."

He reached for my hand and kissed my fingers and whispered, "It's from my heart."

His tender words laid claim to me. His attraction to me was so strong it drew me in. Was I giving him all the attractive qualities of my favorite movie star, or were they really present in Russell? Who was this boy? Why was it so hard to resist him?

"I care very much for you, Russell." The impact of my own words stole my breath. They were true. *I'm giving my heart to a young man from the other side of the Atlantic Ocean. What am I thinking? It'll never last.*

His eyes were liquid blue, and his gaze held me, searching. "We're so different. Our lives and our families are different. It's not just different countries; my world isn't like yours at all." His voice caught.

Why? How are we so different?

I waited for him to go on. He took a deep breath. "I'll be rejoining my ship soon. I don't want to lose you. Will you wait and let me write you?"

"Yes." I wrote lots of servicemen. It was a common enough request.

"No, I mean will you wait?"

Things just went from peaceful to complicated so fast it made my head spin. "I don't understand. Wait? I'm not going anywhere."

"Don't give your heart to anyone else. Wait. We can write, get to know each other." He blew his breath out like he'd been holding it. "It might be easier to say things in letters without those big, beautiful chocolate eyes looking right at me."

The wind whipped my long hair into a tangled mess. He released my hand and reached up to push it out of my face. His expression was so tender as he said in almost a whisper, "God, how I love looking into those eyes."

I didn't tell Russell I'd wait for him, but I said I'd write. That last night before they shipped him out, he came to our house for dinner. My parents were polite but reserved. They were friendly but kept darting glances at each other and at me. Deep down inside, I think they'd seen a change. I felt it too. This wasn't someone to befriend and send on his way. This was someone who mattered to me.

After dinner we walked back to the town hall for a concert. He said, "Your mom's a great cook. Don't know if I'd ever get used to tea, though." He grimaced. "I miss a cup of good, strong coffee. Or a cold beer."

"You must miss your mother's cooking."

He halted. "Now there's where you're wrong. I'm surprised we survived our childhood. She's a horrible cook." His smile was slightly lopsided.

"Are you teasing me?"

"Not on your life." He slipped his arm around me. "Let's not go to the concert. I want you all to myself."

I nodded. "Let's walk on the Esplanade."

"Not what I'd really like but okay." I peeked at him, and he blushed. This was unexplored ground for me. All my interactions with young men had stayed strictly on a friendship basis with me relegated to the protective status of a little sister.

Oh, quite a few young men had kissed me goodnight. I'd heard the girls talk about things that happened on dates. Della for one. But it'd never been something I'd had to deal with. Russell's deep blush told me he meant something, oh, I don't know, more than a kiss. Warning lights flashed in my head. This was a guy who lived halfway around the world. My world was here with my family, friends, and the deep love I had for my country. I had to do a better job of guarding my heart. I searched for a safe topic of conversation.

We walked and talked. "When Felix Mendelssohn's grandson came to town, he saw me dancing. Do you know his band?"

I was never sure he was really listening when he looked at me with his mouth so ready for a kiss, but I pressed on. "They play Hawaiian music mostly. I'd love to visit the islands."

"We should go there together."

I rolled my eyes.

"They asked if I'd like to join their band—as a dancer, you know." My face heated with the pleasure of being singled out by this celebrity. "He said I looked more Hawaiian than some of his dancers, but my mum said no." I still felt the bite of disappointment.

Russell stopped. "I'm glad she said no. You'd never have tripped me on the stairs if you were off with some band."

"I didn't trip you. You weren't watching where you were going." We laughed.

"Well, I'm glad I fell in more ways than one."

Boys. Where do they come up with lines like that? But his face was so sincere I almost believed him. Yes, I was in danger of losing my whole heart for good. When we kissed goodnight and goodbye, unexpected tears ran down my cheeks. He wiped away a tear and smiled.

"You'll miss me?"

"You know I will. Do you think they'll send you back? Back here, I mean, to Greenock. To me."

"I heard we'll be back, but I can't say when." We stood on the Esplanade, the wind picking up off the water. He held me at arm's length. "Here's the thing. I know I don't deserve you, but I can't help it. My family—we didn't have much growing up. Your folks . . . well, they're not poor."

"What does that matter?"

He pressed on. "I think I love you, Chrissy. Think of me and write."

Young men going off to war often said things like this. I'd heard my girlfriends talk about it. But it hadn't happened to me. Still, he'd broken down the walls I kept around my emotions. Russell shipped out, but I thought about him all the time.

I'm not sure why, but I painted scenes of sandy beaches and palm trees and used them as stationery. We talked about everything. He was affectionate and funny, but there was an underlying sadness in his reminiscences. Not melancholy but almost. Still, it didn't show up all the time, only when he remembered his childhood on the prairies of Saskatchewan. I don't think he was a happy child.

He asked if his sister Margie could write me. No one had ever asked me to write a family member. I wondered why but thought it was sweet of him. I said I'd love to write to her.

Margie was curious about life in Scotland, and she shared what it was like in Canada. She was her brother's advocate, always talking about his abilities and noble traits. From Margie, I learned Russell had a fabulous sense of direction. He tracked and hunted with the best of them. My imagination pictured him as a cowboy.

I dreamed of a life in a wilderness with Indians and log cabins. It must have been those American movies. I was in love with Westerns, and the way she described their lives, he seemed to fit right into my picture of life on the North American prairies.

A few months later, Russell's ship was back for two weeks, and he came into the store as soon as they gave him shore leave. I was working in the dispensary restocking supplies in our closet. I thought I was imagining things when a familiar voice said, "I got tired of waiting outside for you to come sweep those steps."

"Russell?" I spun around to find him standing in the doorway to our little supply closet. I was in his arms, and he held me so tight.

"Christina, I've missed you. Did you think about me?"

I didn't answer him. My throat closed with emotion. He backed me into the shelves. They'd fire me if anyone saw us, but I couldn't help myself. I wanted him to kiss me. When he did, it felt as if the entire world melted away. Nothing mattered. Russell was safe.

When he pulled back to look at me, I was shaky. "Will you be here long?" Everyone was talking about some big offensive. I hoped he wouldn't be going back to the front.

We heard voices coming from the store. It seemed there was a world beyond our little closet. He took my hand and led me out into the everyday world. I held his fingers up to the light. "Looks like these healed well."

Nurse Graham came around the corner. "Do we have a new patient?" She stopped and looked from one of us to the other and extended her hand. "You must be Russell."

He stepped forward and shook it. "Yes, and you must be Nurse Graham."

We were all smiles when Nurse gave me the afternoon off.

It was a warm autumn day. "How long do we have?"

He was positively glowing, and I was as well. "All the way till my seven thirty curfew."

I grabbed my jacket and his hand. "I want to take you for a hike."

"A what?"

"You'll see." We walked up the hill from town, past my Grandma Cowan's house on Wellington Street and into the hills. All the time we talked about the things we'd written in our letters. At the crest of the hill, I paused. The wind blew his sailor's cap off his head, and he had to scramble backward to catch it. When he straightened, he stopped, his eyes traveling over the view of the hills, our little town, the wide River Clyde, and the Highlands beyond.

"Now that's really somethin'."

I reached out and took his hand. "It's my special place. From the time I was a wee lass, whenever I was troubled, I'd come here." I pointed to the slope on the other side of the hill. "Doon there is an old watchtower ruin. I used to pretend it was my fortress."

"You mean that's where you hide your heart?" His tone was almost accusatory.

I pulled back. "Why would you say that?" I was angry and confused.

He folded me in a hug. I struggled to break free with the full intent of marching back down the hill toward Grandma's house. But his words whispered against my ear. "You've built walls around your feelings. I understand that. But not between us, right?" I froze. His words demanded my attention. "No walls between us."

I knew he was right. It was part of this alone feeling that had been with me since Isabelle died. Every time I let down my defenses, I lost someone I loved. Now Russell was asking me to let down my walls for him, and I didn't want to lose him. I couldn't resist the force of my feelings.

"Aye, no walls." My voice sounded like a pitiful child. "I want to, I do, but I don't want to lose you."

"You won't." He sounded so sure. "I promise. You'll never lose me unless you send me away." And I believed him.

"Come on," he said. "I want to see your fortress." We followed the path down the hill and crossed the small stream. Vines grew up the old stones of the watchtower. I remembered the Gypsy family who'd camped here once and smiled.

"What are you smiling about?"

I told him about losing my sister Isabelle and climbing the hills behind Grandma Cowan's house to this spot. I described the small caravan wagon and finding the Gypsy family camped down in the wee glen next to the tower.

"We have small trailers in Canada too. Lots of people live in them." I thought of the movies I'd seen.

"You mean like wagon trains?" He threw his head back and laughed. He sobered at my reaction.

"No, not really. They're more like small houses on wheels."

"But you don't pull them with a horse?"

"Horsepower but not horses."

I quirked my head to the side, trying to understand. "The Indians don't bother you?"

Something I said amused him again but he only said, "No, not really."

He was being so cryptic, but I decided not to pursue it in the joy of having him here with me. I took his hand, and we crossed the stream by stepping from rock to rock. He'd written to me about his love for the out-of-doors. He was at home in the little wooded glen.

He stopped me at the door to the old, ruined watchtower and backed me to the ivy-covered wall. His arms were around me in an instant. His lips covered mine before I said his name. Warmth flooded me. Every nerve in my body came alive. When he drew back, I moved without conscious thought closer to those lips. Little warning voices sounded in my head, and I thought of things Della had said now becoming clear.

I pulled away, taking his hand in mine. We climbed the old stone steps to the top of the tower. The steps were mostly intact as they circled the inner wall to the top of the battlement, only twenty feet from the ground. We stood for a moment looking down the wee *cleugh*, or gulch, with the stream running to the River Clyde.

"I've always wondered why they built this tower below the crest of the hill. Seems to me it would have been a much better watchtower up there." I pointed to the top of the hill.

He looked back at the hill behind us and down the length of the *cleugh*. Pointing toward the Clyde, he said, "This would be the perfect landing for an enemy to approach." His eyes squinted as he spoke. "An enemy could come up from the river inland quite a distance, hidden by the hills on either side of the stream." He turned around. "From here, one man could watch the river and send a warning to others long before an enemy reached him."

I shook my head. "All these years, and I never figured that out."

We spent a perfect day together, and when we said goodnight, he planned to come for me after work the next day. I hated to mention anything that might ruin our time, but I had to know, so I asked him how long he'd be back. He shook his head. "No one's saying much."

We had a wonderful week of stolen moments between my work and his duty shifts. It was my turn to memorize him, every expression, the way he turned his head to hide his laugh when he thought something I said was funny. His broad shoulders and small waist, even the dimple in his chin, I seared into my memory.

One afternoon he was waiting for me after work. He stood at the bus stop, looking at his watch. There was something different about him. A tenseness. It all changed when he turned to see me come down the stairs. His face relaxed into a beautiful smile as if relief at seeing me washed away the worry creases between his brows.

I was so focused on him, I stepped off the walkway into the street only to jump back when an automobile sounded its horn. As soon as it passed, I was across the street and into his arms. He engulfed me in a fierce hug and kissed me with the same intensity. "I didn't know if you were still at work or gone home for the day." He pulled back and took my hand. "Let's walk."

"Why didn't you come in?" His manner was a bit off, and I stopped.

He paused and turned a few steps ahead of me.

"What is it? You're scaring me. What's wrong?"

"I want to walk to the water and talk. We can sit on those benches on the, what do you call it, Esplanade."

I nodded, and we fell into step. He was still quiet when we turned onto the wide walkway along the river's shore, always a favorite of mine. The fresh breeze from the water lifted my hair. When we came to the first empty bench, I pulled him over. "All right. That's far enough. What's wrong?"

We sat, and he stared out over the river. "I've been trying to think how to say this is all."

"Out wi' it." Even as I demanded an answer, I knew what was wrong. "You're leaving, aye?"

He bit his lip. "Yes."

"How long?"

"I have to be back on the ship in an hour."

"An hour?" I would not cry. I wanted his last memories of me to be happy. I battled back my fear for him and attempted to be positive. "But you'll be back soon, won't you?" I searched his eyes but didn't find any reassurance.

He had such pain in his eyes. "No matter what happens I promise I'll come back to you."

"I'll hold you to it, Russell Beckman. Wild Indians can't hold a candle to an angry Scot."

He laughed. "You know we Canadian commandos have a reputation for being tough, but I'd hate it if you were mad at me, Scot or not." He stared at me with such an intensity before turning away to wipe his eyes with his sleeve. I touched his chin, and when he looked back, my lips met his.

When we separated, I whispered, "No, you wouldn't want to make me mad, so keep safe and come back."

He nodded once and stood, offering me his hand. "Walk back with me?"

We strolled in silence until his ship came into view. People filled the dock. Uniformed men guarded the gangway. "There's a crowd ahead. Let's say goodbye here where it's quiet."

My lips trembled, but he kissed me one more time, our tears mingling.

"I love you, Chrissy. I want us to be together always." He searched my face, and I knew he was waiting for me to answer. I had so much to say, but we had so little time, and I didn't know where to start. He added, "But I'll never regret this time I've had with you."

How could I echo his words? To say I love you would mean leaving my family, my country. He turned to walk away. I grabbed at his sleeve to stop him. "I want to spend my life with you, too. Come back to me. Keep safe."

His expression was alight with so much love it stole my breath and made my chest ache. Then he turned and walked away. Back to his ship. Out of my life but not forever.

Yes, I was in love. I'd lost the battle.

Wendy—Seattle
1968

Little bubbles floated into the air from the sudsy water as Mum ran her hands over the mixing bowl in the kitchen sink. Her expression was warm, even dreamy. I realized how young she looked. Her hair was that shiny blue-black. The thick curls tumbled this way and that, but the effect was beautiful.

It must have taken so much courage to leave her life in Greenock and cross the world to marry my father.

She fixed her gaze on the darkening sky beyond the kitchen window. "You really loved him," I said. It wasn't a question. But it hit me. "You were so young."

How old do you have to be before you know, really know, who the right person is? I thought of John and realized I needed to get it right or I might—what? End up like her?

She sensed my thoughts because she looked me in the eye. "Yes, I loved him, even that young, and I still do."

My thoughts began to drift. Mum's life didn't have a "happily ever after." Dad was gone so much. It seemed like he had to work all the time, and we were still poor. She came from a well-provided-for home. Her life had been full of extended family. Here we were alone. Dad's family didn't embrace her or us, for that matter. Now if she got her hands on some fabric, she was busy making us clothes. Her own closet had two house dresses. They were nice enough but nothing so nice as the clothes she made during the war. But she was always cheerful. Now there's something to try to live up to.

Chapter Twenty-Two

Christine—Greenock, Scotland
1943

I watched Russell walk away, tracking him through the growing crowd. Every few steps, he'd look back over his shoulder and share a tender smile. I knew he was trying to encourage me. His eyes said, "Believe with me. It will all work out. We'll be together forever." My smile may have been tearful, but I tried to keep up a brave front and show him I believed with him.

As the staging area filled with Canadian sailors, I lost him in the sea of young men. It surprised me as I turned to leave that quite a few lassies stood behind me. Some were waving and smiling. Others clearly wore the grief of parting on their sad faces.

I walked home, wondering if I'd ever see Russell again. Even if I did, his home was on the other side of the world from mine. Did I love him that much? Could I leave my mum and dad and live a completely different life?

I came through the door to find Mum home early. The house smelled wonderfully of shin o' beef soup and freshly baked bread. But I didn't feel like eating. So, this was what it was like to say goodbye to someone you love. All I wanted was to go to bed and shut out my world of hurt.

As much as I wanted to trust him, my heart kept whispering, "I loved Isabelle, and she died. I treasured Moddy's friendship, and she died. Bad things happen to people I care about. Better forget Russell, or he'll die too. No, I'm alone again. Best stay that way." I wanted to cover my ears, keep those thoughts at bay. I kept telling myself it wasn't true, at least the part about Russell.

I put my head down, meaning to go straight to my room, but Mum came from the kitchen with a plate of sliced bread and a crock of butter. She glanced up with a welcoming smile, but it faded as she looked at me. Her brows pulled together. "Come have a cup of tea."

I shook my head, walking past her to my room. "No, thanks." I closed the door and fell onto the bed fully clothed. Mum rapped on my door lightly and didn't wait for my answer. She slipped into the room and sat on the edge of the bed.

"He's gone then?"

I bit my lip hard, trying to hold back the storm. "Aye."

"Well, if it's meant to be, he'll come—"

I pushed my face into the pillow, wanting to shut out any words of comfort. Mum stopped. She stood and slipped my shoes off. With a mother's touch, she helped me out of my coat and pulled my big quilt over me. Her fingers pushed hair back from my face, and she planted one kiss on my forehead. The bedroom door clicked shut behind her. My storm broke with fat teardrops and a torrent of sobs.

Much later I fell asleep and slept the night through in dreamless exhaustion. When I woke in the morning, I walked to my bedroom window. I thought, *My street's still mostly the same.* Bridie's house was across the street. They'd repaired the big hole left by the Blitz. I looked to where Mrs. Munn's tenement home used to be. It still lay in ruins.

I was in ruins. All the parts of me that kept me strong were crumbling. I took a shuddering breath and said to myself, "You stop this. Stop it now." I ordered myself to pull it together. "You're not the only girl to say goodbye." I remembered all the other lassies who stood behind me on the dock. "If Russell's brave enough to go to war, you're brave enough to wait here." My voice sounded stronger. I whispered, "Alone." My teeth caught hold of my lower lip as my eyes filled with tears.

That's when I heard a small inner voice. Not my own but familiar.

"You're not alone."

I felt strangely comforted, and I looked down at my little rose. It would soon outgrow its wee space in the bomb-casing planter. It had survived all kinds of hardship, and still it thrived. I could too. I had to. I began life again by changing out of yesterday's clothes.

Wendy—Seattle
1968

I WASN'T sure what to expect when Fred came to interview my mum. College had changed him. He was still that tall, lanky young man I remembered, but now he seemed serious, settled, mature and so polite. He was a totally different person. It made me explore my feelings toward him. If this was the Fred I'd known two years ago, would I have stayed with him? The answer was a resounding no. I'd never cared about anyone like I now cared for John.

I apologized for accusing him of following me. He accepted with grace, sounding concerned when he said, "Thanks, but are you sure you're being followed?"

"I remembered the feeling from when you did it." I tried to keep the blame out of my voice.

He flushed right to his hairline and cleared his throat. "Guess I can see why you suspected it was me. But thank you for setting this up. It came just in time. I'm leaving for Pullman in the morning."

He turned from me to Mum. "Has Wendy told you I have a psychology class that touches on people who've had paranormal experiences?" He nodded at me. "When we were dating, she told me some of your experiences."

Mum only smiled. He started the interview by asking, "Can you start by talking about some of your experiences? Tell me everything that led up to the events if you don't mind. I won't use all of it in my interview, but it will give me a sense of the time and who you were back then." He had a pen and notepad ready. As Mum started, his face was a study in concentration. I listened with him, wanting to remember everything she said for my own notebook.

Chapter Twenty-Three

Christine—Greenock, Scotland
1943

A fter Russell left, I continued to work in the canteens, and while I enjoyed dancing, I felt my heart was somewhere near Italy. The Canadians were very active in that theatre of operations. His letters didn't tell me anything specific, but from the radio news, I felt sure that's where he must be.

During the month that followed, I tried to harden my heart with thoughts about the harsh realities of war. You never knew if you'd see someone again. So many people were dying in battle. I tried not to wait for Russell's next letter. But I had little luck with building back the walls around my heart. It helped that there was always so much occupying my mind and keeping my body busy till I dropped into bed exhausted. I increased my visits to the Canadian hospital. I worked as many hours as they would give me. I volunteered at the Canadian Overseas Club, church socials and the Y.

I pretended to be the old Chrissy. Even if I felt like an empty shell, at least I was doing my part for the war effort.

This Thursday I worked in the kitchen of the Canadian canteen making sandwiches. One of the older ladies handed me a large tray filled with ham and cheese on freshly baked bread. She said, "Will ye take this out to the fuid table?"

Hungry Canadians swarmed me; my tray was almost empty within minutes. Someone stood close behind me as the lads crowded round reaching for the last sandwiches. I set my tray on the table and tried to back out of the crowd.

A familiar voice whispered in my ear, "*Ti amo, la mia bellezza. Non ti dimenticherò mai.*" He added for me in English, "I love you, my beauty. I'll never forget you."

"Lee." I grinned. Over the last month, we'd become good friends. He had blue-black hair like my own and said I looked like his little sister. I knew his dark eyes must be twinkling with mischief, and I thought his large Italian family back in Vancouver must miss him so much. I felt his arms circle my waist from behind.

"Don't dance your feet off while I'm gone." He spun me around and gave me a fond kiss on the forehead right there at the food table. I shot a quick look at the manager. Thank goodness she didn't catch him doing that. I wasn't sorry, but Mrs. Wagner didn't tolerate open affection.

Lee's nature was to be exuberant. He was a dance instructor back home, and we'd hit it off from the start. As passionate about dancing as I was, we looked for each other at every dance. We'd practice steps. I learned a lot from him, but I like to think I taught him a thing or two. He often called me *sorellina*, little sister.

I was laughing when I looked up into his eyes. "I will miss you, Lee. Keep safe. I hope they send you back here soon."

He asked, "You have my address?"

I nodded.

"You'd better write." I nodded again. He reached out to take my hand, and we walked to the door. "I wanted to say goodbye here with the music playing."

I was used to not asking questions. It was war. They couldn't say much at any rate. He wiped my cheek, and I realized I was crying. "Don't cry, little sister. I'll be fine."

I looked up at my friend and caught my breath. A mist or film floated down to cover his face. It was without color, grey, like a shroud that masked his features. Only his bone structure hinted at the vibrant, living Lee.

Dread and panic settled over me. I hadn't felt this way since that night walking home with Moddy. No, no, not now. Not Lee. I rubbed away the tears and looked again. The lighting was poor, but I saw everyone else. It was like a veil was drawn over him. My heart started beating so fast.

"Don't worry, Chrissy. I'll see you soon."

I nodded but couldn't seem to get any words out. Then he was gone.

That night I left early. I tried to tell myself I was over-tired and needed to sleep, but loss and grief settled into my heart. I said nothing to my parents or anyone else. They'd think I was having a breakdown. The memory of that experience stayed with me. I couldn't seem to shake it off.

A week later, on a Wednesday afternoon, I was up at the Canadian canteen getting ready for my weekly dance lessons. The hall was empty, and I was in the back picking out records for the afternoon. A few sailors arrived.

"Hi, Chrissy."

I looked up and smiled. Then one more young man burst through the doors.

"Did you hear? It's just come in. They sunk the St. Croix."

I looked up. The St. Croix was Lee's ship.

"Shhh," a sailor said. "Chrissy's a friend of Lee Torino. How bad was it?"

"The HMS Itchen picked most of them up. But then two days later the Germans sank her. Only one of the St. Croix men survived that, and he wasn't Lee." I dropped the records and grabbed my coat to run for the door.

I realized the veil had been his death mask. Inwardly, I railed at heaven. Why, God? Why would you tell me ahead when there was nothing I could do to save him? Just like Moddy. No one answered me.

The next time I saw the veil, it happened again with a nice young American named Jack from someplace called Ohio. He had a fresh-washed, healthy look to him like he was straight off a farm. Not a bulky lad, more the lanky type, but strong. His honey-colored hair was hard to miss in a group of sailors. I spotted him often when I volunteered at the canteens in town.

He talked a lot about his home. He was from a big family, and my first impression was right. They were a farming family. I liked the way he called me ma'am and talked about his favorite horse, Buster.

Tonight, we danced the last dance together, and he asked if he could kiss me goodbye. He was being shipped out in the morning. I think the men often needed the comfort of tenderness before going into battle. As odd as it sounds, I thought it reminded them of their mother's arms around them as a child.

I said yes, and we walked down the hall toward the door. He was so self-conscious but determined to have his kiss. His manner changed from talkative to quiet. He looked to be losing his nerve. He blushed, and I was thinking that saying goodbye was going to take a long time. So, I reached for him and drew him to me. It was a sweet kiss, tender, not at all passionate or demanding, but when I drew back the same white shroud covered his face. All color disappeared. Only the bones of his face stood out under the veil. My heart raced again as dread settled over me.

I stiffened.

"What's wrong, Chrissy?" He sounded alarmed.

I forced a smile. "It's nothing, I'm just sad to say goodbye. I'll be praying for you."

He asked me to write and bent his head to scribble his name and address on a slip of paper. I froze in place, waiting for him to finish, afraid of what I'd see when he looked up at me again. This time I saw him clearly, and I let out my breath in relief. He folded the paper and slipped it into my hand and left me standing there with shock and fear as my company.

I didn't want to save his note, but I did. I tried to forget his name. I couldn't bring myself to write him a letter. A fortnight later, I was walking home from shopping when my friend Moira caught up with me.

She'd had a letter from a friend at the front. He said a young man in his unit was always talking about a girl named Chrissy he'd met in Greenock. "The boy's name was Jack. Did you know a lad with that name? My friend shipped out a few weeks ago."

"American?" A sinking feeling was forming in my stomach.

"Aye, ye ken him then?"

My free hand slipped into my coat pocket, fingering that small, folded paper with Jack's address. "Why, Moira?" Afraid of her answer but needing to hear it all the same.

She looked at me with troubled eyes. "My friend says he died in battle. Och, Chrissy, I'm sorry to be the one to tell ye."

I pulled out the note and read his name aloud. "Jack Tillman." And thought, Lord, not again. My legs felt weak.

Moira stopped and patted my back. "Sorry, Chrissy. I'm sae sorry. Did ye care for the lad?"

I shook my head no and got a few words out. "It's all right, Moira. No, I hardly knew him. I don't know why he talked about me, but he was a likeable lad. I'm sad he's gone, that's all. I'll be fine."

What I wasn't saying was that I hadn't even written him a letter. In fact, I'd tried not to think of him at all, not even praying for him. I felt like I'd failed Jack, failed God.

I realized the veil was a sign. Those were the boys who were about to lose their lives. It was always the same. Within a few days or weeks, I'd hear about their deaths. Thankfully, I didn't see the shroud often, but when I did, I lived in torment.

Now I prayed for those lads, but not even prayer would change the outcome. Word would come to me somehow about their deaths. I'd grieve and try to put the experience behind me, hoping it would never happen again.

It all came to a head when Russell's sister Margie wrote and asked if a young friend of hers could come visit me. "His name is Eddy Garl. Nice kid but really frightened. When he wrote where they were sending him first, I gave him your address. I hope it's all right. It's just that I know you're kind, and he's afraid. Maybe you could talk to him. You've been living with the war for a long time."

When Eddy Garl didn't show up, I almost forgot about him. I was home alone on a Monday afternoon doing some cleaning for my mum. I'd been sweeping, and I'd covered my hair with a scarf. A knock came at the door. A young man, little more than my age, stood with his sailor's cap in hand.

"Could you be Christina Finlay?" I knew from his accent he was Canadian.

"Yes, can I help you?"

"My name's Eddy Garl."

I smiled, and his boyish face relaxed into relief. He reminded me of the film star Mickey Rooney. Short, not much taller than me, but with the look of the man he was becoming showing on his features. I liked him right away.

"Margie said you'd be by. Come in."

We spent the afternoon talking by the fire. He had a transparency about him. His questions were open and honest. His face showed everything he was thinking, and I became fascinated watching his reactions to what I said even before he responded verbally.

I made him tea and served him some of Mum's wonderful

scones. Mostly I listened, but occasionally I spoke of the times we'd been bombed and how I dealt with the fear.

"I've always been more afraid that I would be a coward when it really counts, ye ken? When I need to be strong." I looked at the fire, remembering the night of the Blitz. "My parents are so strong and brave, and I'm always afraid I won't measure up, that I'll let them down. But then I hear a little voice."

He quirked his head to the side, and I laughed. "I'm not daft; least I don't think I am. Ye ken it's not like I hear it. More like it's a whisper in my thoughts. Could be me own self saying it." I stopped. "No, that's wrong. I think it's God whispering to me, or that's as near an explanation as I can come to.

"He tells me I'm not alone. Then I just seem to do what I think I must." I reached out to take his hand. "I know you'll do the same."

He smiled back, and we talked of other things. I asked if he knew Russell. His smile faded. "Not well." For the first time, a look of wariness crossed his face. It only lasted a minute, and then he added quickly, "Seems nice enough, but I really only know his sister."

"I see." But I wondered why his manner changed at the mention of Russell. I didn't have time to ask much more because the mantle clock chimed out the hour.

As Eddy rose to leave, he took my hand once more. "Thank you. I feel much better now." He had such an honest face and a friendly smile, and I couldn't help but like him.

Then the veil fell, and all I saw was a whitish blur. Why? Why would I give him confidence to fight when he wouldn't make it? I don't remember what I said or even his leaving. It turned my thoughts inward. Stop this. Stop it now. You're just imagining it because he was so afraid.

Two weeks later, it was near closing at work. I had my coat on and was saying goodnight to Nurse Graham when a Canadian sailor came in with a cut above his eye.

He looked at me. "Sorry, I thought you were still open."

He was turning back toward the door when I heard Nurse Graham say, "Come in, laddie, and sit ye doon. We've a minute to tend ye." He smiled in relief, and I could understand why. The cut on his brow was really bleeding.

She glanced at me apologetically. "Chrissy, can ye get me a basin of water and a bit of the disinfectant? I'm all out of what I had here." We never said iodine or Mercurochrome, because even the big brawny lads seemed to blanch white as a ghost at the mention of those words.

"Right." I shrugged out of my coat and went to fetch her supplies.

When I returned, the sailor was saying, "It wasn't much of a fight. I just saw red and hit the fellow."

"Looks as though he hit ye back." I could see the hint of a smile on Nurse's lips. Then she sounded more like a mother than a stern ward nurse. "And why do ye need to fight? I'd think you'd have enough of it on the battlefront."

"I just heard a good friend of mine was killed." He winced as Nurse dabbed his cut with the Mercurochrome. "Then a guy said something—well, I can't say what he said, but it made me mad."

Nurse Graham was drying the area and putting butterfly tape across the cut to keep it closed. She said with such tenderness, "I'm so sorry about your friend."

"Thank you, ma'am. His ship took a direct hit. Sunk almost right away. He was a swimmer at school. Won medals and such."

"Oh, aye?"

"That's how I know him. We grew up together. He saved the lives of four men, pulling them onto debris after a torpedo hit their ship." I waved my goodbye to Nurse, not wanting to interrupt her patient. Sometimes a wee chat is better medicine than all the Mercurochrome in the world.

She looked up and nodded I should leave. The sailor was saying, "My friend dived into the sea to save one more man floating unconscious nearby. My buddy went under but never surfaced again. Eddy Garl died saving four other guys."

I stopped, stunned. It's not like I wasn't expecting it, but that didn't make it any easier. He'd been so afraid. Did I help him risk his life? Make him feel like he could save everyone? God, no.

I don't remember catching the bus. I don't remember the ride home. My eyes blurred with tears as I stumbled up my steps and through my front door.

I found my father alone at the table with a cup of tea. I remember coming to him and sobbing. I told him everything from the first time I saw the veil and all the other times, ending with Eddy's story.

"You need to talk with my mother."

"No, Da, I can't tell anyone. They'd think I'd gone dafty."

"Get yer coat, Chrissy. We'll pop round now, and believe me, you'll be that glad you did."

He came with me, and we found Grandma Finlay in her rocker napping by the fire. Her golden-red hair was loose today, spilling over her shoulders. She smiled when she saw us.

Grandma was born on the Isle of Skye where they still mostly spoke Gaelic. Her father sent her down to Port Glasgow to work as a cook and learn English when she was a lass of sixteen.

The old ways are stronger in places like Skye; they rarely doubt superstitions and tales of magical creatures. I guessed if anyone would accept my story without question, it would be my Grandma Finlay.

Still very spry, she was out of her chair, calling us into her large kitchen and insisting on making us tea. My dad started by saying, "Mam, Chrissy has something I think you should hear." He pulled out a chair by the kitchen table for her to have a seat. She gave him a quizzical stare but sat with us and waited.

Da gave me such a direct look, and I realized he would brook no detail omitted. I told Grandma Finlay everything.

She sat at the table and listened with her eyes half closed.

When I finished, she didn't move, and I thought maybe she'd fallen asleep. I looked at Da, but he put a hand up to stop me from speaking. I realized he was waiting, and I did as well.

Finally, a tender smile spread across her worn face. It transformed her. I could see the beauty she'd been as a girl. Grandma's hair looked golden in the afternoon sunlight. Unruly curls framed her face like a halo.

She lifted her chin and deep blue eyes rested on me with what seemed like a fierce pride.

"We call it the Sight, ye ken. It runs through our bloodline as far back as history is told. Usually naught but every other generation has the gift." Her eyes changed, and I thought I saw pity. "I have the Sight, and now so do you, my Chrissy."

"They used to call us seers or heather witches. But it's not like that. We're not Gypsies or fortune tellers." She paused, thinking, then said, "It's like God lifts a veil."

I drew in my breath.

"Stay then, luv, not like the veil of death you've seen. I mean He lets us peek past the curtain of time into the future. Gives us a glimpse of what will come."

My body stiffened in protest. "I don't want to know. It doesn't make any difference if I pray for them. They still die."

Grandma Finlay reached across the table and took my hand. Her skin felt smooth and thin over the bones of her fingers. She squeezed an encouragement. "Ye canna ken what those lads did before they died. Could be like the young one who saved four men from drowning. Maybe the others made their last minutes count. What courage or kindness you gave them might have meant all the world to them."

"Aye, but why me? Why do I have to know?"

"I canna say, lass. Maybe the Lord is just getting your attention. When He lifts a veil between us and Him, sometimes it's to save us now, and other times we never know. It's no our place to question His reasons. It's a gift and a curse, and now it's yers ta live wi'."

Wendy—Seattle
1968

Our ordinary living room came back into focus as I left my mum's first life behind. Her last words were still ringing in my ears. "It's a gift and a curse, and now it's yers ta live wi'." To hear her experiences shook me to my core. That was my mum. She amazed me. But I was grateful I didn't share her second sight.

Fred closed his pen and clipped it to his notepad. "Thank you for sharing all this. Wendy talked about you having second sight, but I had no idea what that would be like." His chuckle sounded forced, and I noticed he'd grown fidgety as Mum told her story.

He glanced back at me. "Does anyone else in the family have the Sight?" I could see speculation in his eyes.

I shook my head. "Not me. That's for sure. I don't think I'd like hearing voices in my head. Not even God's."

Mum broke in. "Grandma said it mostly popped up every other generation. But this isn't Scotland. Americans are scientific. They must analyze and figure out how things work."

Fred cleared his throat. "I was going to ask if I could perform a few tests suggested in some books I read."

"Second sight isn't something you can call on when you need it. Like Grandma Finlay said, it's a gift from God. He decides when to give it, not me."

Fred put his hand up to stop her protest. "I get it's not like the Sight has ever been a good experience. I'll forget the tests." He stood, gathered his things, and thanked us both for the chance to hear her story. Then he left.

As the front door closed, I asked, "Was there ever a time you got it all wrong or thought you knew something and found you were mistaken?"

Chapter Twenty-Four

Christine—Greenock, Scotland
1943

A few nights later I was leaving work at Boots Chemist and walking to the bus stop when my Uncle Angus stopped me. "I'm glad I caught ye afore ye went home," he said. "I wanted to warn you that our killer-spy is still in country." The sun was already setting, leaving his face in shadows as he spoke.

He said, "Ye ken we had Bofors gun batteries along the coast of Aberdeen. The Germans were hitting the city hard, coming at it from the North Sea. That's why our army installed the big guns pointing right out to sea to protect the town. The guns never fired a shot. As soon as they were installed, the Germans stopped coming from that direction. They came from every other approach. The army moved the guns, scattered them at different locations, but the next German raid came straight in from the coast. That's when our boys knew there must be a spy."

Cold crept up my back, but I was careful not to show my fears.

Uncle added, "Right after that a lovely lassie turned up missing." He looked at me and touched one of my long black curls.

"She had long dark hair like the others. Like you. Be careful, Chrissy."

"But, Uncle, why would a spy want to kill girls?"

"He's no just killing them, luv, he's doing other things first then strangling them to death." Uncle blushed down to his collar. Clearing his throat, he said, "They found her in the dunes of Balmedie Beach."

"Oh." I swallowed the bile rising in my throat. "Is there anything else that links the girls?"

Uncle thought for a minute. "Near as we can figure, all the girls worked at a canteen. I'm thinkin' the fiend is posing as a serviceman." He spread his hands wide in frustration. "Every town in Scotland is full of men in uniform."

He continued in a hushed tone. "He must have a motor car, though, to take the lass eight miles north to the beach. My captain thinks the bloke took her for a picnic. Balmedie's a picturesque place, secluded but a lovely spot."

I gave him a direct look. "Ye mean ta say he's no just spying and trying to stay unnoticed. He's killing. I still don't understand what would make him take the chance?"

Uncle pushed his cap back on his head. "You're asking me if someone working for a madman like Hitler could be mad as well?"

I shrugged. "Guess yer right. But mad or no, he must think he's a deal smarter than the rest of us to get away with being sae bold."

Uncle looked at his watch. "Where are ye off to this evening?"

"The Canadian Overseas Club." It made me uncomfortable to think those other girls might have met the fiend while volunteering their time. It also made me mad the spy used their goodwill to his advantage.

Before he left, Uncle Angus gave me a hug. "Keep yer eyes open, lass."

I stood waiting for the bus, trying not to look at everyone as if they might be a German spy. Keep my eyes open? For a man able to lure a girl to a lonely beach for a picnic? For a serviceman who wasn't really a serviceman? Keep my eyes open for someone who thought he was above being caught? My head filled with the impossibility of finding such a person.

I said aloud, "He's not a Scot. No, we've never had such things happen here."

As soon as I came through the doors at the Canadian canteen, Mrs. Wagner put me to work making sandwiches. She said, "It's going to be a busy night. We've another ship in port, and the base is full."

I was still thinking of Uncle Angus' words when I spotted a smallish man. I'm not sure what drew my eyes to him. He didn't stand out in a crowd. He wore the uniform of the Canadian military, but it was missing all the special insignias that identified which unit he was from. Instead, it had a fat patch shaped like a red spearhead with USA embroidered in red across the hilt and Canada down the blade. I'd seen nothing like it.

I grabbed the arm of a passing sailor. "Toby, what insignia is that?" I didn't point but nodded toward the young man sitting in the folding chairs along the wall.

Toby squinted, and I added, "The guy with brown hair and the red patch."

"Oh." Toby bent to whisper in my ear. "He's a member of the Black Devils."

"What? Are you making fun of me?"

"Well, you Scots have the Black Watch, right?"

I gave him a skeptical look. "Sure, they're the fierce fighters of the Royal Highland Regiment. But I've never heard of the Black Devils." Toby shrugged and walked away. I asked several other people if they knew the man, but no one seemed willing to say.

It piqued my interest. I made a point of observing him, only to find he constantly sat on the side of the dance floor watching everyone else.

Finally, I took a seat next to him. "Hello, my name's Christina."

He had a friendly smile, but it didn't quite reach his eyes. "Tom Gorsky."

I'd met Free Polish Forces before, so I asked, *"Polski?"*

His mouth flattened before he answered. "No, my parents immigrated after the last war. We live in Ontario."

"Oh."

I waited to see if he'd say more. He didn't, so I did. "Would you like a sandwich or some biscuits?"

"No, but thanks for asking."

We sat like that for a bit. Then I asked, "Do you dance?"

He looked at me with mild amusement. "Not really, but you go ahead. I enjoy watching. Quite good, aren't you?"

It made me uncomfortable to think of him keeping an eye on me, but try as I might, he wasn't interested in talking. I got back to my duties making sandwiches and talking to the other lads who sat alone.

Possibly he was suffering from some sort of emotional distress. I'd listened to the doctors talking about the ward of men who were "shell shocked." As I understood it, those were the men who came back from the front traumatized by the experiences they'd had in battle.

After my last talk with Uncle Angus, I couldn't help looking for signs of a spy who preyed on young women. I learned Tom was a patient at the hospital. But I didn't see any outward signs of battle wounds on him. He was unremarkable in every way. Average looking—probably under thirty but not by much. I would say he was bookish. Shorter than most of the lads, but he was very strong. I saw him once carry in a load of heavy boxes for Mrs. Wagner.

There was something off about him. Over the next week, I asked several other Canadian servicemen if they knew him. It was the same reaction every time. The laddie would look over his shoulder and shake his head. "No. No, I've never met him." Several times they'd say in low tones, "Chrissy, he's not a very nice sort. Best stay away."

Oddly, it was that warning that made me wonder if Tom Gorsky was the spy, the fiend who stalked young women. I searched my feelings to see if they would warn me about this peculiar man. But evidently second sight wasn't something I could call up anytime I wanted to know something. I made it my mission to study him.

Some things didn't make sense. I saw no sign of rank or branch, but the other men treated him with the respectful aloofness given to higher ranks. The only insignia on his sleeve was that odd, fat spearhead patch. If Uncle Angus was right about the fiend killing girls and spying for the Germans, wouldn't Gorsky show interest in one girl?

The next time I saw him, he was dancing, *dancing* with Sanga. It was a slow dance, but they seemed to get on well. Sanga was new. Her family had moved to Greenock after her father was discharged from the navy with a severe leg injury. She started volunteering at some of the same places I did. Our paths had crossed several times, but we hadn't exchanged many words. With her dark brown hair, she could easily fit in with the other girls who'd gone missing. I looked for an opportunity to ask her about Tom.

Later, I took a chance when she headed for the kitchen. I was afraid for her, but she treated my questions as if I were interested in Gorsky for myself.

"Why are you askin' about Tom?" She put her hands on her hips and stuck her chin out belligerently. My temper flared. How dare she accuse me when all I wanted was to keep her safe?

Her next words stopped me. "You should quit now. He's interested in me, not you."

When I found my voice, I said, "You're wrong. I was wondering how well you know the lad."

"Well enough, if that were any of your business." She turned on her heel and left the kitchen, stopping to speak with another girl. They both looked back at me.

This wasn't going well at all. It didn't matter. I couldn't put down the idea that something was wrong about Tom Gorsky. The longer I studied the little man the more reasons I found to be worried for Sanga. Whether or not she liked it, I wasn't about to take a chance with her life.

The next day, I left work on my lunch hour to see Uncle Angus. Luckily, he was coming out of the constable's station when I arrived. He suggested we take a short walk. We headed to a nice little park down the street and sat on a bench. I laid out all my observations about Tom Gorsky. To give Uncle credit, he listened to the complete case I'd built.

A week later I was stocking shelves at Boots Chemist when my uncle came by. "Can ye come by the station after work?"

I nodded. Uncle's manner was stiff, and I wondered what he'd discovered. But the store was full of shoppers. Not the place to discuss spies.

I skipped my bus ride after work and went to see Uncle Angus. He was waiting for me and showed me into a small office. His expression was grim, and it was really worrying me.

"Uncle, what? Did you find out anything?"

"Aye, Chrissy." He paused, and I waited, getting more and more worried about his stiff manner.

"I put a lot of store in your good judgement." He paused. "Here you were dead wrong." I felt myself shrinking back. I couldn't find words to ask what he meant.

"The man's a hero." He leaned closer. "Ever hear of the Devil's Brigade?"

"Is that the same as the Black Devils?"

"Aye, it's a special unit made up of Yanks and Canadians. They take all the most dangerous missions behind enemy lines and such."

I interrupted. "But there's something off about him."

"And you'd be right. His last mission was a disaster. They didn't tell me the details. I spoke to the base commander." He cleared his throat. "The man's no our spy."

"Are ye sure of that?"

"Aye, Chrissy, he's Jewish wi' family in the Warsaw Ghetto."

"Oh," I said, getting sick inside. We'd all heard about the extermination of Jews in Poland.

"The Germans call them the Devil's Brigade because they're ruthless. When they lose someone, they take their revenge. That kind of thing changes even a good man. Tom Gorsky is at the hospital for observation." Uncle looked pained, as if he were seeing the scene he described. "A teammate died in his arms. When they brought him in, Doc says he wasn't speaking. They say he's doing better every day. It's all a matter of perspective. What seems off to you is still a significant improvement to where he was."

Uncle's expression became sympathetic. "I ken ye meant well, but the man's a hero. His actions in battle saved the rest of his platoon. Let's respect his privacy."

I left my uncle's office feeling like I'd done something that could have really hurt a man already damaged. I thought of Sanga's defense of him. Maybe she knew what he'd been through. Maybe all my questions made people uncomfortable. Now Sanga's words seemed protective of him instead of being unfair to me. I felt terrible.

I found it hard to go back to my work at the Canadian canteen. When I did, I went straight to Sanga and apologized. I couldn't tell her about the spy because I'd promised my uncle not to say anything. Instead, I said, "I'm so sorry, Sanga. I thought Tom Gorsky was someone else. A very bad person, and I worried for you."

"Well, he's not bad."

Her words bristled with indignation, but I pushed on. "No,

he's not the same person at all. My mistake." She nodded curtly in acknowledgement. I didn't speak to Tom. I wasn't sure he was aware I'd been watching him. Instead, I kept a low profile for a week or two, feeling like a foolish schoolgirl. Never again. I would never point my finger at someone else.

Wendy—Seattle
1968

Mum handed me a short grocery list. "I need a few things. Not much. Thanks, love." I threw on my coat and was down the steps on the way to Larry's Market. As I crossed our front yard, I felt eyes on me. The skin on my neck tingled, and I looked around.

Our house sat on a large lot. To one side of us was a rural neighborhood, mostly older houses on large lots or acreage. To the other side were businesses, the bowling alley next door and Larry's Market across the street. Both parking lots were crowded. No one watched me.

I thought that let Fred off the hook for sure. He'd left for school last Friday. I realized Fred was my Tom Gorsky. I'd been foolish for accusing him. Still, the feeling of eyes on my back made all my nerves fire up. I tried to put it out of my mind as I walked across the street to shop.

Within thirty minutes, I was almost done. I reached for a can of corned beef on the top shelf. Straining my five-foot-two frame as tall as I could, my fingers barely touched the edge of the can. A hand closed over mine. I jerked backward, pulling away. Off balance, I would have fallen but for a solid body behind me.

A familiar voice said, "Steady, I've got you."

"John? Good Lord, you scared me." I was unreasonably angry.

"Would you rather I let you drop the can on your head? I thought you might climb the shelves to reach the thing."

There I went again, thinking people were doing something sinister. I stuck my hand out for the can, but he held it back. "If I give it to you, you're not going to throw it at me are you?" A smile broke through his annoyed expression.

"Sorry." I tried to change the topic. "What are you doing here?" That's when I noticed the golden rose bouquet in his small shopping basket.

He grinned like a kid caught in the act of some secret errand. "I was bringing you flowers."

Did he just blush? "I'm sorry for being jumpy. That's so nice of you. But why, I mean?" I reached for them, but he pulled his basket back.

"Tell me what's bothering you first."

I didn't want to talk about it, not here in the canned-goods aisle of Larry's Market, but those brown eyes held me with a direct stare. "It's that I've had the feeling lately I'm being watched."

"What? You mean some guy's trying to pick you up?" He looked around for a likely culprit.

I put my hand up to cover my grin. "No, I think I'm being followed."

He turned serious and gave me his full attention.

"Followed?" It surprised me he didn't laugh. I think I would have. His dark brows pulled together. "How long's this been going on?"

"On and off for most of the summer."

"And you never told me?" His body visibly stiffened.

I rolled my eyes in complete frustration. "You broke up with me. Remember?"

"Oh." John blew out his breath and at least some of his over-protective, pompous air. I knew I was right but said nothing more. We were both locked in silent stares.

Finally, I said, "Why the flowers?"

I won a tender smile from him. "I wanted you to know—that is—I think about you all the time."

I whispered back, "Me too." My anger melted away. "Do you

have more shopping to do?"

"No, only this." He held up the flowers.

We each checked out, and he walked me back home. This time I didn't feel anyone watching. I only felt the warm glow of John's affection.

He couldn't stay long; he had a night-school class at South Seattle Community College for his Ford apprenticeship, and I had to go back to school in a couple hours for rehearsal. Before he left, he asked me about my schedule and gave me a kiss that claimed ownership. Things were changing fast with him, and I liked that very much.

I came through the door with a beautiful bouquet of yellow roses and a bag of groceries. Mum looked at me. "John?"

I buried my face in the heavenly rose petals and smiled my answer.

"I'm liking that laddie more and more."

Before I left for school, I asked her again about the serial-killer spy. I needed to settle my mind, and listening to her took me out of my head and into her past.

She said, "It's a long story. Don't you have to go soon?"

"I do, but I have a little time. Go ahead."

"A lot happened before that."

"Please, just start at the beginning." She looked oddly resistant, but I did begging eyes, and she relented.

Chapter Twenty-Five

Christine—Greenock, Scotland
1944

There's something about spring that makes your heart lighter, gives you hope. Maybe it was spring fever or wishful thinking after the long, hard slog of war, but it felt like something important was coming. Even the lads spoke in low tones about rumors of a big offensive.

Russell still wrote regularly. His letters were mostly upbeat. But I'd catch that same hint of sadness when he remembered things from his youth. But it wasn't often. I wanted to ask him why but couldn't think of a tactful way to frame my questions.

Otherwise, his descriptions of life in Canada fit my picture of a Western frontiersman. He told me his family had moved to a small village called New Westminster near the port of Vancouver, Canada.

For as long as I could remember, I'd heard stories of my seafaring grandfather. Grandpa Cowan and Aunty Tina both had the courage to make a life far from home. That was something I wasn't sure I could do.

I looked it up on the map and pictured what life would be like living on the other side of the world. Russell said the country was very much like Scotland. That might not be so bad. No wonder Grandpa felt at home there, although he always came back to his wife and children in Greenock.

I stood at my bus stop a block from our house thinking about Russell's last letter. It was all about the benefits of living near Vancouver. There would be lots of excellent job opportunities after the war. He meant for us to be together, but he hadn't asked me to make a commitment. I was thankful for that, but it didn't stop me from considering the possibility. At least he seemed to be away from the action for the moment. I was thankful for that as well.

He was still on my mind while I waited for my friend Moira at the bus stop. A group of people waited for the bus this morning. Lost in my own thoughts, I hadn't been paying much attention. I glanced up and saw Moira walking around the corner. We were so much alike, people often assumed we were sisters. We were about the same height, a little over five feet. We both had long black hair. Her eyes were a soft grey, and mine were brown. She waved, and I smiled my greeting. A young man standing next to me must have thought she was waving at him, because he waved back at her.

I almost laughed. It was like that with my friend. I used to tease her she was a prettier version of me. But if I was honest, Moira was beautiful. She looked like Elizabeth Taylor. Except Moira never noticed the men who noticed her. That's part of what made her so dear to my heart, her total lack of self-importance. We'd been in the same class throughout our school years.

I walked past the young man to meet her, and Moira quickened her pace. She looked all lit up with pleasure when she said, "Good, you two have met then."

I looked at the lad and he at me. We both said, "What?"

Moira was grinning. "Chrissy, this is my friend Kevin, Kevin O'Brien."

My designer's eye noticed he wore a suit and overcoat. It wasn't often we saw young men who weren't in uniform. My dressmaker's eye took in the expensive fabric and extra touches of his suit. Judging by his clothes, Kevin was someone important. How in the world had Moira met him, and why hadn't she said a word to me? Questions I intended to find out as soon as we were alone.

"So, this is Christina." Kevin turned the full force of his charm toward me. His hair was dark auburn. Long black lashes framed brilliant green eyes. He was slender and average height, but his smile was infectious. By the way Moira was glowing, it was clear she was really taken with this young man, and I could see why. I liked him right away.

He took my hand formally. "I'm so glad to meet you. My darlin' here has said so many nice things about you."

"Thank you, and do I detect an Irish accent?"

"Donegal born and bred." His green eyes sparkled.

"I've been to Donegal as a young lass with a friend," I said. "Where 'bouts did you live?"

"Oh, you have, have you?" He put his arm around Moira and gave her a squeeze. "I'd love to show it to Moira. A beautiful place to be sure." She looked up into his eyes.

I didn't think she was even listening.

"And what do you remember about the place?" he asked.

"The crossing was quite rough. I remember almost everyone was sick. We stayed with the Donoghue family at Butter Hill Farm."

He nodded. "A lovely place that." He turned to Moira. "I have to report early, so I'll see you later?"

He reached out and gave her hand a squeeze. Her eyes were dreamy as she answered, "Later."

As soon as he left, I asked, "Where did you meet him?" The

bus came, and we got on. We could have walked down the hill into town. It was only two-and-a-half miles, but we liked to travel into work together. It gave us time to talk, but this morning Moira was quiet.

"Well, out with it."

"He's sae braw, isn't he?"

I grinned at her infatuation, but an uneasy feeling crept over me.

"Who is he? I mean, he isn't in a sailor's rig. But did he come in on one of our ships?" There hadn't been a British ship in port in a fortnight. "Come on, Moira." I was badgering her, but I couldn't help myself. "How did you meet him? And, for the love of God, why didn't you tell me about him?"

She'd been looking out the window with a wistful smile on her bonnie face. Then she turned. She put her head down, and I did the same as she whispered, "I didn't tell you because he asked me to keep our friendship to myself."

"What? Why?"

"Well, he's attached to some commander, and they don't want to make his presence in town known."

"Oh," I said. We all knew to keep our mouths shut regarding the movements of high command.

"I met the lad at Gina's restaurant."

We'd been in school with Gina. Her father owned a small Italian restaurant on Hamilton Street.

Moira started twisting her ring, a carved Celtic silver ring with a perfect emerald embedded in the center, a gift from her grandmother. She always fiddled with it when she was excited.

"I'd been doin' a bit of shopping before headin' home. I was that thirsty, decided I'd stop in for a wee chat wi' Gina and a cup of tea. It was busy, so I sat at the only empty table. She served the tea and visited for a few minutes before she left.

"When the bell above the door rang, I glanced up to see Kevin come in. The room was sae crowded. He asked if he could share my table. He ordered a cup of tea and two tiramisu desserts. I thought he was expecting someone else, but when Gina brought them, he slid one over to me."

"That was nice, forward but nice."

Moira was twisting the ring on her finger again. "Oh, aye. And we talked forever. He's sae sweet. He hasn't asked me out yet. We just seem to meet at odd times and talk."

"He's a handsome laddie."

Moira's eyes drifted back to the window. She was like that all day. It was busy in the infirmary with two earaches plus the symptoms of a severe cold going through the naval base and one very nasty black eye from a sailor who was a repeat patient. The laddie had a bit of a temper.

Every time a customer came through the door, I saw Moira's head shoot up.

But it wasn't until closing that Kevin appeared. He was waiting for her on the street with a bag of tablet; it's sort of like Scottish fudge, buttery and sweet but without the chocolate. It's very rich and my favorite candy. He offered us both a chunk. "Nice that, a candy store below you."

Moira shot me a look, and we both laughed.

She said, "Oh aye, we thought so too when we first came to work here. Within a week we couldna bear ta even look in the windows. We may have made ourselves sick of candy for life."

After that, he met Moira after work every day.

Sometimes they'd go for a walk and ask me to come along. I didn't want to intrude, but Kevin often insisted, saying, "I wouldn't want Moira's reputation to be in question. If you come, we're only three friends out for a walk." I looked into those sparkling green eyes and saw his concern.

Moria reached out and took hold of my hand. "Come wi' us, Chrissy. It'll be fun." Her voice was light, but her eyes implored me. Maybe things were getting too serious. So, I came whenever they asked. I tried speaking to Moira about it later, but she acted as if she didn't know why I was asking.

As for Kevin, he was happy to include me. I was positive he wasn't losing interest in my friend. He seemed fair smitten but always attempted to include me in their conversations.

Once he suggested we all walk to the Esplanade and watch the boat traffic on the Clyde. That was a favorite of mine. He led us to a bench and sat between us girls. We watched as a British naval submarine motored up the river toward the shipyard. Kevin said, "Moira here tells me your da works at Scotts. He must be important if he's the man who takes the new subs out for their shakedown cruise."

I looked past him to Moira. It was understood between the two of us I didn't speak about what my da did beyond saying he worked at the shipyards. She shrugged her apology.

Kevin continued, "She says he supervises repairs as well." I shot her another dagger look, but she looked away quickly. "He's an engineer, right?"

"He never talks about his work."

"Oh." Kevin looked crestfallen. Much later we were all eating fish and chips when he asked, "I heard they've been testing a new underwater radar using sound." He said it like an afterthought. "Have you heard about it?"

I had learned a bit about it. Da explained to me how it worked, but it wasn't something widely known. I shook my head. "No, sorry. Do you serve on submarines?"

Kevin's smile was amiable. "No, but my uncle does. He has for years. When I was a lad, he used to regale me with stories. I'm only interested. Does your da only work on subs?"

I was getting annoyed. "Sorry, I must get back. Duty at the Overseas Club." I had an uneasy feeling. I shoved my hands in my pockets as I turned to walk toward home.

Once, to change the subject, I asked, "Do you know the Donoghue brothers well?" I must have caught him off guard because his face looked completely blank.

I said, "Butter Hill Farm? Tom and Paddy? You'd be about the same age. Were you not in school together?"

He smiled. "Donegal's as big as Greenock, could be a wee bit bigger." He looked at his watch and said with a start, "Sorry, Moira, I report to the commander at half past five. Got to run." He reached for her and gave her a tender kiss on the lips. He lingered, searching her eyes as he pulled back. I looked away. Things were getting a bit more serious between them.

"*Slán go fóill, mo stór*, an' ye as well, Chrissy." When he walked back down the Esplanade, he didn't seem in that much of a hurry. But he was walking toward the admiralty. I shook my head.

Moira watched him walk away. "What's that he said?"

I laughed. With a grandmother from Skye who had family ties to Ireland, I'd learned enough Irish to be pretty sure of my translation. "He said, 'Bye for now, my darling.'" Moira's face flushed. "You'll be dreaming of a life in Donegal."

Things continued that way for a week. He'd show up after work, and they'd go for a walk. Once we all attended the cinema. Then one morning we woke to a British destroyer in port. My dad said she was an old girl, the HMS Scimitar, left over from the last great war. "Everyone's being pulled in to work on her." I got the impression he was excited for the change of pace.

Kevin didn't come by after work that day. By the end of the week, there was still no sign of him. It upset Moira. She came to work with her eyes red on more than one occasion. I felt that sorry and tried to console her. "He probably shipped out with his commander sudden like."

A month later, I remember coming home to find my father with his head in his hands, sitting at the kitchen table. Mum had her hand on his back, and she looked up when I came in and shook her head. I walked past them down the hall to my bedroom but stopped short of closing my door. Instead, I left it cracked open. I knew I shouldn't bother them, but I couldn't help listening discreetly. In my defense, I worried that one of my uncles had been killed. I needed to know for sure.

Da's voice was low, above a whisper, but somehow I heard him say, "It was top secret. They called it Exercise Tiger. A practice for some upcoming offensive. The Germans got wind of it.

"One of our destroyers had a problem with her steering. Some mechanical failure. She collided with another vessel. They had to turn back to Plymouth for repairs, leaving the troop ships unprotected. German subs came up from the rear of the convoy as the troops were landing on the beach near Slapton. Hit our lads wi' torpedoes. How did the Jerries find out?"

"But, Jim, how do you know all this?"

"Cause my crew worked on the ship earlier this month—the HMS Scimitar. I certified her in perfect running order. We were all questioned."

"Do they think someone botched the job?"

"I assured them we didn't, but I'm to take the night train to Plymouth and have a look at the problem. They're guessing someone sabotaged it."

I put my hand over my mouth to keep from making a noise in my surprise. Sabotage? There was never any news of the incident, and my dad was away for a few days and then came back without saying more. I wondered who in our town was responsible for the problem that sent the British destroyer back to Plymouth, but I couldn't ask without my dad knowing I'd been listening when I shouldn't have.

Much later, I learned Operation Tiger was a dry run for D-Day. The Allies lost nearly a thousand lives in this secret exercise.

Wendy—Seattle
1968

"You suspected the spy sabotaged the British destroyer?"

Mum seemed thoughtful. "My dad did. I overheard him. Funny

thing, even with so many men lost, the news said nothing about the attack. You'd think it would have been on a broadcast or at least rate a newspaper story."

I found myself deeply interested. "If a spy was responsible, that made it even more likely to be top secret." I reflected for a minute. "This spy, if he was the same person responsible for the murders and Operation Tiger, he was really evil."

Mum's face looked bleak, but she only said, "Yes."

I lifted one of my books, and a pamphlet slid to the floor. Mum picked it up and looked it over before she handed it back to me. "This is about the women's liberation movement. Where'd you get it?"

"A group on campus was handing these out. They're recruiting members for a march coming up soon. Not something I'm really interested in."

Her reaction surprised me. "It's a good thing. Women can do so much more besides get married and have babies."

"Agreed." I wondered where this was going.

"Did I ever tell you about my great-aunt Madge?"

Chapter Twenty-Six

Christine—Greenock, Scotland
1944

D a's mood was grim for a week or two after his secret trip. I reasoned if he'd found poor workmanship or something missed by his crew, he'd rant for days. It must have been sabotage. That was something you didn't speak openly about. I wanted to ask him, but if Dad discovered I'd been eavesdropping, he'd be furious. Worse still, he would be as disappointed in me as I was myself. I'd never know for sure what happened to the HMS Scimitar.

The possibility of sabotage tormented me as I went over what I could remember from the day I saw the Scimitar. None of my friends were interested in talking about the ships in port. Well, except Kevin but that was the day he left town. The men who worked at Scotts Shipyard were all local, mostly older with years on the job, and everyone had family in the war. Surely not any of them. I was full of unanswerable questions. But it was clear my uncle was right; a spy was working here in Greenock.

Growing up during wartime, you learn to accept disturbing

facts and push your fear aside. I wasn't about to get involved in another spy hunt. After what happened with Tom Gorsky, I was staying out of the matter. There were plenty of other things to keep me occupied, like the big band playing at the town hall dance that night. Everyone was talking about it. Even Moira had perked up.

I was getting ready for work that morning when Mum called out, "Aunt Madge is coming to dinner tonight so be sure to come straight home from work."

"There's a dance at the town hall tonight." I'd finished the makeover of an old formal, and I was proud of the results. My tap shoes were polished. I had everything ready to change into after work. "There's a new band playing tonight."

"They're not playing for you, dear. I want you home. Your Aunt Madge doesn't come that often, and she's bringin' her doctor friend wi' her." Her voice was firm. Even my father gave me the look. The look could easily mean "I completely sympathize with you," which I rather thought it did, or "Compliance is not optional," which again, I'm sure it was intended to convey.

My mood didn't get any better by the end of the day. Della and Moira left early, talking about what they would wear. Nurse Graham had one last customer, and I stayed to help her. I missed my bus and headed up the hill toward home at a determined pace. That's all right, I thought. *A brisk walk is what I need to work up courage.* I'd won so few arguments with Mum over the years, but this time I was adamant about having my way. After all, I was seventeen, not a child to be ordered about. Very fine sentiments until I thought of the look on Dad's face. Mum may have been all of four-foot-ten, but she was a force to be reckoned with. And she admired Great-Aunt Madge.

My heart fell as I came through the door. Aunt Madge and another woman I'd never seen were sitting on the sofa talking with my dad. I realized there was no escape, no way to slip out ahead of our company. Even Dad had come home early. Mum poked her head through the kitchen door, asking me to come give her a hand. I greeted everyone and turned toward the kitchen.

Once through the door I whispered, "Mum, if I help with the table, may I go to the dance?"

"No, luv." She stacked plates in my arms and set napkins on top. Her voice was little more than a whisper as she added in a lecture tone, "You know well as I, especially in these times, we have to treasure our time wi' family." Her expression softened. "Aunt Madge is an amazing person. I want you to know her better."

I looked into those deep blue eyes. This wasn't an ultimatum. It was a skillful use of guilt, pure and simple.

I sighed. I'd lost the argument before it'd even begun.

After setting the table, I glanced over at my dad's conversation with the two women. Aunt Madge was all of two inches smaller than my mum. She was my Grandfather Finlay's youngest sister. I couldn't fathom what was so extraordinary about the tiny woman. She pulled her grey hair into a bun at the nape of her neck. She was the picture of a stern governess. Her black dress looked like something from thirty years ago. It was positively Victorian with its high neck and mutton-chop sleeves. But Aunt Madge's eyes were sharp and clear, her voice tinged with good humor. Despite my disappointment, I liked her too.

Her friend was heavyset with what appeared to be a man's suit jacket over a matching skirt and crisp white blouse. My mother called us all to the table.

Aunt Madge greeted me and introduced her friend. "Chrissy, this is my good friend Jane Sutherland. Dr. Sutherland."

"Pleased to meet you." I extended my hand, and the doctor shook it heartily.

"I'm pleased to meet you as well. Your aunt has often mentioned you in her letters." That stunned me. What could Aunt Madge know about me? She was my dad's aunt, but I knew it was my mum who wrote to her.

Once a governess, Aunty had retired years ago. But she still lived on the large estate of the family she'd served. It was somewhere south of Aberdeen on the coast near Stonehaven.

Mum was positively glowing with pleasure. Madge said, "Dr. Sutherland is trying to talk me into coming to live at their home in Paisley."

"Oh, aye," my mum said. "That's only a short bus ride up the coast."

I tried not to roll my eyes, thinking that Aunt Madge could visit more often if she lived in Paisley. I knew it was unkind, but really, I'd rather be out dancing.

Dr. Sutherland's smile broadened. "My husband inherited a large estate. We use part of it for our work. With her experience, your aunty could be a great help."

My curiosity got the better of me. "What?" I looked at Aunt Madge. "I didn't know you were a nurse as well."

"I'm not, dear." But she didn't explain further.

Mum asked, "So you're still in private practice, Dr. Sutherland?"

"No, we're not practicing medicine in Scotland. With the war on, our mission activities are even more needed. The travel can be harder to arrange."

"Sorry," I said. "I don't understand." I forgot my resentment, caught up in understanding what little old Aunt Madge could help with.

Dr. Jane looked around the table but directed her question at Madge. "You never told them?"

My aunt shrugged. "It happened so long ago. Old business, no one would be interested."

I sat up straight. "I'm interested."

Dr. Jane grinned. "Let me tell you how I met your aunt. My husband and I were in private practice here in Scotland. But occasionally we liked to take a few months off and go to an undeveloped country and volunteer in villages. We usually had a registered nurse who traveled with us, but on this trip we couldn't find any nurses willing to travel. We put the word out for someone new.

"In 1918, the Spanish flu was raging across the globe. It was hard enough to survive with proper medical care and nearly always fatal without. Your Aunt Madge came into my office for a physical exam. And I swear she was just as she is now. You look at her and don't think she could do that much. But she was healthy. And she seemed strong. As I finished, I pronounced her in perfect health.

"Well, then. Your aunt held out the paper and pointed to the advertisement and said, 'I'd like to apply for the position to accompany you on your trip to the Congo. You've certified I'm in perfect health. I speak German and read and write in French.'"

My mouth dropped open, but my mum beamed, giving Dr. Jane her complete attention.

"We had asked for a registered nurse or at the very least someone with a first-aid card. Madge pulled out a worn-looking card. That this little woman could carry packs of medical supplies through the jungle was preposterous. So I said, 'You don't speak Swahili though, do you?' And what did ye say ta me, Madgie?"

"I'm a quick learner, and I'm not afraid of hard work. I have a current passport as well." Even now I could hear the determination in her voice. She seemed so much younger.

The doctor continued. "There was something capable and positive about her. I hired her on the spot. We left in two weeks. On our way to the Congo, she found a crewman who spoke Swahili and paid him to tutor her. By the time we reached our destination, she was very proficient."

Aunt Madge chimed in. "Nice young man. He was glad to see us going to help."

"We hired packers, but we all carried gear. Even your tiny aunt carried her pack without a word of complaint. We took a boat up the Congo River and offloaded at a trailhead."

She chuckled. "Well, I say trail, but it wasn't much more than a rough path, so overgrown in spots that we had to hack our way through with machetes. We had a guide, and he always seemed to get us back on the right heading. Not long into our hike, we found a native by the trail. He was just a young lad, maybe fourteen."

Madge looked so sad. "He was such a funny color; his skin was grey with a blue tinge. That's when we knew what he had."

"The Spanish flu did that. The patients turned bluish. I don't mind telling you we were all alarmed."

"Mind, Jane, all our packers ran off."

"Aye, only our guide stayed. We made camp right there and nursed the lad. That was the first wave of the virus. Not as lethal as the second but bad enough. He was very ill. As he recovered, the boy begged us to go back to his village. Most of the people were sick. He feared they would all die without our help. We put the young man on a stretcher and all took turns carrying him. Thank the Lord, it wasn't too far as we followed the boy's directions to the village.

"What we found was horrifying. We decided this was as good a place as any to serve the people. That's what we did. We were able to save most everyone in the village. It took long hours each day.

"Your Aunt Madge was tireless. She organized a group of children and started a small school. On Sundays she taught Sunday school. She held classes for anyone who wanted to understand the scriptures better. And her children's choir was amazing. Many people came to know God because of her kind, straight-forward encouragement, including my husband and myself."

"How long were you there?"

Aunty answered, "Nearly three months. The day we left the village to return home, it was empty. We thought they might be herding the goats or hunting for food. The only one in the village was the chief."

The doctor was smiling when she said, "He'd given us such a hard time when we arrived, but after Madge nursed his son back to health, he became our close friend. He gave us many gifts and invited us to return and live with them. He even told Madge he was sure he could find her a husband, or she was welcome to become one of his wives."

Aunty's eyes sparkled with amusement.

Dr. Sutherland said, "The whole tribe lined the trail, singing to us one of the beautiful hymns Madge had taught the children."

Madge's eyes grew very bright, and her smile was beautiful. "Mind ye, Jane, that was such a delight."

"Aye, Madgie. Aye, it was."

I forgot about the dance as I sat at my own dining room table soaking in the stories those two women told us. I will never forget what a gift I received from my Aunt Madge. This was my heritage, strength and determination. One more of my people who left home to follow her dream. I wondered what my future would be.

Wendy—Seattle
1968

That story about Aunt Madge gave me so much to think about. It also made me wonder if my mum might have been happier having adventures like her great-aunt. For that matter, would I be better off with or without John? Amidst the demands of my classes and the play, my mind still asked that question. How do we know which way to go?

After a long day of classes, I found myself spending an evening fitting costumes and making sure everything was back where it belonged. I walked out of rehearsal with Mrs. Wilson, our drama director. She shut off all the lights and locked the door behind us. "I'm headed for the teacher's lot. Where are you parked?"

"The upper lot." The campus landscaping cast dark shadows

on an already poorly lit path to the parking lot. Mrs. Wilson said, "Campus security should be around. Need help getting them?"

"No, I'll be all right but thanks."

As she headed across campus to her car, she called back, "Good job tonight."

Alone in the dark, I decided I'd feel foolish asking a security person to walk me a few hundred feet. I trudged up the hill to my car, muttering to myself, "It's stupid to be afraid." But I kept glancing behind me and stayed as far from the bushes as possible. "Think of Mom during the war. She walked through blackout conditions. That meant no light after dark."

I reached the almost empty upper parking lot only to see the most welcome sight ever. John was standing by my car. For a moment, it reminded me of the night we broke up. But that faded from my memory as he greeted me with a wave. Even from here, I could see a smile on his face. As I neared, he reached out and pulled me into a warm embrace. "I thought you were never coming out."

"What brings you here?"

"You." A long kiss followed that took my breath away.

I said softly. "Me?"

"I came out to drive home behind you. I wanted to make sure you were safe. After what you said about being followed it, well, it worried me."

How do you react to someone who does that kind of thing? I was speechless. I stretched up to kiss him again and finished with a whispered, "Thank you. But you don't have to do that."

"I want to. Come on, let's get out of this place." He chuckled. "It's creepy."

"Not anymore." I gave him a squeezy hug.

He followed me all the way home and even up the drive. A quick kiss goodbye and he left. I climbed my stairs with a bemused feeling. It was true. He only wanted to make sure I got home safely.

Mum rose and turned off the TV when I came in. "What's up? You, my dear daughter, have the oddest expression on your face."

"Only a few months ago, I was sure John was done with me. Now I . . . I feel loved. John drove all the way to Highline just to follow me home. He said he wanted to make sure I got home safe."

She looked as pleased as I felt.

We didn't talk about the war again for a few nights. I was glad to have time to catch up my secret notebook of Mum's life.

Even though it was time for bed, I sat in the big rocking chair, tucking my feet up under my flannel nightie. "Mum, I wanted to ask you something."

She put down her book. "What's on your mind?"

"During the war, did you know anyone named Seamus?"

"That's an Irish name."

"Right, my friend from the Highland Games Association."

Her blank expression clearly said she had no idea who I was talking about.

"Didn't I tell you about Seamus? You saw me talking to him at the Highland Games."

"That official you spoke with after your dance?"

"Yup, that's the one. He volunteers at the campus library."

"A bit old for a friend, isn't he?"

Her concern caught me off guard, but I wasn't willing to be sidetracked. "He said he was all over Scotland during the war. Did you ever meet him?"

"I don't remember that name. But, Wendy, he's old enough to be your father."

I felt chastised, and my comeback was defensive. "He's a funny, charming man who I sometimes stop and chat with. That's all."

I searched for a way to change the subject. "I remember reading about D-Day in Mr. Armburster's history class in school. What was that like for you? Was Dad at Normandy?"

Chapter Twenty-Seven

Christine—Greenock, Scotland
June 6, 1944

What good is second sight? Especially when you're sure
something is coming but you have no idea when or even
what?

God was silent.

Greenock had been unusually quiet for weeks. Our docks sat
empty, and there were no servicemen in the shops or canteens.
Only the Canadian naval hospital at NIOBE remained busy. I
don't know if it was more unnerving to walk empty streets or
struggle through crowds of sailors. I wasn't the only one uneasy
with the quiet. People whispered rumors that something big was
coming. Maybe I wasn't having a bout of second sight—I might be
letting the rumors rule my emotions.

Every time I tried to make excuses, the warning voice said one
word: "Pray." And I did but couldn't find the peace I'd hoped it
would bring.

My inner storm raged on. Fear and dread stayed on me like a
blanket. The weather seemed to match my emotions. We often

had late spring storms, but this proved to be fierce. Tree branches whipped in the wind. Storm clouds rolled across the River Clyde, dumping rain over everything. One storm front after another came through Scotland. Finally, the sky cleared. I looked out my window at the little fairy rose planted in the empty shell casing. It had bloomed overnight. White petals unfolded, soaking up the sun. That was worth a big smile. Fluffy clouds floated across the deep blue sky. That was worth a smile too.

I came to the breakfast table at eight ready for work. Mum stirred the porridge. Dad had a later shift, so he ate breakfast with us. He said, "Helen, can you turn on the BBC?"

Mum put the porridge pot on a hot pad and turned to our radio. It sat on the sideboard where it resonated through our small house. I built that radio myself. Dad supervised, but he always wanted me to understand how things worked. And it worked perfectly. We kept it tuned to the BBC to catch the latest news.

A familiar voice said, "Here is the eight o'clock news for today, Tuesday, the sixth of June, read by Frederick Allen."

"Do you want some tea, Jim?" Da nodded, his mouth full of porridge.

"Supreme Allied Headquarters have issued an urgent warning to inhabitants of enemy-occupied countries living near the coast." My spoon froze on its way to my mouth.

Mum turned up the sound as Frederick Allen continued. "The warning said that a new phase in the Allied air offensive had begun."

My pulse raced. So, the rumors were true? Russell's face flashed through my mind, followed by my uncles and boys I'd befriended at the canteens. I reminded myself; you didn't see the veil. That's something, isn't it?

There'd been no veils for quite a while, no letters either. People mumbled about an information blackout. Russell's letters had stopped weeks ago but so had letters from my uncles.

When the newscast ended, we all went our separate ways. I prayed all the way to the bus stop where I met Moira for the ride into work. She was quiet. I looked around the bus and saw the same worried expression on everyone's faces. I prayed silently.

We turned up the radio at work. By midday, a familiar voice interrupted a Glenn Miller song to make an announcement. All activity in the dispensary stopped. Momentary static and then, "Here is a special bulletin read by John Snagge. 'D-Day has come. Early this morning the Allies began an assault on the north-western face of Hitler's European fortress. The first official news came just after half-past nine, when Supreme Headquarters of the Allied Expeditionary Force, usually called SHAEF from its initials—'"

Moira grabbed my arm. "Oh, Chrissy, do ye think that's where Kevin is?" I looked at her enormous grey eyes, but I couldn't offer comforting words. My heart cried out for Russell. We missed part of what they said, and I motioned for her to be quiet.

"It was announced a little later that General Montgomery is in command of the army group carrying out the assault. This army group includes British, Canadian, and United States forces."

When the news finished, music filled the store, but it did nothing to help calm us. I fought to keep panic from over-whelming me. I told myself to stop it. But I knew Russell was wounded. I walked away from stocking shelves and found a quiet corner in the back room. And I prayed for Russell, for my uncles, and for the boys from the canteens. Still, peace didn't come. I told myself I was foolish, but I couldn't shake it.

Moira wasn't doing any better until I thought of something and said to her, "Kevin's attached to high command. He's not likely to be in the fighting is he?"

Relief washed over her face. "You're right. Thank ye, Chrissy. I dinna think on it that way."

I smiled at her lovely face, but in my heart, I knew for sure Russell had been right in the middle of this. She must have read the worry on my face. "Oh, Chrissy, I didna think on your laddie. I hope he's aright." I managed a weak smile, but the feeling of dread crept over me.

At one, the music stopped again. "Here is the news read by Frederick Allen." He reported on a speech Prime Minister Churchill gave as he addressed the Commons. It sounded as if everything was going well with losses lower than expected. There was a collective sigh at this statement.

That was good news. Maybe Russell was unhurt? But I didn't have time to dwell on his fate as Churchill disclosed they had committed four thousand ships and two thousand smaller craft to battle, and that, since dawn, eleven-thousand Allied aircraft had entered German airspace.

Churchill's familiar voice said, "This vast operation is undoubtedly the most complicated and difficult that has ever occurred." But we were making headway, and forces were already several miles inland. The enemy was taken by complete surprise. I remembered that a spy was in our midst. But this time no one found out our plans. Men were alive now because of secrecy.

Please, God, let Russell be alive. And Uncle Tommy, Uncle Jack, Uncle Willy, Uncle Davie. All of them and all the laddies fighting so hard.

We lived from one news broadcast to the next. By nine o'clock that evening, we were getting a better picture of the operation.

Churchill said, "The outstanding feature has been the landings of the airborne troops on a scale much larger than any that has been seen so far in the world." Overall, he reported that, "Many dangers and difficulties which last night appeared extremely formidable are now behind us." He said that losses were much less than expected. I was so encouraged.

Russell. But even as I thought his name, I prayed, *Please don't let his wounds be serious.* I repeated that prayer often.

Everyone was saying this was the beginning of the end for Hitler, but it was still only a beginning, and there was a long way to go before peace. Now I waited. Even though Churchill proclaimed our losses were lower than expected, we still lost so many. Sunday dinner at Grandma Finlay's was a quiet affair. We were all worried about my dad's brothers, and even my Aunty Agnus had her beau John MacDonald in the thick of fighting.

I'm not sure how we got through the next week, waiting for some word of how our loved ones fared. Every day at the noon hour another broadcaster would update the latest news. Interwoven with the stark numbers of wounded and dead were stories of courage and valor.

Today Boots was very quiet. We turned up the radio during our lunch hour and heard about a young piper, Bill Millin. When our troops landed on the beaches of France, he piped them into battle. It'd been the custom for centuries that the pipes would accompany the troops into the fighting. This brave young man carried only his pipes and a *sgian dubh*, our traditional small knife tucked into our knee socks. His kilt was the same one his father wore during the First World War. The soldiers called Millin "Piper Bill." He followed the men into the ice water of the English Channel and onto the killing field with his division. Bullets flew around him, but he never missed a note of *Highland Laddie*.

We sat in the little infirmary with our tea and sandwiches. It was empty. No servicemen to patch up after a fight. No colds to medicate. I imagined everyone was storming the beaches at Normandy. Waiting was terrible. Everyone had family there, people they loved. Even Nurse had a nephew serving in the RAF. I looked over at her stern face. Tears rolled down her cheeks. Her face blurred, and I realized my own eyes were full of unshed tears. We shared watery smiles full of pride in our country, our traditions and our fighting laddies and the women who waited at home for word.

The announcer said, "Captured Germans said they didn't shoot at the piper because they felt sorry for the poor, mad soul." Piper Bill wasn't mad. He was following in the footsteps of so many other brave pipers, giving courage to the men who stormed the beaches. For those who lay wounded and dying that day, the pipes called them home to heaven.

Most of us tried to catch news of the front from the radio and newspapers. On the twelfth, I took in the cinema but not for the film that was playing. It was packed. We all came to watch the newsreels. I couldn't imagine a more horrifying attack. Big ships stood offshore, bombing the dunes where German bunkers were hidden among the tall seagrasses. The camera followed the men in one landing craft as it bounced over choppy waves toward the sandy beach.

We'd had a holiday at the seacoast in France when my sister Isabelle was still alive. I remembered blue skies; soft, tawny sands and a very blue ocean. Now that ocean was covered with boats filled with men.

The camera did a close-up as the commentator spotted one young Canadian. I'd been hoping for some glimpse of Russell, but now I was just as glad not to see him. The quality of film from the battle photographers was poor, but I saw fear and anguish on the boy's face, and it made my blood run cold. The image on the film rocked as the commentator announced, "Our troops hold on tight despite being strafed by enemy fire." A nearby troop carrier exploded.

On the beach, Germans were machine-gunning everyone. The reporter's voice shook as he hurried off the landing craft, saying, "As the carrier hit the beach, the front dropped away. Men"—no, these were still mostly boys, not much older than me—"poured out of the small boats and ran toward the German machine-gun batteries in the cement bunkers. They were running into the fire-fight, lobbing grenades at the bunkers." Soldiers were falling in the sand, and they weren't rising. I ached for what Russell was going through. I reminded myself this film was from six days ago. Where was he now?

The announcer was talking about what a victory this was. I rose and left the theatre. A victory but at what cost?

If it was a victory, it was still only a foothold. We continued to follow news about Allied forces pushing across France. Our papers were full of it. Even reading between lines meant to encourage civilian populations at home, the cost of victory was dear in lives. Still, the Germans were being forced back.

Again we waited for letters telling us our loved ones were still alive. And they came. One by one, all my uncles checked in. Greenock canteens filled again with men being rotated out of battle for rest and with new recruits, replacements coming in to join the fight, taking the empty places left by the dead and wounded.

Life began again. It was still war. Within a week of D-Day, the Germans took their revenge out on the people of southern England by bombarding them with German V-1 rocket bombs nicknamed "doodlebugs." I was busy volunteering and working, but I hadn't stopped worrying. A month passed and still no letter came from Russell. I wondered if I'd ever find out what happened to him.

I lived in constant fear I'd hear from his sister Margie that he'd been killed. For a solid month, I rushed home from work and headed straight for the mailbox. Today I wasn't going to torture myself any longer. If he wasn't writing, the news must be bad. I had to stop waiting for the other shoe to drop. It was my mum who met me at the door with a letter in hand. I held my breath when I recognized Margie's writing. Standing right there in the entry, I tore open her letter.

She wrote, "They sent Russell home with a severe head wound. They say he still has a piece of shrapnel lodged in his skull. An operation to remove it could kill him." Tears rolled down my cheeks. The words blurred, but I wiped my eyes to clear them and read on. "Oh, Chrissy, they riddled his body with shrapnel. The doctors removed it all except the piece in his head. We're not sure what will happen next. Russell has terrible headaches. I can't bear to see him suffer so."

But he was alive. Alive. I was so relieved until I thought, *alive and home in New Westminster, British Columbia*. So far away. I'd never see him again. I longed to go to him, but with the war on it was hopeless. There was no way I could travel halfway across the world. Not to mention my parents would never allow such a thing.

I told myself it didn't matter. Russell promised he would come back to me. His last words before he got on his ship were a plea for me to wait. His voice came to me as clearly as if he stood before me. "I love you, Chrissy. I want us to be together always." He'd be back. But for now, my only link to him was Margie's letters.

I was home alone on a Saturday afternoon when I pulled a letter from our mail slot. Finally, it was Russell's handwriting. I held it to my heart and ran for my bedroom.

I sat on the bed looking at it. I was afraid. *Take a deep breath and open the damn letter*. I did.

He wanted to explain how things were different now that he was back from the war. I shouldn't wait for him because his injuries were so bad they weren't returning him to the fighting. And I shouldn't worry about him because his old girlfriend was visiting and helping him to recover.

I read his letter again and again. Despite the pain, I couldn't help myself. It didn't seem real. But I finally had to accept his words.

That's it then. I felt hollow. Empty.

That old saying was true. You don't realize how much you love someone until they're taken away. Tears clouded my vision, and I wiped them away with an angry gesture. *No. You always knew this might happen. It's not like you were ready to immigrate to Canada*. A sob escaped my lips, and I clamped my hand over my mouth. But it did no good. The dam had broken. Deep, racking sobs shook my body. I couldn't see my bedroom for the tears that flooded my eyes. Hours later, I heard the key in the lock of the front door and remembered Mum and Dad had gone to visit the grandmothers.

I brushed my face with the back of my hand and looked in my mirror. My eyes were red and swollen. My nose too. I stood there thinking of all the things Russell had said to me. Lies, every word. No, it couldn't have been. I believed him. He'd made me love him. A spark of anger flared to life. And if he really meant what he said, he'd find a way back to me no matter what happened. Old girlfriends be damned.

Mum called out to me.

"I'll be right there." I picked up my brush and ran it through my tangled curls. Somehow it seemed important not to share my loss. I was sure I'd see relief in their eyes. They knew I was serious about Russell, and that worried them. I didn't blame them. I was the only daughter they had left, and they wanted to keep me nearby. I just couldn't face their reactions.

I tucked Russell's letter into my pocket and slipped into the water closet to wash my face. This time I looked better, but my eyes were hard, sharpened by anger. My mind still strayed to the young man with sandy-blond hair and sparkling blue eyes. He'd changed me. I wouldn't be that naïve ever again.

Wendy—Seattle
1968

When Mum finished, I could see the hurt of her loss still close to the surface. Nearly twenty years ago and her pain was still real, even knowing it had all worked out in the end. I thought about her all week.

During a break between classes, I stopped by the cafeteria to get a cup of tea. Thank goodness for tea. Must be my Scottish side, but it always revived me. There was Seamus. He was staring into his own steamy brew, so he didn't see me walk up. He jumped when I started talking. "Something floating in your tea?"

When he looked up, I wondered at his cross expression. That wasn't like him.

"I'm sorry to bother you." And I really was. But his face transformed into pure pleasure. The sudden change gave me an uneasy feeling.

His voice was cheery. "Not a'tall, not a'tall. Have a seat, my darlin' girl." I slid into a chair across the table.

"If you don't mind my asking, is everything all right? You don't look yourself." But he had transformed into the lovely, funny man I called my friend. I relaxed, thinking that whatever was wrong, it couldn't be that bad.

"A minor setback is all. It's sure to come right in the end. And tell me what's up with you. I walked to my car last night, and who should I see standing next to your car but that imposing young man of yers."

"How do you know which car is mine?"

"Oh, and wouldn't it be that fifties-something, pink-and-orange Buick with the daisies all over it?"

"That's me."

"Really, you Americans." He was chuckling. "I saw you leave once. Not a car you'd forget." He took a sip of his drink, his expression expectant. I realized he was waiting for me to explain.

"That would be John, and he's back." I felt myself blush as I remembered how sweet it was of John to worry about my safety. I still couldn't quite believe how quickly things had changed.

"The lad who broke up with you. Are you sure it's wise to trust someone who let you down in the past?" His expression was grave, and his comment took me back. He seemed to read my reaction. "And don't you know I've come ta think of you as a dear friend? Never mind that. I don't want you to get hurt is all."

I changed the subject and talked about my classes and the play, but as soon as I could, I excused myself to go to my next class. I couldn't help feeling something was not quite right about his reaction.

I had told John all about my friendship with Seamus, but John thought the man was out to seduce me. That made me smile. John was jealous, and I liked that, but he was wrong about Seamus. Wasn't he?

Deep down, I was afraid both Mum and John were right. God, I hoped not. That would be awkward. It's so hard to judge intentions. Sometimes you can't go by what people say. That thought had been haunting me since Mum told me about my father's letter. She'd believed him. Second sight hadn't warned her Dad was lying. I was glad he was away driving his bus. I think I'd have to have a serious talk with him.

Was Seamus only pretending to be my friend? I had to admit it was hard to tell.

And then there was John.

I lost myself in WWII. That night I asked Mum, "Tell me more about the war and what happened to you next." She rolled her eyes, but I added, "Please."

"What do you want to know?"

"Only everything." I smiled at the face she made. "Just tell me what happened after Dad's letter. How did you get back together?"

Chapter Twenty-Eight

Christine—Greenock, Scotland
Summer 1944

I hardened my heart. I wouldn't give Russell one more tear. The thought haunted me that maybe God didn't mean for me to marry, like Great-Aunt Madge. She found adventure and fulfillment in a life of service. But I wasn't tramping the jungles of Africa saving whole villages from the Spanish flu. My service was right here in Greenock. I sighed. It would have to be enough for now. The war was a constant reminder nothing was permanent.

From one week to another, Allied forces struggled to gain ground. We all watched the newsreels, read the paper, and the BBC was on in every home and every store across the country. One headline really hit home. They dubbed the battle for France the "battle of the hedgerows."

Here in Scotland, farmers often separated their fields with short, stony fences. They piled the stones they dug up in their fields along the edges. It was the same in France, but French farmers often planted actual hedge roses or brambles.

It gave Nazi snipers the perfect place to hide and pick off our infantry as they battled to push the Germans back. Progress was slow. I was sad when I heard that Robert, my friend from school, lost his father to a German sharpshooter hiding behind one of these rose hedges. We lost many of our lads to the snipers' bullets. The battle of the hedgerows was a pleasant name for a deadly game.

In the south of France, things were progressing much better. We all felt it was only a matter of time until the Allies liberated the entire country. I'd seen General de Gaulle once as he came through our town with his Free French battalion. We cheered wildly for them as they marched past. I tossed a rose at him and waved. He stopped for a minute and looked up. I was at a window on the second floor of the Canadian Overseas Club.

He smiled and blew me a kiss.

When the Germans took France in 1940, they set a puppet government at Vichy. But one general refused to surrender. De Gaulle's spirit of resistance inspired the French people. Gradually fighters flocked to him from all over the world—French nationals living abroad but also from French colonial territories in Africa, India, and the Pacific. Eventually his force swelled to over 300,000 regular troops. The Allied command recognized him as the leader of the Free French government in exile. He united the "French Forces of the Interior," otherwise known as the underground resistance.

I remember thinking how brave they all were. Their families were all living under German occupation. While working at the Y in town, I'd talked with some of De Gaulle's fighting men. One young man named Francois spoke quite good English. He couldn't have been over seventeen, so young and vulnerable. He didn't want to dance, so I brought him some food and sat with him, letting him talk.

He said, "When the Vichy government surrendered, the people thought *possiblement* it wouldn't be so bad." He shrugged in a typically Gallic fashion. "We began to see things change. France wasn't France anymore. Everyone was afraid. Food was scarce, and friends and neighbors were taken. You know. They were just gone. The Germans took them, and they didn't come back.

"We heard stories about this civilian band of freedom fighters. They mostly caused mischief. You know, *petit désastres*. I was still only thirteen, but I saw things." He looked past me as if watching some horrific scenes unfold before his eyes. "The Germans were vigilant in their efforts to root out the partisans. If they caused too much trouble, the Germans would pick people at random to execute in the streets."

I was incredulous. "They'd kill anyone? Not the guilty parties?"

"*Oui*, men, women, old ones, even children. *N'importe quelle personne.*"

I shook my head in disbelief. Few of us thought about the dangerous balance forced on the French people.

"De Gaulle unified and directed underground actions. They started making more of a difference. As soon as I could, I escaped to join them," Francois said proudly.

"Is your family still in France?"

His face clouded, and I wished I hadn't asked him such a stupid question. "*Oui.*"

I couldn't get that conversation out of my head. I'd heard that on D-Day ordinary French men and women, at monumental risk to their own lives and even those of their children, did everything they could to aid the Allied forces.

After D-Day, French troops fought on French soil, and de Gaulle called for the French underground resistance to rise and continue to cause as much trouble for the Germans who occupied their country as they could. They had to be successful, or the enemy would snuff out many innocent lives.

Free French fought alongside Allied forces from the beginning and were instrumental in battles of North Africa. Now they were fighting at home. In August, they eradicated the great darkness of

Hitler from the City of Light. France was finally free of German occupation. The world celebrated this amazing victory.

The Allies were making genuine progress, but unfortunately, I was not. I wanted to forget Russell and move on, but I was still hurt and angry he'd led me on and then dismissed me. I slept badly, my dreams filled with tender moments in his arms. When I woke, I'd be so angry with myself for wanting him; it would put me in a sour mood all day long.

Our town hall hosted special dances. It was a time when we all came together and celebrated being alive. We invited all the different servicemen to join us. In July, the Queen Elizabeth ocean liner docked in Greenock. She brought the American 404th Field Artillery group and other reinforcements for the war effort. Our town threw a big dance to welcome the Americans and celebrate the Allied victories. The women of Greenock decked out the town hall.

I loved this grand old building. One of its nicest features was the wide balcony that ran around the dance floor one story up. From there you could look down and watch the action. I wandered around trying to find Della after the first dance.

Mounting the stairs to the balcony, I made my way past little tables with flickering lamplights. By the look of the men on the dance floor, practically every branch of the Allied forces attended.

I found Della sitting at a small table by herself at the far end of the balcony, staring at the dancers.

"Where's that boyfriend of yours?" I asked.

She looked up at me with sad eyes but didn't answer.

"Della, what's wrong?"

She stared off into space, her expression bleak. "I was thinking what rotters men can be. Maybe it's a good thing Russell showed his true colors before you followed him to Canada."

Before I could respond, a very masculine voice asked, "Would you like to dance?"

She said, "No, tired."

He touched my shoulder, and I turned to face a very handsome lad. He wasn't much taller than me, dark brown hair and dimples when he smiled.

"What about you?" he asked in a deep, smooth voice. He was the opposite of Russell in every way imaginable. Canadian, too, but with none of Russell's boyish innocence. No, wait, Russell couldn't have been as innocent as all that with a girlfriend at home he'd forgotten to mention. In that split second, I realized I needed someone who was completely different.

But if Della wasn't well, she might need to leave, so I said, "Are ye all right? I don't want to leave you alone."

She waved her hand in front of her face as if to wave away her mood. The old Della grinned up at me. "Och, I'll be fine."

I looked closely at her, but she shrugged away my concern. "Been under the weather is all. I'll sit for a while and enjoy the band." She looked at the young man. "Andy Brown, this is Christina Finlay. See that you treat her nicely." She whispered to me, "Go ye ahead. Really, I'm fine."

I was reluctant to leave her, but she shooed us away. Before I realized it, he'd taken my hand in his, and we were walking downstairs to the dance floor.

Andy danced like Fred Astaire. When you love dancing, it's especially wonderful to discover someone who loves it as much as you. We clicked, anticipating each other's moves. My feet were in heaven. I couldn't help but be impressed with this laddie. I didn't see Della again until it was time to go home.

I found her at the coat check. "You two hit it off?" I blushed and apologized, but she stopped me. "I knew you would. He dances almost as well as you do."

Dance brought me to life again, and Andy was just what I needed. It was no wonder I spent as much time as possible in the arms of my dream partner. He was a Canadian naval officer stationed at NIOBE attached as an aide to some high command. That meant we had his off-duty time together. We saw each other at every liberty. We became such good friends, went for walks and talked. He even came to meet my parents, and they loved him.

But mostly we danced. It's hard to describe the feeling when your partner knows what you'll do next. We were in sync with each other, both on and off the floor. I wasn't in love—my heart was still reeling from Russell—but Andy and I were wonderful friends, and there was an attraction between us.

One night the canteen was full. Everyone was sitting around at tables while the band took a brief break. We were all talking at once. But Andy leaned into me and said, "Tell me something about your family."

"What?"

"Oh, anything. No, something you don't tell other people." Lord, he had a bonnie smile. Andy's family had French ties. He had brilliant hazel eyes that twinkled when he smiled.

"Something I've told no one, hey? My mum told me this. She was only a girl, and her father was a shipwright. He worked out of Vancouver for the Canadian Pacific Rail Line. That's odd, isn't it?"

"Not really, they run shipping all over. But he worked aboard ship?"

"Oh, aye. The Empress of Asia. He made several large models of his ship and the Empress of Japan."

Andy sat up straight. "They wouldn't be in the Vancouver Rail Station, would they?"

"You've seen them then?"

"Well, one of them, not sure which, but Empress of Asia sticks in my mind. Anyway, go on."

"My grandfather was home on leave, but when it came time for him to head back to his ship, they booked his passage and sent his trunks ahead. He missed his family and wanted to stay till the last minute, so he took the night train to Southampton to catch the sailing. A few days later, a town crier came down the street announcing a disaster.

"You see, he was booked on the Titanic. The boy was selling

newspapers, and the morning edition announced its sinking. My Grandma Cowan nearly fainted when she heard the lad call out, 'Titanic sunk.' She sent my mum to get the paper, but before they could even read a word, my grandfather's telegram arrived letting them know the night train from Scotland was late as usual, and he missed his sailing. He was waiting for another."

"So your grandfather's trunks went down with the Titanic."

I matched his smile with my own. "And that, my dear laddie, is not something I tell many people."

"Why not?"

"Because my mum says every time her father came home it was like Christmas with all the treasures he found in faraway places, but his telegram was the best gift of all." I looked away from him. "It's personal, you know, tender. A treasured family story."

I rested my chin in my hand and looked back into his handsome face. "Your turn."

Wendy—Seattle
1968

"Don't think I heard that story of my great-grandfather before." It was an oddly personal connection to the past that fascinated me. "I remember you talking about your seagoing Grandfather Cowan, but his trunks really went down on the Titanic?"

"Yes, he died much later and far from home in Vancouver from the flu." Mum sighed. "But Grandma Cowan told me all about him. So much so, I felt I knew him."

My mind floated back to Mum's story. "Tell me about Andy." I grinned at how her face lit up.

"I thought of him as my Gene Kelly, but he was the spitting image of the movie star Tyrone Power."

Mum and I watched all the old black-and-white movies from the war years together. I loved the styles, the music, and the deep romanticism of that era. Mostly I loved all the little things she'd share about her experiences from the war years. Both were handsome leading men.

"Sounds like Andy was impressive, and you had so much in common." I let that thought dangle in the air, not wanting to think how opposite Mum and Dad were. Kind of like John and me.

I knew the way things were going with John, I'd have to make some important decisions in my own life.

"Sounds like you might have married him instead of Dad." Again, her eyes focused on the past as she recalled something troubling. "What? What happened? Did Andy die?"

"No, the Sight happened."

Chapter Twenty-Nine

Christine—Greenock, Scotland
1944

T he customs of Hawaii always fascinated me. It was fanciful, but when I was going to a dance, I often stopped to buy a gardenia. I wore it in my hair the way Islanders do in the movies, behind my right ear to show I'm an unmarried young woman. I was probably the only one in Scotland who was aware of the significance, but it made me smile. I remembered all the letters I wrote to Russell decorated with palm trees and sandy beaches, and my face slid into a frown. Maybe someday I'd move my flower to the left.

Aunt Tina in Canada sent me a parcel with fabric and, best of all, new shoes with a label that said Hollywood. It lifted my spirits, and I couldn't help thinking wait till my friends see these.

The fabric was a red-and-white check. By the next evening, I'd made myself a dress that looked a lot like the one in the movies, adding a few touches of my own. I had a rule about not copying costumes exactly.

I was so pleased when Nurse Graham said, "Did your aunt in Canada send you a new dress?"

"No, just fabric but, thanks, I made this last night."

"Last night?" She looked at me skeptically, picking up the hem of my skirt to examine the stitches. "Do you own a sewing machine?"

Moira was passing us and said, "She does not. That's all done by hand."

I smiled back at her compliment.

Nurse looked up at me, and I nodded. "I wish I had such a wonderful thing. No, I only have scissors, some tailor's chalk, a needle and thread and a good imagination." Long ago I'd perfected the ability to sew even little stitches at a pretty good clip.

Andy picked me up at work, and we walked to the town hall. Its tall spire was visible from all over town. But it was the ornate entry hall with beautiful, tiled floors and carved panels along the walls that made me feel like a princess entering the royal ball.

As we walked through the double doors to the auditorium, one of our local bands was playing to a packed house. You could barely see the polished dance floor for all the young men in uniforms, each with a lassie in his arms swaying to a pretty good rendition of *I'll Get By*. I knew the trumpeter worked at the train station, but tonight he sounded like the famous Harry James himself.

We paused at the door, enjoying the sight. There were little tables all along the edge of the room and more in the balcony above. I spotted Della and her boyfriend Rodney.

"Look, there's Della. She said she'd save us a place at their table."

But as I entered the room, the band stopped playing and started into Glenn Miller's *In the Mood*. All heads swiveled toward us. A slow smile spread across Andy's face. "That's your signature song, isn't it?"

I looked up at him, my eyes bright. "They started doing that after I won a dance contest a year ago."

"Wow, I didn't realize what a celebrity you are."

Heat rose to color my face. "Don't be silly. They're only teasing me. My mum would box my ears if I took them seriously."

"Maybe," he placed a kiss on my head, "but they don't stop for anyone else." He took my hand and led me out onto the floor. We finished *In the Mood* and danced till the last dance.

"I don't want to dance this one," he said.

I was amazed. "You're tired?" I'd rarely met anyone who loved dancing as much as I did.

"No, Chrissy. It's the last dance, and I don't want to ever dance the last dance with you."

I thought of Russell. If there were anyone who could help me forget Russell, it'd be Andy. But a sailor with sandy-blond hair and bright blue eyes still lingered in my heart. Och, it made me so mad at myself that everything came back to thoughts of Russell. I whispered under my breath, "Well, I hope his head is hurting." But I didn't really, and that was the problem.

Andy took my hand, and we went to get our coats. He leaned down and kissed me. I wanted to remember how his lips felt on mine, how good his arms felt around me. Instead, I remembered Russell's voice saying, "Can you wait for me?" *But you didn't wait for me, did you?*

We met Della and her boyfriend. I was glad things were better between them. I didn't know what the tension was, but at least for now they seemed happy.

The four of us walked up the hill toward Dempster Street. The cobblestones were damp with dew, so we stayed on the sidewalk as we wound our way past the darkened windows of little shops then past a small park on Trafalgar Street. It was only a twenty-minute walk to my house, but there was an eerie silence as we passed bombed-out homes. Not to say that our mood was dampened; we were merry after the dance, Della and her beau behind

Andy and me. We were all tired but in good spirits. Rodney must have said something funny because Della was laughing.

A deep, commanding male voice roared in my ear, "Stop, now."

I whirled to look at Rodney. "What's the matter?"

His expression showed a fair degree of bewilderment. "What? Me?"

"That's not funny. What did you say?"

"Not me, I can't get a word in edgewise with this gabbler." Della cuffed his shoulder.

I turned back to Andy. "Didn't you hear a loud voice?" He shook his head.

Andy started talking about the Arthur Murray Dance Studio in Vancouver.

I was only half listening, still trying to puzzle out what I thought I'd heard. We were climbing the steep bit up the hill when the voice spoke again.

"Stop now. Turn around or die." It sounded urgent, nearby.

It had to be Della's beau, so I swung around to give him a piece of my mind. But Rodney had his face next to hers, and it looked like he'd just kissed her.

She flinched and sounded annoyed. "What's wrong with you, Chrissy?"

"Sorry, thought I heard something." I looked at Andy. His dark brows pulled together. "You didn't hear that?" I was nonplussed.

As we fell in step together, he said sympathetically, "I didn't hear anything."

I looked around, but the street was empty except for the four of us. "I don't know what's wrong with me. I heard a voice, and it was so loud."

I was feeling like a fool, wondering what was wrong with me but afraid I knew. My pulse raced, and I panicked. Then the voice boomed, "Turn now. Run or die."

The urge to race back down the hill overpowered me. I

grabbed Andy's hand and pulled him to a stop. Della and her lad bumped into us.

"Run. Now." I kept a firm grip on Andy and ran as fast as I could, screaming, "Run, Della! Run." They followed. When we came to the corner, I pulled us all around just as the blast knocked us down. It felt like my eardrums exploded. Dust and debris covered the ground.

Andy helped me stand. "Are you all right?"

"Aye, I think so. How about everyone else?"

Della's beau helped her up and brushed her off. But Andy was just staring at me. "How did you know?"

I shook my head weakly. The movement hurt. "You didn't hear the voice?"

"What voice?"

Della looked at me, tears in her big blue eyes, and put her hand on my arm. "I should have listened to you. Sorry, luv." Then to Andy she said, "Chrissy has the Sight." The air was full of dust, and there was an unnatural quiet. I saw bewilderment on his face. Della said, "Ye ken, the second sight. She knows things."

Rodney was brushing off his clothes but stopped. He looked at me as if I'd grown a set of horns and crossed himself. Della swatted him with her purse. "Stop it. She just saved yer hide, laddie."

Andy said with accusation in his voice, "You never told me anything about this Sight thing."

"And I wouldn't, would I, not with the way people react." I motioned to Rodney.

"Does it happen much?"

"No, and I never know when it will happen again." There was no concern or tenderness in his stare, only accusation. But that was so unfair. God had saved our lives.

Self-conscious, I didn't want to see his reaction, so I walked past him to look up the street we'd just run down. The houses we'd passed were gone. They had already been bombed during the

Blitz. Although unfit to live in, they were still recognizable as once being homes. Now rubble lay in their place from what must have been an unexploded bomb. I felt Andy come stand behind me.

He let out a low whistle. "You saved our lives."

I remembered what Grandma Finlay said, that the Lord pulls back a curtain and lets us peek behind, sometimes to see the future and sometimes to save our lives. I said, "No, God did. I only listened."

Della never mentioned it again and neither did Andy. Few people knew I had the Sight. Only a few of my friends. For a while Andy was much more reserved in his attitude toward me. Sometimes I caught him giving me a strange, sideways glance.

The Sight's like that. Some people think you have a power. You can tell them it's not you, but they don't believe it. I was afraid that incident would change how Andy saw me. Did God close another door?

Wendy—Seattle
1968

I didn't have time to ask any more questions about Andy's reaction to the Sight because Dad came home unexpectedly. All summer he'd worked out of the Greyhound bus station in Portland. He said it was a busier assignment. Now that peak travel time ended, he had to bid a new run.

When he bid a run like Portland, he stayed there, and on days off we rarely saw him. He said he was tired and spent his free time sleeping. Even when he was home, we had to be quiet because he slept so much.

This year was the first time I really noticed the difference in Mum with Dad home. I would have expected her to be more relaxed, but she hurried around catering to his every need. He didn't like noise, so the music that filled the house when he wasn't home was now silent.

I couldn't help wondering if this was the life Mum expected from her young John Wayne sailor. I didn't think she had changed much. She was still quite beautiful, but my father's long days driving a bus showed in his expanded waistline and bloated face.

I scolded myself for thinking such thoughts. We all change with age. But I couldn't help wondering if life with Andy would have been all about dancing and laughing. She didn't laugh much with my dad.

It made me wonder about who I was in love with. What kind of life was I choosing for myself? And how would I know now what life would be like in the future? I decided to ask her about it when Dad left again.

One week later we all drove him to the Greyhound station in Seattle. He had his bags packed for another long tour out of Portland. I wondered why working out of Seattle wasn't just as good. Not a question I felt comfortable asking.

When we said goodbye, Mum looked sad. But I was relieved. Life could go back to our normal. Mom encouraged us to have friends over, play music, and then there was Heather and her love of board games that seemed to collect on every flat surface. I felt guilty for being glad he was gone. Still, that's how I felt if I was honest.

When things settled down, I asked Mom, "Why didn't you marry Andy? He seems so perfect for you."

There was sadness in her voice when she answered. "Like I said, the Sight has a way of changing how people see you."

I blew out a long breath, feeling bad for bringing up old heartaches.

With a melancholy smile, she added, "Or maybe God was showing me Andy wasn't the guy for me. Not sure. In the end, the Sight changed our relationship."

Chapter Thirty

Christine—Greenock, Scotland
September 1944

The Allied Forces liberated Brussels on the fourth of September. Europe was being released from Nazi domination. Almost every day we heard about another European city that was free. Finally, we were pushing back the Germans at a record pace.

Even with so much good news, the war wasn't over yet. People were still dying, and we all lived with constant anxiety that someone we loved would be killed. Hitler used every opportunity to strike fear into our hearts. He developed new self-guided bombs called buzz bombs for the sound they made. Cinema newsreels were full of their destructive force that decimated the south of England and especially London.

Sound was one of the most powerful weapons. Hitler's bombs screamed through the air on their way to their intended targets then went silent as the rocket motors on the bomb cut out. The V-1 buzz bombs would fall to the ground, and a thunderous explosion would follow. We were told if we heard this terrifying sound from above to run toward the scream, letting it pass overhead. When the sound cut out, the bomb would blow up anyone under its fall. Once again, we feared the Clydebank was a prime target for Hitler.

I tried not to worry about losing my parents or family, but it was impossible to push fear out of my mind altogether.

Since the night God told us to turn and run, Andy had distanced himself from me. That reaction was the reason I didn't tell people about the Sight. Still, I was crushed. I loved his company. I guess he missed me too, though, because in a few weeks he started showing up after work. Then we'd meet at dances. It took a while before he stopped giving me speculative glances.

He relaxed and so did I. We went back to spending every minute we could together. If anyone could help me put Russell's memory behind me, he was the lad. Mostly we danced, but we had time to talk during intermissions, and he always insisted on walking me home. During those quiet times, we talked about everything. He seemed as interested in what life was like for me growing up in Scotland as I was in finding out about his childhood in Canada.

I asked him to dinner, and he accepted without hesitation. He got on wonderfully with my parents. I was certain you could set the lad down at the queen's table, and he'd be able to make pleasant dinner conversation.

Mum asked, "Do you come from a large family?"

"No, ma'am. Only the four of us. I have an older brother serving on a sub hunter." He ducked his head, realizing what he'd said. "Sorry, sir. I know you're a submariner. I don't imagine any submariner likes to hear about sub hunters."

"Quite all right. Did ye hear we caught a German sub right here on the Clydebank? They ran afoul of our submarine nets." Dad was proud of this because the government had given him free rein to go over the German sub to discover what he could about the German U-boats.

"I did. I'm stationed here as an aide to Captain Hunter. He's a fan of yours."

"Me? I dinna think so. I'm sure I've never met the man."

"Maybe not, sir, but you have quite a reputation."

I saw red creep up Dad's neck and realized he was enjoying the compliment.

"There now, Jim." Mum turned to Andy. "Don't get him started on the subject. Ye'll never make it back to yer base before curfew."

Andy turned to my dad. "I love the stories Chrissy tells me about your family."

Mum chimed in. "Jim, tell him about Miss Spencer's hero."

Andy perked up. "I'd love to hear it."

Mum served us tea and cakes. One bite of Mum's tea cake, and Andy beamed appreciatively.

I rolled my eyes. You'd think he had to win them over the way he was buttering them up. But secretly I was pleased.

Dad said, "My younger brother Jack is a character but a good-hearted lad."

Mum smiled. "On Sundays, the entire family would go to Grandma Finlay's for dinner. While we women were busy in the kitchen, the men sat in the living room talking."

I couldn't help adding my bit. "Me and my cousins waited for Uncle Jack to settle himself in the big chair by the fireplace. We'd find a spot on the rug beside him. I remember how anxious we were for the master storyteller to begin."

"Aye, that's right, luv." Mum's eyes looked very bright. "I still remember how your wee sister used to climb onto Jack's lap."

I reached over and squeezed Mum's hand. Every memory of my little sister Isabelle brought with it the reminder of grief and loss. I pushed on, wanting to turn the story away from sad thoughts.

"So, you were a tyke?" Andy said.

"Yes, but I remember those times as if they just happened."

The clock on the mantle ticked away the minutes. "Uncle Jack was our hero, and he fit the part perfectly."

Dad sounded proud of his brother. "See, our Jack was an apprentice bricklayer. His job as a bricklayer kept him outdoors, so he was lean, muscular, and tanned."

Mum added, "Jack's a soft-spoken man with a kind face. He has his mam's reddish-blond hair."

Talking about Uncle Jack always made me smile. "All the cousins were in awe of him. He achieved impossible deeds that none of us questioned. For a half hour he transported us to faraway lands where new conquests waited. Sundays were something to look forward to."

Andy patted my hand. "That sounds wonderful. None of my grandparents are alive and both my parents are only children, so I can't imagine what that would be like."

Dad leaned in to pick up the story. "It all started this one Sunday. Jack was weaving this tale about being shipwrecked in the Pacific."

"We sat enthralled as he explained how he'd fought the sharks off with his knife in one hand while his other hand clung to a coral reef," I said. "He showed us a chunk of coral, pointing to the indentation where his fingers had hung on. A passing boat finally rescued him, but he still had the chunk of coral.

"To my delight he held it out and said, 'This is for you, Chrissy.' It was about eight inches long, quite heavy. It took both my hands to hold it.'"

Andy interrupted me. "He sounds like quite an adventurer."

Dad added, "Oh aye, he is, but it backfired on him. Go ahead, Chrissy, tell him."

"The next day it was show-and-tell at school," I said. "I took my piece of coral with me. When it came my turn, I walked proudly to the front of the class, holding it up for everyone to see.

I repeated Uncle Jack's story word for word. It was a big hit with all the children, but my teacher, Miss Spencer, lit up like a Christmas tree."

Later she gave me a note and asked me to give it to my uncle. She said, "I should love to meet this brave man. Perhaps he might be persuaded to come to school and tell us more. Please try to talk him into it."

Andy chuckled, but I held up my hand. "There's more. That night I showed my parents the note from Miss Spencer."

I could see Mum enjoying the memory. "Jim went into fits of laughter and Chrissy sitting looking at him, her eyes all agog."

"When Da stopped laughing," I said, "he told me Uncle Jack's stories were only make-believe, something to keep us kids entertained. In truth, Uncle Jack had never been more than twenty miles from town."

Andy's expression was sympathetic. "I'll bet that upset you."

"It was almost more than a seven-year-old could bear. Part of me still wanted to believe all his adventures were true."

Mum shook her head. "I remember the look on his face that next Sunday when Chrissy handed Jack the note and explained about show-and-tell. All the adults at the table burst out laughing, but Jack's face turned bright crimson."

Dad chuckled. "Our mum was sitting beside him. She's a wee, small woman, but ye dinna want ta make her angry. Very feisty when riled. She gave Jackie's shoulder a good shaking. When she was mad, she'd break into a string of Gaelic. Which she did before scolding him in English, too, saying, 'There now, do you no see the trouble yer big imagination has gotten ye into?'"

I finished with that same odd sense of letdown I'd felt as a child. "He looked at us kids and said he was sorry for getting carried away. He threw the note into the fireplace. Miss Spencer was waiting for me the following Monday. She asked what my uncle said. 'He isn't coming,' I answered. When she didn't say anything, I felt awkward, so I added, 'He's really a quiet man.' I thought she'd be angry, but she smiled with a faraway look on her face and muttered, 'A true adventurer.' Several more notes followed, but they all went unanswered."

Dad rolled his eyes. "That's my brother, a born storyteller."

We'd finished our cakes, and Dad asked Andy to come sit by the fire while Mum and I cleared away the dishes.

Later, I walked Andy to the corner of our street. I guess I wanted him to myself for a few minutes. We held hands. "Do you know American Westerns are popular in Scotland?" I asked.

He shook his head.

"Och aye, we all love them, especially Uncle Jack. Most of my dad's family are quite musical. Even my dad can pick up any instrument and soon start playing a song. And they all have great voices."

Andy's face lit up with admiration.

"Oh, not me. I canna sing a note. In fact, the choirmaster at church asked me not to join." Andy laughed. "But Uncle Jack bought himself a guitar and learned to sing songs from the American West. He even found himself a ten-gallon cowboy hat."

"Really, you love western music?"

"Well, I loved the idea of the wide-open West. And so did Uncle Jack. I helped by making him some things they wear over their pants."

"Chaps?"

"Aye, I cut up an old piece of upholstery fabric. Anyway, it surprised no one when they asked him to sing on musical nights at the town hall. Dad and Uncle Tommy made him a fake mustache and glued it to his upper lip. I remember sitting in the front row giggling because the mustache kept slipping sideways. No one seemed to care. They loved him. Even with the fake fire and thick-accented western songs, Uncle Jack weaved his magic once again, and we all could imagine him on the prairie singing to the stars."

"Where is he now?"

"In a field hospital somewhere in North Africa." I sighed at the memory. "Grandma and I saw him off to his unit the last time he was home. He looked so handsome in his regimental kilt with his rifle slung over his back. He looked the part of a true adventurer."

I held up my wrist to show Andy my bracelet. "He's sent me things from all over. This came from Gibraltar. And there was a necklace from India and a little handmade leather camel from North Africa. Uncle Jack saw the world. Then his letters stopped coming, and my dad made inquiries. During a battle with Rommel, Uncle Jack was seriously wounded. Almost his whole Highland regiment was wiped out. Only a few escaped. The doctor said he had no idea how Jack did it, but he managed to carry another soldier to safety before he collapsed. My uncle's had two surgeries, but the doctors say he should recover."

Andy's eyes twinkled with amusement. "So, your Uncle Jack really is Miss Spencer's hero."

I thought of all the stories he'd told us. "Aye, that he is, and my hero too."

Andy looked at me with such tenderness and reached out to draw me closer. His kiss when it came was sweet. I leaned into the kiss, wishing I could feel more, but my heart had been so guarded since Russell. I wanted to love this man. Everything about him was perfect.

When we parted, he squeezed my hand. "I had a good time tonight. Your parents are great."

I pushed his shoulder a bit in jest. "And don't you know how to butter them up."

He laughed as he turned to walk down the hill to the bus stop, calling over his shoulder, "And don't you know it takes years of practice."

As I walked back to my front steps, I felt deflated. When was I going to get over Russell?

Wendy—Seattle
1968

Listening to Mum's story opened my eyes to the depth of her love for my dad. But I knew how life with my father had gone, and I was sure it hadn't been what she expected. Her first life was full of music and dancing. Dad never took her out dancing. I wondered if she would have been happier with Andy. Then I thought of John.

"We're both so different," I said to Mum.

"Yes, you are." She knew right off who I was thinking of, but she lightened the mood, taking our conversation in a whole different direction. "I think he looks like that actor from *West Side Story*."

I smiled. Mum had a habit of comparing everyone to a film actor. You could usually tell if she liked a person depending on her choice of actors who played heroes or villains. This time I wasn't sure how she felt. "The one who dies?"

"Don't they all die in that movie?"

"George Chakiris."

John looked like that actor, and he had the persona of Bernardo, the leader of the Sharks, right down to the hair and the bounce in his walk. And he always carried a knife.

It was his other qualities that stole my heart. "He's not like Bernardo, really. He's kind and always ready to stand up for the underdog." I hesitated, adding, "And he's not as hotheaded except he never backs down from a challenge." I was proud of that last quality more than I'd admit to my mum because I always felt safe around him. Protected.

I didn't realize Heather was passing through the room until she giggled. "That's why no one would date you when they found out you were Mutton's girl."

I had to smile. Heather had a good point. I turned to Mum. "How do we know we're making the right choice? The one that will make us happy?" I couldn't help thinking she would have been much happier with Andy. Dancing was such a big part of her past life. I knew she still loved it because she often put on a record and tapped up and down the hall. I realized she only danced around the house when Dad was gone. He didn't like music or dancing much.

Mum's voice was soft and wistful. "We don't. We must make the best decision we can with lots of prayer and our hearts." She looked at the clock. "You'd better alter those costumes if you hope to do them by tonight." I knew she didn't want to talk about Dad anymore, but I wanted to know what might have been. "I can sew while you tell me more. What happened to Andy?"

Chapter Thirty-One

Christine—Greenock, Scotland
January 1945

I n December, the Germans began their last major offensive. The Battle of the Bulge lasted five bloody weeks that ended with Germany's troops in retreat. The victorious Allied forces pushed them back, liberating town after town.

Afterwards, we heard of a secret German mission to wipe out all Allied air support for our ground forces. On New Year's Day, the German Luftwaffe sent most of its force to fly over Allied bases in Belgium, the Netherlands, and France. That day, they bombed over 400 planes. But we didn't lose many pilots because the targets were often unmanned planes parked on airfields. The mission was such a well-kept secret that German high command failed to notify the German Air Defense. When the Luftwaffe pilots returned home, the Germans thought they were Allied planes attacking Germany and shot down many of their own aircraft, killing scores of experienced pilots. Nazi secret operation *Bodenplatte* was meant to secure air superiority for the ongoing

Battle of the Bulge. Their secret raid failed because it was too secret. Stories like that gave us hope God was hearing our prayers.

Andy often talked about wishing he was fighting with his friends instead of writing reports and looking into legalities for Captain Hunter. I knew it bothered him, but I was glad of every day we had together. Gradually, I was losing my heart to this sweet man. Then one ice-cold Wednesday afternoon in early January, Andy came by my work just before closing for our half-day. His handsome dark features were alight with happiness.

I looked at him, wanting to know his news. He gave me a crooked smile. "I'll tell you when we can sit and talk."

"I'll get my coat."

We were walking down Main Street when he turned us toward the Esplanade. I nearly stopped, remembering that the last hour I'd spent with Russell was down by the water. I wanted to plant my feet on the sidewalk and refuse to go any further. Andy didn't seem to notice. His hand closed over mine as we crossed the street. I found myself pulled along in more ways than one.

The afternoon was breezy. Waves on the River Clyde crashed wildly against the breakwater wall. When we came to one of the little benches, he sat. The wind still whipped around us. He gathered me close, but his eyes were looking out across the water.

I remembered how I'd sat with Russell on one of these benches. Finally, I couldn't stand it. "Andy, what is it? What's happened?"

"Did I tell you I'd been away at school to finish my law degree when the war came? I left a month short of my finals."

He looked to me like a person with a wonderful secret. "Andy Brown, I always knew you were an intelligent man."

He pulled a letter from his coat pocket. "The army has a special program for people who were close to finishing their degrees. I didn't think I had a chance." He smiled with joyful pride. "Can you believe it? Harvard Law School." He handed me the letter to read.

I scanned the contents. "This is an order to report to Harvard. They want you to go back and finish now?" I was excited for him but afraid I'd never see him again. "Why would they need you to be a lawyer?"

His eyes sharpened as he scanned the river. I realized he wasn't looking at the water but into the future. "There are lots of legalities about ending a war. Conditions of surrender, the decommissioning of bases. Soon the legal war will begin and, from what I'm hearing about the discovery of prison camps, there are going to be quite a few people tried for war crimes."

We'd all heard about the prisoner-of-war camps, not to mention what Hitler was doing to his own people. Terrible rumors about things happening to Jews and Christians, really anyone who didn't fall in line with the Nazi Party. Even with Andy's arms around me, I felt a chill. It was hard to keep desperation out of my voice. "But you'll be back, won't you?"

I was coming alive again inside, and now he said he was leaving. As if he could sense my distress, his arms tightened around me. His face buried in my hair, and he whispered in my ear.

"The letter doesn't say so, but my superior recommended me. He says they're sending me back to sit for my final exams. It'll be a lot of studying, but I promise, Chrissy, no matter what we'll see each other again." His promise sounded too much like Russell's. Then he added, "Hunter says I'll be back with him for a while after I'm done."

My heart lurched. I couldn't help comparing Russell's heartfelt plea of "Wait for me." Andy knew he was coming back, but it wasn't for me.

Confusion swirled around my brain. I'd been afraid I'd hear echoes of Russell's hollow promises. I wasn't sure if this was better. But I forced myself to look him in the eye and put on a bright expression. "I'm so happy for you. And I'm that relieved you won't be in the thick of fighting. They don't need lawyers on the front lines, do they?"

I saw a troubling thought cross his face.

"I know you think you're supposed to be with your friends out there." I put my hand in his and squeezed. "But, Andy, maybe you're supposed to be right where you're going. I'll be thankful if you're out of danger and doing what you're meant to do."

"Thanks for that, Chrissy."

He walked me home and talked, not about our relationship or missing me. He was excited about what the future held for his career. He talked about the direction he'd wanted to go before the war. He explained what a prosecuting attorney does and how a public defender would be the same but different. I heard about the legalities of the military and the reasons he thought they were sending him back to school. I realized with a sad heart he didn't once talk about our future as a couple.

Andy was the perfect partner on the dance floor. Now I had to admit that didn't mean we would be the perfect couple for life. Neither of us had professed love. But with a little more time, I thought I might be able to love him. At my doorstep we kissed one last time. I wanted to hold him there, but life was sending him on, and nothing I could do would stop that from happening. *Why him too, God?*

I didn't see him again, but he sent word to me he had to leave suddenly. There wasn't a chance to even say goodbye. I heard later from his friends that, yes, he got off all right. Then his letter came in the mail beside one from Russell's sister Margie. Mum handed them to me. I'd been setting the table for dinner but sat down for a minute to read. I held them both, wondering which to open first.

Without examining my reasons, I tore open Margie's letter. It was full of news about her life, and I skimmed it quickly for any mention of Russell. There it was at the end. "Russell is still having terrible headaches. The doctors say it's because of the brain trauma. They put a steel plate in his skull. They said it's the reason for the headaches." I read it all again. And one more time.

"Chrissy?" Mum's hand was on my shoulder. "Is it bad news?" Her sweet face looked so worried.

I slipped my hand over hers. "No, Mum. It's only a letter from Russell's sister. She says he's had a steel plate put in his brain from the injury on D-Day."

"Well, if you ask me, he needed his head examined afore now, leading ye on as he did." She humphed and went back to fixing our meal.

I put Margie's letter by my plate and turned to Andy's, almost afraid his news would be bad as well. It wasn't.

"I'm studying day and night, but I wanted you to know how much I love this. It'll be worth every minute. This may be the only letter I can get out while I'm here. I miss you. Don't go finding a steady dance partner because I can't wait to take you to a dance at the town hall. Makes me feel like Gene Kelly when I'm with you and the band stops playing and breaks into *In the Mood*. Keep safe. I'll see you in forty-five days and counting." I closed his letter.

"There now, Chrissy. That letter was guid news. I can tell from the smile on yer face." Mom's hand patted my shoulder. "Go on wi' ye and get your da from his book. Both of ye need a guid washin', and we'll have our fuid."

Two months later, I was coming down the steps to the street after work when I heard a double buffalo tap step somewhere on the sidewalk below. Andy danced into view at the bottom of the stairs.

I ran into his arms and hugged him shamelessly. "You're back. I can't believe it."

"Well, I am here, and you look as beautiful as ever." He took my hand. "Can we get some dinner and talk?" For all his attempts at lightheartedness, his face showed signs of sadness.

"Aye, let's, and you can tell me what's wrong."

"Is that your second sight speaking?"

I reached up to kiss his cheek. "No, laddie, I'm just your average canny Scot."

We walked down the street arm in arm. I felt like dancing. I was so happy to have him back.

"I've missed you, Chrissy, and I missed this place. Nowhere else on earth are the fish and chips as good as right here. Let's get some at that little place next to the quay and go sit out on the rocks by the Cloch Lighthouse."

"Sounds good to me." It was quite a walk to the fish and still more to the lighthouse, but the view was wonderful.

He started imitating a Harvard accent. "I was an upperclassman, you understand. They let me audit a few classes to finish my law degree. They had all my transcripts from before, so you are now looking at a graduate of Harvard Law School. I'll have to pass the bar. That's still ahead, but it looks like the Navy is getting another lawyer and soon, by the sound of it." He smiled sadly. "Mom's so proud."

"Your da must be busting at the seams with pride."

Andy took a deep breath and blew it out slowly. "My father's serving somewhere in North Africa. You hear about Dear John letters, but he sent my mom a Dear Mary letter." My puzzlement must have been evident because his expression fell into a deep frown, and he added, "He wants a divorce."

"Oh."

"Mom's really broke up about it. She's all alone at home. My brother and I are so far from her."

I put my hand on his arm. "I'm sorry."

"Yah, me too." He covered my hand with his own. "Thanks." We were silent for a bit more just watching the waves, and I remembered the last time I was here with Russell. *God, does that mean something? Am I losing Andy too?*

Panic rose in my throat, and I pressed my lips together to keep from crying. If we'd only had a little more time together, things might have been different. Maybe it was pride or the realization that being almost in love is not the same as being deeply in love. If I was sad at being parted, I knew I wasn't heartbroken. I swallowed the lump of emotion rising in my throat.

Andy was talking again. "Captain Hunter is being rotated back to Canada to get ready for post-war litigation, and I'm to go with him. It'll put me closer to home. I don't know. I hope I can help Mom get through this." He looked me in the eyes. "I'm not sure what's ahead, but the war's still on, so it might be a while before the legal battles begin."

It's true. I am losing Andy too.

Wendy—Seattle
1968

"Andy chose his career over you."

Mum gave a slight nod. Her expression clouded with sadness. I wanted to tell her how sorry I felt. But that didn't seem right. I mean, if she hadn't chosen my dad, Heather and I wouldn't be here.

Mum often said my face gave my thoughts away. It didn't surprise me when she said, "I love your dad. I always have, and I'm grateful for both you girls. So, no worries. I'm happy in my life here." She got up and gave me a hug that said, "We're done talking about this now."

She flipped the TV on to the early news as she walked toward the kitchen. "It's getting close to four, so you'll be leaving soon. I should make you a sandwich or something before you go."

The sound of a solemn news anchor turned our attention to the screen. Someone had strangled another college coed in her dorm room. This time her roommate had come home minutes before the man left. The announcer said, "A window was open. The roommate saw someone running away. Unfortunately, it was dark, and the young woman couldn't give a description."

Mum turned back to stand by me. "Thank goodness for John following you home."

I took her hand, both of us reacting to the horror of someone doing such a violently cruel act. "That was a long way from my school. I'll be all right." But I thought of John's headlights in my rearview mirror, and I said my own silent thanks.

Her voice was intense. "Be careful."

I could see she was serious, and it chilled me.

She added, "I have a terrible feeling. I remember a time I ignored this kind of warning."

"Moddy?"

She shook her head, and I could see the stark fear in her eyes.

"What? Tell me."

"It's a long story, and you have to go to school."

"Forget the sandwich. You can't leave me like this." Now I was afraid. I had a lifetime of listening to her warnings, and not once was she wrong. "At least start. I have half-an-hour."

She sat back on the couch, looking out the window like something or someone would materialize in front of her. "It was toward the end of the war. I've never told another living soul. I gave my word I wouldn't. But I remember wondering if someday it would catch up with me."

I could barely breathe. "Tell me."

Chapter Thirty-Two

Christine—Greenock, Scotland
Spring 1945

The Battle of the Bulge ended on Jan. 25. Now the German army was retreating across German soil. On March 22, Allied troops crossed the Rhine. Fighting continued. Defeated and disheartened, more and more German troops surrendered. We were winning the war.

I was happy and relieved but guarded in my outlook for the future. Two heartbreaks in one year were two too many. Andy left within a month for his posting in Canada, and from his letters, he was quite happy with his new life. No mention of his love for me or any promise to return. Had I misread him completely? I realized I missed him more as a companion, a friend, and a dance partner.

I was done with men, bonnie looking or not. I spent more time with my friends. Della had her own worries. Her romance had changed her as well. I finally discovered the reason for her bouts of fatigue and sad eyes. She was expecting. It might happen to any young girl caught up in the drama of living in war times. It makes you do things you normally wouldn't.

Della was the oldest of six children. When she discovered she was pregnant, her father threw her out, saying she was a bad example for her younger brothers and sisters.

They sent Rodney back to the front. He seemed like such a nice, likable lad, but a letter came later saying he couldn't marry Della. He had plans for his future, and they didn't include a wife and child. I told her that was something he should have thought of earlier. Everyone blamed her as if she were the only one who'd made this child.

My mum, ever practical, helped Della find a wee flat in Port Glasgow and a better job. After that, I didn't see her as often. But Moira and I didn't abandon her. We sent her little baby things and ration coupons. Sometimes we'd take the bus into Port Glasgow to spend a Saturday afternoon with her. We didn't tell Moira's parents because they didn't want their daughter spending time with that kind of lassie.

If you ask me, Della was the very lassie every girl should spend time with. It would make them think twice if they knew how poor her surroundings were and how alone she was. Only shame was her constant companion. So, I came up with a story. Something to tell people.

Was it a lie? Well, most of it was true. Except, of course, her marriage to Rodney on a quick trip to Gretna Green, the traditional destination for all couples wishing to elope in Scotland. One thing I realized: life goes on. Even when things didn't turn out the way you hoped. Life goes on. Do the best with what you have. Della's troubles made me treasure my friends even more. She and Moira were the people who knew my deep heartache over Russell. I never had to pretend with them. I tried not to be melancholy, but they understood why I struggled with my emotions.

On April 2, Moira and I had plans to go to the cinema after work. When I looked up from stocking shelves, there stood Kevin.

Handsome as ever. I fell back on my bottom. Moira hadn't seen or heard from him in months. I put a hand on my heart. "Och, Kevin, you startled me."

He reached out and gave me a hand up and a friendly hug. "It's good to see you again, Chrissy. Is Moira here?" I grinned and nodded toward the other end of the store where she was helping a customer. As soon as the woman at the counter left, she looked up and saw him. Her face crumpled, and she began to cry. She was around the counter and in his arms in seconds. Through hiccup sobs she said, "I thought you died on D-Day."

Nurse Graham, usually so stern, came up alongside Moira. "Moira dear, take your lad out, and don't worry about coming back this afternoon. It'll be all right. We're that slow."

Kevin reached for Moira's hand and led her out of the store. I was so happy for her, but I wanted to know the reason Kevin hadn't written. Secrecy or no, it seemed unconscionable to go so long without even a quick note letting her know he was alive.

The next day I met Moira at the bus stop as usual. "Tell me?" Another rider walked up, and Moira looked past me to the woman who'd joined us. "You can't leave it at that. I have to know."

She didn't speak again until we were on our way into town. "Kevin says most of what he does is secret, but I think he was behind enemy lines."

"All this time?" I put a hand to my mouth as it dawned on me. "Kevin's a spy."

"Hush, Chrissy." She scowled. "I don't know for sure. Only that he says his commander sends him on special assignments."

I whispered, "For our government?"

"Oh, aye. He's Irish, and ye canna tell if he's from Donegal or Dublin. Ye ken the country of Ireland is neutral." She looked fearful. "What have I done? I shouldn't have said a word. Ye canna tell another soul."

I put my hand on her arm to stay her fears. "You know I wouldn't do that. Kevin will never know you've told me."

Her smile was pure relief. We spent the rest of the ride talking about how much she cared for him. But I kept thinking about the possibility that Kevin was a spy. Imagine how brave he must be to go alone into enemy territory. Moira was saying, "He's coming by after work to take me for a walk. Will you come too?"

"Why would you want me there? Don't you want to be alone with him?"

Moira sighed. "I can see how things might have gone with Della, and I don't want that to happen to me." I understood her fears, so I agreed. They spent time together regularly for about a week. He'd come into work to pick her up and always stopped to talk to me. I couldn't be with them all that often, but they seemed to do fine.

I was heartsore after Russell and Andy, soured on romance and off men. But Kevin was sweet, and he tried so hard to make friends. Eventually, I let down my guard and relaxed around him. I told myself, He's a nice guy, and Moira's really taken with him. Be happy for her, you old curmudgeon. Still, I never lost that inner reserve. He said once, "You know, you and Moira look like sisters."

"No, and we haven't heard that before," I teased.

"You both have beautiful black hair."

Moira came back from getting her things. I said, "Can you believe it? Kevin says we look like sisters."

She laughed. "Oh, my darlin' laddie"—she copied him right down to the Irish brogue—"and don't ya know, we hear that all the time?"

Kevin and I were laughing too. He gave her a sweet kiss on the forehead. "You sound like me own sister, Katie." His next words were whispered in Moira's ear. I don't know what he said, but they made her blush.

As he helped her with her coat, she said to me, "Come with us. We're going for a walk and fish and chips."

"No, I—"

Kevin stopped me. "With a beauty on each arm, I'm sure to be the talk of the town."

I looked from Kevin to Moira, and she nodded encouragement.

"All right, then. I'll just get my things." Maybe if I spent some time with Kevin, I'd get over whatever was bothering me about him. Besides, it was Wednesday half-holiday, and Mum and Dad would still be at work. Usually, I'd fill the day with volunteer time, but today fish and chips sounded very tempting.

It was a fun afternoon. Kevin was charming, but he had a vulnerable side when he spoke about his humble beginnings and how he still sent money home. That made me like him a little more. We talked about everything. The difference between Ireland and Scotland. The war. He didn't seem like someone who was afraid of fighting. There was much more to him than I suspected. It was the beginning of several afternoons spent with Moira and Kevin.

Late on Friday, I came on Moira in the back of the dispensary. We only had one mirror, and she was standing staring at it with an intent look on her face.

"What are you looking at?"

She jumped. "Oh, I'm asking myself why I'm falling so hard for Kevin." She grimaced at her reflection.

"Could be he spends every spare minute with you. Seems like he's doing some falling as well."

"Do you think? I've tried to bring him home to meet my parents, but he's always got an excuse." She turned to face me. "I can't help wondering if it's one-sided."

I wanted to encourage her, but I still had an uneasy feeling about him. Instead, I said something my mother might say. "Time will tell."

Nurse Graham popped her head around the corner. "Miss MacDonald, your young man is here, and I don't think he's looking for plasters."

We grinned at each other. Nurse Graham sounded gruff, but I knew it was her attempt at humor.

"Where are you going this evening?" I asked.

"He says he has a special surprise for me."

"Have fun. I'll see you on Monday." But Moira was already hurrying past Nurse Graham.

We both looked after her. I barely heard Nurse Graham say, "When something looks too good to be true—"

"It generally is," I whispered back.

Wendy—Seattle
1968

I glanced at my watch. I was going to be late. "Sorry, Mom, gotta run. I want to hear the rest when I get back." I grabbed the two altered costumes for the college play and literally ran out the door. As I passed the living room window, I caught sight of her still sitting on the couch staring off into space.

I couldn't shake my anxiety over her words: "I have a terrible feeling, and I keep thinking of a time I ignored this kind of warning." But I told myself I'd be careful. It would be all right. I only had a week before performances, so all my attention had to be focused on the play.

At rehearsal, I wasn't on stage till the last scene, so I sat in the audience. The costumes looked great, and I was proud of that. I'd only been sitting for a minute when Seamus slid in beside me.

"Came to see the costumes." He smiled. "You must take after your mum."

I gave him a double take. I didn't remember telling him about Mum's sewing skills.

"Sure'n you haven't been by much. Did I say something to upset you?"

I blew out my stress. Most of my work was finally over, but that wasn't the reason I'd been avoiding him. His reaction to seeing John and me together had made me uncomfortable. I'd wondered if I'd read our friendship all wrong. "Sorry, the play's been keeping me busy."

"Don't suppose you've seen your young man much either?" I looked at him, wondering where he was going with that comment. "Hard on a relationship being too busy, isn't it?"

Nonplussed, I didn't respond. We watched the whole run-through until it was time for my small part.

"I must go. It's my turn on stage." I smiled, trying to keep things light, and left before he could say another word. I felt intense relief, and I wasn't sure why.

I danced with the chorus in the last scene and looked out over the house seating. Seamus wasn't there.

When I came home Mum was restless, unable to sit still. She rubbed her arms as if a chilly wind passed through the room.

"What's bothering you?" I finally asked.

She sat next to me on the couch. "Talking about my life."

"You don't want to stop do you?" I knew I was being selfish, but I couldn't stand the feeling of walking away with so many questions unanswered.

Mum took my hand. "I know you want to hear the rest. It's just so hard to talk about."

"Even after all these years?"

"These memories have stayed buried a long time."

Chapter Thirty-Three

Christine—Greenock, Scotland
Spring 1945

After a cold winter, the weather was unseasonably warm for early spring, but Monday morning I woke to rain pelting my bedroom window. By the time I made it to the bus stop, my coat was soaked. Moira wasn't there, but occasionally she took an earlier bus so I sat alone, feeling as gloomy as the weather. This was a dismal way to start my work week. I told myself, If it were bright and sunny, you wouldn't want to go to work.

Heaviness hung over me as I walked down Hamilton Street and up the steps to work. My new coworker Betts was taking off her coat on the way to her locker. Nurse Graham had hired her to take Della's place. I knew Betts from volunteering at the canteens. We'd always got on well, but I still smarted at losing Della to a new life and motherhood.

I followed Betts to the small room at the back of the store and sat on the bench facing the employee lockers. The only light in the room filtered through windows near the ceiling. I had peeled off my wet coat and rubber boots when Nurse appeared in the doorway. She looked even more austere than usual. Her square shoulders rounded forward. Even her grizzled grey hair escaped from its usual tight little bun. I felt my stomach clench. Something was very wrong. She cleared her throat, and all movement stopped.

"The constable is here to talk with you both. He's using my wee office." We looked at each other in complete bewilderment. "They'll call you in one at a time. Until then, go about your regular duties." She pivoted to walk away.

I called after her. "Nurse? What's this about?"

She stopped. Her stern face turned my way for the barest moment. It took my breath away to see such sadness in her steel-grey eyes. Her frown lines, always present, pulled down into deeper creases. She didn't answer me as she left the room.

I realized one of our number was absent—Moira.

Betts looked over. "Chrissy, ye go first. I promised the chemist I'd be right up front to help him." That suited me fine. When I'd first thought Moira's name, dread overpowered me. I couldn't tell if it was the Sight or my own fears, but I wouldn't wait for them to call me back. Instead, I hurried to Nurse Graham's small office.

It was my Uncle Angus who stopped me outside her door.

"Uncle, I'm that relieved to see you." I gave him a brief hug. "What's this all about? Is it Moira?"

He turned back at my question. "What makes ye say that?"

Vexed that no one would tell me anything, I struggled to sound coherent. "We usually ride into work together. Sometimes she takes an earlier bus. She wasn't at the bus this morning, and she's not here."

"Oh, aye?" He took my hand, giving me a sympathetic squeeze. "Sorry, lass." We filed into the wee office behind the dispensary. A small middle-aged man in a black suit and tie sat at Nurse Graham's desk.

Uncle Angus said, "This is my niece, Christina Finlay." He turned to me. "Chrissy, this is Inspector MacNeil."

The man rose and took my hand for the barest moment and motioned for me to sit.

"Has something happened to Moira?" I blurted.

He raised a brow, directed at my uncle.

"The lass asked me if it were about Miss MacDonald."

I broke in. "She's my friend. We work together." I spread my hands in frustration. "And she's not here." I wanted to shake the wee man. "Can you no tell me what's happened?"

He plopped back into his seat. His voice sounded disheartened. "Aye, she went missing over the weekend."

"Missing? No."

"That's what we're trying to determine. Her parents say she didn't come home from work Friday night. At least, she wasn't there when they came in later, and it didn't look like she'd been there. They've tried asking everyone, but no one's seen her." He took out his little notepad and licked the lead of his pencil. "I take it you weren't that close if they didn't ask ye as well?"

"But we are," I stammered. "My da took us to Kirkcowan for the weekend."

"An odd place for a wee holiday."

"We used to live there after the Blitz." I looked away, thinking of how second sight hadn't been able to save my friend Moddy. "We go back from time to time to stay with friends." I choked out the words. Occasionally we'd get an invitation from Moddy's mum asking us to come down for a weekend. She said how much it helped her, and how, with Eddie off to war, her house was too quiet.

"When was the last time you saw Miss MacDonald?"

"On Friday as she left with Kevin near the end of the day."

"No one's mentioned him afore. Who is this laddie? Boyfriend?"

"Kevin O'Brien. He recently came to town on business, I think. Could work for the government, but I'm not sure about that."

"You say they were together Friday night?" Something about his question seemed insulting. His tone implied Moira might have stayed with Kevin. Then again, maybe I was being sensitive, but after what happened to Della, we were all very careful.

My cheeks burned with a fiery heat. I unclenched my hands and tried to calm down. "She isn't like that. It was a date. He had a surprise for her. Moira's not . . ." I couldn't finish.

"Where's he staying? Do you know?"

I shook my head. "But he'll be here at four to pick her up. When he's in town, they spend a bit of time together almost every night after work."

They looked at each other. Uncle said, "Can you think of anything else that will help us?" I shook my head as uneasiness crept over me.

I'd always had a funny feeling about Kevin. But I was wrong about Tom Gorsky. Thoughts roiled through my head. I wondered if Moira had run off with Kevin, or maybe there was an accident, and they were both hurt somewhere.

It was a long day, but before four, the inspector and my uncle showed up at work again. I realized they were waiting for Kevin. *Well, if he comes, we'll know she isn't with him, and if not?*

The bell above the door sounded at four. Kevin strolled in, a peaceful smile on his face. My uncle motioned toward the young man. I nodded, and they moved in. "Kevin O'Brien?"

"That would be right, sir." Kevin's voice sounded friendly and casual.

"You're an acquaintance of Miss Moira MacDonald?"

"Right again." He looked from Uncle Angus to the inspector. "Why? Say, is Moira all right? What's this about?"

That was not the face of a man who'd run off with a pretty girl. He was as shocked as we all were.

"Miss MacDonald is missing."

Kevin staggered backward and braced himself on a nearby counter. His gaze searched us all. "When? How?"

The inspector cleared his throat. "That's what we're hoping you can tell us."

"Me? No, I mean I want to help but—"

Nurse Graham approached the inspector. "Would you like to use my wee office again? I think you need a bit more privacy." It was more a direction than a question. The inspector ushered Kevin into the small room they'd used this morning.

I stood frozen and clamped my hand over my mouth to keep from crying. Uncle patted my back. "You too, Chrissy."

We all crowded into Nurse's office. I was the last through the door, and I moved to Kevin's side. The inspector sat at Nurse Graham's desk, and my uncle stood beside him.

The initial shock seemed to be passing. Kevin raised his voice and demanded, "What do you mean missing? She was fine the last time I saw her."

"When exactly was that?"

Kevin sank into the only other chair in the room, his head cradled in his hands. He looked up finally, his face flushed and worried. "I planned a picnic for us Friday after work. It was a surprise. I had my superior's car for the afternoon. I met her here, and when we came downstairs to the street, a messenger was waiting for me. My superiors had called me to Edinburgh on official business, so I had to cancel our date."

"Your superior's name?" MacNeil's face was hard, even skeptical. "What is it you do?"

I felt like crying. *Give the laddie a chance. Can't you see how upset he is?* But I clenched my jaw to keep from interfering.

Kevin seemed not to notice. His response was flat. "He's high command, sir. I'm not at liberty to disclose his name." I knew that meant his superior was high-up in our government.

Inspector MacNeil wasn't impressed. "You'll have to do better than that. We'll at least need a contact in his office to verify your story."

Kevin nodded absently. "She was fine when I took her home.

There must be a mistake." He looked hopefully at me. "Could she have stayed with a friend or relative?" He ran his hand over his face. "God, if only I hadn't been called away. I was gone all weekend."

Everything was quiet. My hand rested on Kevin's back. I'd had the day to get used to the idea that Moira wasn't where she should be. Kevin struggled to grasp that fact.

"You're Irish. Northern?" Derision lingered in the inspector's tone.

Kevin's voice took on a hard edge. "Right, born in Antrim."

But I remembered him saying he was from Donegal. I guess I stopped listening for a minute before I caught the inspector saying, "And did you leave Miss MacDonald at her door?"

"I'd never been there before, but that's where she said she lived."

MacNeil looked doubtful. "And why would that be?"

"Moira thought her folks wouldn't approve of her dating a Catholic is all."

But I remembered her saying she'd asked him to meet her parents several times, but he always had an excuse.

Kevin looked from my uncle to the inspector. "There must be some sort of mistake. Her parents can tell ye she came straight home."

"No, 'fraid not. She wasn't there when they got home later." Both men were focused on Kevin's reactions.

"God." A cascade of tears ran down his cheeks.

"Moira MacDonald's been gone all weekend." My uncle's tone was gentler. "Her parents exhausted every other possibility before they called us in. I'm afraid there's no question. There's been foul play."

Kevin's head sank to rest almost in his lap, his auburn hair falling over his face. "I think I'm going to be ill." Occasionally we treated someone whose stomach rebelled, so I knew all the signs. I slid our waste bin in front of him with not a second to spare.

Nurse appeared and handed him a tissue and called out for Betts to get a glass of water.

"I can't believe this is happening."

"Do ye have witnesses who can verify your whereabouts this weekend?"

Kevin nodded mechanically. I picked up the waste bin to clean it. When I came back, the office was empty.

So, it was true. Moira was missing. Really gone. She could still be somewhere, couldn't she? But a small voice whispered, "Moira's with me now." My heart lurched.

I needed to talk to someone. Da was my steady compass. When I finally got home, I found him nestled into his favorite chair with the evening paper in his hands. "Where's Mum?" I asked. The last thing I wanted was to get my mum into a stew about what might have happened to Moira.

"She said she'd a wee bit of shoppin' to do before she came home. I 'spect she's at it."

I pulled up a chair. He lowered his paper with a look on his face that said there had better be a good reason for interrupting. I blurted out, "My friend Moira is missing."

"Missing, what do you mean missing?"

"Uncle Angus was at my work asking all kinds of questions. No one knows what's happened to her."

Da set the paper aside. "Oh pet, I'm sorry. Could she no be wi' friends?"

"Dad, I don't think she's alive."

"An' how do ye know—" He stopped and looked at me. "The Sight?"

"I hope I'm wrong."

"We were just down wi' Moddy's mum for the weekend. Do you not think you're remembering what happened before?"

"I hope it is, Da. I hope it is."

Wendy—Seattle
1968

In the grey morning light, rain pelted the house. Wind whistled around its corners. It reminded me of Moira's story. I'd been sitting on the big chair with my feet tucked up under my flannel nightie, but I shivered involuntarily as Mum finished talking about Moira. "I'd bet my next paycheck you didn't let it go until you had answers."

She smiled. "You're not so different from me, are you? It's surprising what you'll do when you're motivated."

It made me proud to hear her say that even if I knew I could never live through what she had. "Well, you didn't let it go, did you?"

"Some things are better forgotten." She rose and took her empty teacup into the kitchen. "I've never spoken of this before. It's not safe."

"Mum, what? I don't understand what the big deal is."

"Drop it."

That brought me up short. It was so unlike her. But I couldn't leave it alone. I had to know the rest. Why was my courageous mother so hesitant to talk about this?

"That happened twenty years ago, but it's dangerous to talk about? 'Cause that's what you're saying, isn't it? You think it's dangerous even now?"

She pressed her lips together and started to walk away without another word. "Mum, please."

She stopped, fear written on her face. "It bothers me. Why after keeping this secret all these years am I telling it now?" She picked up her sweater and slid her arms into it, rubbing them for warmth. I knew her chill wasn't from the cool morning air. She looked at me for a long moment.

"Seems to me there's always a reason for secrets to come out."

She gestured to the TV. "It's probably those college girls getting murdered bringing up memories better forgotten."

I didn't believe it had to do with the murders. Maybe that's what started her thinking about Moira, but there had to be another reason for the fear I saw on her face. I couldn't leave it at that. "Please tell me what happened," I pleaded. "If you told me all this after twenty years of silence, there must be a good reason. Wouldn't it be safer to tell me?"

Chapter Thirty-Four

Christine—Greenock, Scotland
April 1945

The whole world mourned the sudden passing of President Roosevelt on Thursday, April 12. It dominated the news and everyone's attention. People were speculating about the new American president, Truman, and how it could affect the momentum of Allied victories. But I mourned the loss of Moira, knowing inside she wasn't just somewhere else. She wasn't alive. Still, I hoped this inner voice was wrong.

During wartime we had the mindset of Churchill: "Keep calm and carry on." I worked and volunteered, but my mind was searching for clues to Moira's whereabouts. After all, if she wasn't alive, her body was out there somewhere. I was sure the police weren't making her a priority.

I began asking everyone when they'd last seen her. During my time at the Overseas Club, I volunteered to serve sandwiches. That way I could go from table to table with the tray and ask questions about Moira.

I noticed Tom Gorsky's girlfriend Sanga watching me with

squinting eyes, and I knew she disapproved. How could I blame her after what happened? This was different, but she wouldn't agree. Before closing, Mrs. Wagner asked me to stop talking about Moira. She said it was upsetting the hostesses. But I suspected she meant Sanga.

By Thursday, I was dragging myself through the day. There'd been no news from my Uncle Angus. At the Canadian canteen, no one remembered seeing Moira since the Thursday before she went missing.

There was always a chance Moira might have gone to Della. I knew it was pointless. Moira wouldn't stay away from home. Maybe she wouldn't tell her parents she was seeing Della, but she'd tell them something. I asked to leave work a little early and took the bus into Port Glasgow to check on Della.

I walked from the bus stop up the winding roads above the wee town. Della's room was in a sizeable house divided into little apartments. I climbed the steps that zigzagged up to a door near the roofline on the outside of the house. It'd started raining, the weather matching my mood. I rapped on the chipped paint of her door and heard her steps hurrying to answer.

When Della opened the door, I threw my arms around her and started weeping. It was the first time I'd let down in front of anyone. She said little but pulled me into her tiny flat and put the kettle on to boil. I sank onto one of the kitchen chairs. There wasn't anywhere else to sit but the wee bed in the corner. I was still crying when she handed me a hankie.

"Oh no, I have one here somewhere." I started fishing through my pockets.

"Take it. That's one thing I have plenty of. I've done my fair share of crying lately." I looked up at her through watery eyes. She was still blonde and beautiful, even though she looked ready to deliver her baby any minute.

Della poured our tea and sat. "Now tell me yer troubles."

I blurted out, "It's not me I'm crying for. It's Moira." Della paled but let me get the entire story out before she started asking questions.

Her face collapsed in grief. "Not Moira, I canna believe it." She pulled another hankie out of her pocket. I slid my hand across the table and took hers in mine.

"I've asked everyone we know. Moira disappeared last Friday, and not a soul's seen her since." We sat and talked for a good hour before I got up to leave. "Thanks, I needed this. But I shouldn't have brought trouble to your door with your baby coming soon."

"And don't you know I would have been vexed if you hadn't." Della's face looked so anxious. "You'll let me know what happens?"

"Aye, sure I will." Riding home on the bus, I fell asleep and dreamed.

I was walking through a glen, following the course of a wee stream. Trees grew down to the edge of the water, and I skipped from rock to rock, trying not to fall in. As I came around a bend in the stream, I stepped onto a grassy glade. It was a familiar place, though I couldn't remember when I'd been there before. A blanket was spread on the grass, and my heart skipped a beat when I recognized the girl lying there. She looked like she was asleep. Her long black hair fanned out over the red blanket. It was Moira. But she wasn't sleeping. She was dead.

I woke, startled by the sudden realization that I knew where that stream and wee glen were. "The hills behind Grandma Cowan's house." I looked around to find myself alone on the bus, and my stop was coming up soon.

What do I do? Who's going to believe I saw where Moira was in a dream? I had to think. I was in agony. I wanted to search for the glen in my dream, but my mum kept me busy all weekend. There was never a time I could get away for a walk in the hills. I think I didn't want to confirm that my friend was truly dead.

On Monday afternoon, my uncle came to me as I was leaving

work. I already had my coat on. His face was so grave it stopped me dead in my tracks. He motioned me to follow him out. We stood on the empty landing.

He cleared his throat. "Chrissy, they found Moira." I drew in my breath, and he put out a hand to steady me. "In the hills above town."

I started crying. I knew she was dead but hearing him say it took all hope away. Hope that I might be wrong.

Uncle patted my back and waited for me to get control again. I stopped myself from asking if there was a wee stream next to the grassy glen. How would I explain that to him?

He leaned closer. "There's no way of sayin' this but straight out. Someone murdered Moira sometime last weekend. There hasn't been a murder in or around Greenock in over twenty years." I looked up at his kind face, but my sight blurred with tears. "It's not a secret. We have notified her parents. It will be in the Greenock Telegraph tomorrow morning." He patted my arm. "What the papers won't say is this is likely the work of our fiend."

I put my hand over my mouth.

"We have special investigators coming in from Scotland Yard to have a look at this murder." His voice grew hushed. "Yer da says you can keep a secret."

"Aye. I won't say a word."

I reached out to touch his arm as he turned to leave. "Will ye let me know what they find?"

"I will." His face softened. "I know you two were friends." I nodded, my throat clogged with emotion.

The story of Moira's murder was in the papers the very next day. As upset as I was, I had to go to work. After all, we were shorthanded with Moira gone, a fact that kept me close to tears most of the day.

When I came out on the street after work to catch the bus home, there was Kevin. His face was a mask of grief. I thought it was only a week and a half ago that we all went for a walk on the Esplanade and had fish and chips.

"Chrissy, would you have time to talk a bit?" I didn't have the heart to say no. His eyes were red and swollen. He looked miserable. "We could walk."

I felt my face blanch in memory of all the walks I'd come on with Kevin and Moira. "No, not that."

"Tea then, just a cup of tea?"

I nodded, and he led the way across the street to the little Italian restaurant where Moira told me they'd met. The bell rang as we entered, and my friend Gina came to get our order. We sat, but he wasn't looking at me. He was staring at the table by the window. I wondered if it was the same table they sat at the first time they met.

"It's only been a week since I saw her last. I can't believe she's gone." Tears were running down his cheeks unchecked.

I felt horrible. He was broken up. To think I'd had a bad feeling about him.

He was saying, "Did I ever tell you how much you look like Moira? Course I did."

I remembered him saying that to me and Moira. He cleared his throat.

"I need a friend right now. I'm alone here." He reached across the table. "We're friends, right? I can't seem to get over Moira's loss. Just need someone to spend time with, talk to."

The tea came, and Gina gave me a questioning look. I felt wrong sitting with Moira's boyfriend. It was like taking her place.

We talked after that. He didn't come into work, but often I'd find him waiting afterward just like he'd done with Moira.

We ended up walking as we talked. I can't say why; it just felt safer to be out where people were always passing by. Once we went to the cinema. I also invited him home for a Sunday dinner, but he never could make it. I remembered Moira saying the same thing.

He left on business several times. But just like with Moira, he'd show up unexpectedly after work. As much as I tried to fight it, I was still a bit repelled by him. Not his looks. They were striking. Not his manner. It was proper, almost sweet. No voices or chills but on more than one occasion I felt something like a warning. I would feel restless when we were alone together. I reminded him of the girl he'd loved, and when I thought about it that way, I felt sorry for him.

Once he stopped talking and pushed a curl from my face. It seemed like the thing a boyfriend might do. Then on another day we went walking along the small beach in Gourock and he stopped, pulled me into his arms and kissed me.

I froze. I think he saw how shocked I was because he apologized right away. More than once I was ready to send him on his way. But sympathy for his loss always stopped me.

As much as I tried to keep him as a friend, it was clear his feelings were changing. I was aware of the first time he reached for my hand on a walk along the rocks near the Cloch Lighthouse. He's just helping me over the loose shale, I thought. It means nothing. But even then, I knew it wasn't true.

I had to face the fact that Kevin wanted me for his girlfriend. He showed it in so many small ways, a sweet smile or an innocent kiss on the forehead. I struggled with a way to let him down easy. Neither of us needed more drama. Every time I worked up the determination to send him on his way, he disappeared. But he always came back.

One afternoon, I was doing a bit of shopping before heading home. When I came out of the market, I saw my uncle talking to a few sailors across the street. They laughed about something, and my uncle turned to walk away. I crossed the street, dodging cars and other pedestrians to intercept him. "Uncle. Uncle Angus."

He didn't look happy to see me. "Now, Chrissy, I know what yer goin' to ask, and I have nae news for ye."

"Did the men from London come to help?" I was sure he'd

take my meaning since the last time we spoke he'd said investigators were coming.

"They did that." I could have shaken him for all the information he wasn't giving me. Instead, I just put on my Nurse Graham impression.

"Well?" I wanted to say out with it or else. Still, I got my point across.

"Aye, well, the facts of the killing fit their profile perfectly except for one important detail."

This conversation was going to take all afternoon if he didn't let go of something. I looked around, wishing for someplace more private to talk. He must have felt the same because he lowered his voice and moved closer. "The war is almost over. They never caught the spy. Some are saying he's likely moved on."

I raised my brow. "But what if he hasn't? This could be their chance to catch him before that happens."

Uncle Angus didn't answer. He pushed his cap to the back of his head and blew out what appeared to be the last of his patience.

"That's it then," I said. "They don't think it's the same person?"

"They're still gathering clues, you might say. That's all I can tell you right now."

I pressed my mouth into a thin line to keep from screaming. Moira was dead, and there was no one to give her justice.

He patted my shoulder. "Now, lassie, not to worry. Something will turn up, to be sure."

"With the war nearly over, could it be our spy is out of support or purpose or whatever?"

"Aye, they spoke about that, but we still have no suspects. We've checked everyone's story, and so far, we can't put anyone with Moira except Kevin, and it turns out people saw him in Edinburgh just as he said."

He looked at me with a censorious expression. "You're stirring up more questions, asking everyone when they last saw Moira, aren't you?"

I put my chin up. "At least I'm still looking for clues."

"Well, we either get to people after they've spoken to you or they complain they're being pestered." His expression softened. "Stop, for God's sake. It's not helping us at all."

"Oh." I was chastised by the thought I might have impeded their search for the murderer.

He left me with a quick hug, more of a dismissal.

Wendy—Seattle
1968

Mum got up from her place on the couch and put the tea back on, a good sign she meant to finish Moira's story. She said, "What do you have going today? Time for one more cup of tea?"

I felt myself deflate. "Was that the end of searching for Moira's murderer?"

"Not the end. The beginning of the breakthrough." She picked up a small throw and covered my lap. When Mum was anxious, she would move from thing to thing. Right now, I could feel nervous energy taking hold of her. Changing the subject again, she said, "You should go put on warm clothes."

I shook my head. "Is it the Sight that's stopping you from telling me the rest?"

Her face paled, and her voice dropped to a whisper. "No." Her brown eyes stared into the past. "No, I'm afraid it's the Sight that's pushing me to tell you."

Chapter Thirty-Five

Christine—Greenock, Scotland
1945

The news was full of startling events. On April 20, the Soviet army reached Berlin. On April 28, Italian partisans captured and hung Mussolini. The war was moving to a close. I wondered if our spy had escaped to safer countries. We heard many wealthy Germans were traveling secretly to South America.

Here in Scotland, people were smiling again. You could sense the energy in the canteens. You didn't often see men sitting alone staring into space, their mind's eye seeing the loss of a good friend or the aftermath of German occupation. Now young men were talking about winning the war and finally going home. I wondered how Kevin was. I hadn't seen him in days. It was hard to picture that sad young man celebrating anything.

Everyone else was upbeat except me. Russell had stolen my light and taken it back to Canada. Andy wrote only occasionally, but I could tell he was enjoying the turn his life had taken. And then there was Moira. I couldn't shake my grief over her murder, and the nagging suspicion that the answers to who'd done this terrible thing were locked in my brain.

Restless, I waited for news that they'd found her murderer, but it didn't come. My uncle was avoiding me. Dad said I shouldn't pester him. "Let the man do his job," were his very words, so I put on a smile and kept my voice light with others. It was exhausting.

After a long day at work and an evening serving sandwiches at the canteens, I was glad to be home, get my shoes off and have a cup of tea with my parents. I let down my guard a bit more at home. It was too hard to keep acting as if nothing was wrong when my heart was still so sad.

I knew my folks worried about me, but they didn't push. They were just there. As I came in the front door, Mum called out from the kitchen, "Jim, can you turn the radio down, and let's have a cup of tea with Chrissy before bed."

"Right, Helen." He usually called her "pet," so I figured it miffed him she'd interrupted his favorite radio program. I set my things down and peeled off my coat. Dad's fingers were on the radio knob when the announcer said, "We are interrupting our programs to bring you a news flash."

Mum came in from the kitchen, and we all stood frozen, waiting. The sound of church bells rang out, followed by the familiar voice of Stuart Hibberd speaking from London Court. "The German radio has just announced that Hitler is dead." He repeated his news. Nothing more. Not how or when but it didn't matter. The monster was dead.

We stood in stunned silence, our mouths open in wordless surprise. Then relief and joy overtook me. For the first time in months, I felt truly happy. I laughed. Mum and Dad hugged each other and pulled me into their embrace. Tears of joy ran down our cheeks.

Dad turned to the sideboard and brought out a bottle of

whiskey. "Turn off the kettle, pet. We'll each have a wee dram to toast the news." I'd tasted whiskey a time or two, mostly on Hogmanay, our New Year's Eve, but never from the hand of my dad. At nearly eighteen years old, I'd lived most of my growing years during Hitler's reign. But you never really feel grown with your parents. Our toast was a small thing. My face flushed, not from the whiskey but from my dad's acknowledgement that I was an adult.

In the days that followed, the papers said Hitler had died in battle fighting the Bolsheviks. In all these years, we'd never heard of him doing any of his own killing. The papers reported that Admiral Karl Doenitz was now at the helm of Germany. He promised the world that the war would continue. Doenitz, an ex-submarine commander, hated us, but he wasn't the leader Hitler had been.

The Germans were losing heart. More and more of their armies were surrendering as we advanced. Churchill hinted that peace was at hand. I wondered what this would mean. Surely they'd continue to search for the spy who'd been murdering young women like Moira.

We heard rumors that many influential Nazis were leaving the country. Where could you hide when almost the whole world had been at war with Germany? People said Argentina had quite a few German transplants. Could the spy be with them? It made my blood boil that he might have escaped to live his life out in some South American paradise.

As far as I could tell, nothing was different in my life. I still went to work, volunteered, and thought about Moira. I was as happy as everyone else that the war would soon end, but it would never be over for me until there was justice for her.

Nurse Graham stopped me as I was coming into work on Wednesday morning. "Chrissy, pull yourself out of this." Her face softened from its normal stern expression. "Really, luv. Everyone's lost someone close to them. But the war will soon be over, and you need to think about what's next for you." It touched my heart that she saw through my mask.

I nodded and looked away, my eyes blurring. "Aye, I know yer right."

"Good lass." As Nurse left me to stow my things in our wee locker room, she added, "I need yer help. We've our first patient in my dispensary."

By the time I joined her, Nurse Graham was patching up a young American with a split ear that was bleeding profusely. He said he'd tripped. You don't get a black eye like his from a fall on the pavement. She was giving him her stern talk about fighting. By the end of the day, we'd patched up three fights and several severe hangovers. Too much celebrating had followed the good news about Hitler's death. As the last sailor left our dispensary, we looked at each other, tired but for my part in a much better frame of mind.

Nurse said, "Go ahead, Chrissy, I'll clean up here. We've had a doozer of a day."

"Thank ye."

I slipped away to get my things from my locker. Most of the room lay in the deep shadows of late afternoon. Only dim light shone through the window near the ceiling. There was movement in the dark corner of the room. My heart jumped as a shape materialized into the shadow of a man. It was Kevin. He whistled a sad tune as he moved out of the shadows. A single beam of sunlight glinted on a camera in his hand.

"Lord, Kevin. It's you."

"Gave you a fright, my darlin' girl?" He looked mildly pleased, which really annoyed me.

"What are you doing back here? This is for employees only." I'm sure I sounded harsher than I intended, and I caught a fleeting look of anger on his handsome face. It left again so quickly I figured I must have imagined it.

"Why, I'm waiting for you, don't you know?" He leaned

against the lockers and sighed. "This was Moira's locker, wasn't it? I think of her all the time, and I remembered something she said."

He hadn't answered my question, but he looked so sad I let it go, asking him only, "Why do you have a camera?"

Again, he sidestepped my question. "She said the cupboards all had wee locks."

"Aye, but we don't use them. No one comes back here—" I started to add "except for us" but realized he'd just proved me wrong.

"Is this one Moira's?" He touched her locker as he walked into the light.

"What's this?"

I couldn't keep impatience out of my voice, but he didn't seem to notice. "Me da gave me this camera. I've some pictures of home on it." He moved closer. "That's why I'm here, actually."

"Oh?"

"I'm being sent out of the area on business. Wouldn't want it to be lost or stolen. Da's gone now, and it's all I have left from him." He looked so pained I felt terrible for being suspicious.

"Your da? Did he die recently?"

Kevin gave a slight nod. "I've just come back, meant to have the film developed." He sighed. "Seems like everyone I love dies." For a moment, his eyes glazed over. He sniffed and rubbed a sleeve across his face. "Chrissy, can you keep it for me? Until I get back? I'll be moving around a lot. Don't want to leave it in an empty room. We could put it in your locker. It'd be much safer there than with me. Please?"

Maybe Moira was right about him working for the Allied high command. And if he needed my help, I owed it to him to do what I could. I opened the door to my locker. Inside, I had photographs of my friends taped to the door. My rubber boots were on the floor, and my coat hung from a peg. I took my handbag from the cubbyhole on top. "All right, then. I guess you could put it on the top shelf."

He smiled and slid the camera to the back. "Thank you. I'll feel so much better with this safe and sound. Don't open it or anything. It'll expose my film. I always want to remember home the way it looked when I left."

"I understand. I want to remember the way Greenock was before the war." I reached out to touch his arm. "Not to worry. Your camera will be safe, waiting for you when you return. But, Kevin, the war is almost over. Where could they be sending you now?"

"Nothing's ever over. It's only now the hunters are the hunted."

Before I could ask what he meant, Kevin put a hand over mine. "You're a good lass. Ye've been a good friend to me. Maybe someday we can be something more."

I had to bite my tongue to keep from saying, "Not on your life." He'd lost his father and his girl, and I was sorry for him. But one thing I knew for sure: we'd never be anything more than friends. Never.

THE MONDAY FOLLOWING Kevin's visit, May 7, the German high command signed unconditional surrender documents at General Eisenhower's headquarters in Reims, France. The Allies declared Tuesday, May 8, VE Day or Victory in Europe Day. Shops were closed, and the townspeople set up tables in the streets. Ladies from all our churches brought food, and many gents dug out bottles of whiskey they'd been saving for better days. And this was a very good day indeed.

Mum, Dad, and I walked into town to join the festivities. We danced in the streets and ate until we were full. Since I'd lost

Russel, I'd had a coil inside me that wound around my heart. On VE Day, it loosened. I felt like myself again.

It turned out Andy was right. The army was still active in peacetime. Our canteens were still open. Ships came and went on the Clyde. The difference was we no longer feared for the lives of the people we loved.

Nurse Graham was right as well. It was time to consider what I would do with my life. For now, I liked my little job at Boots Chemist even if it reminded me of Moira. Her memory lingered, along with the feeling that something had to be done to find her murderer.

Wendy—Seattle
1968

I COULD SEE my mum was stressed. She barely finished her tea, and now she was moving round the kitchen like a cleaning maniac. I knew I needed to give her a rest, but I was afraid she wouldn't finish her story.

"I'll go get ready for school." I stopped her from wiping down the countertops. "But will you please tell me the rest when I get back?" I was driven to know the details, and that disturbed me almost as much as the tale itself.

HOT APPLE STRUDEL was waiting for me when I came home around three. I wasn't sure if Mum was trying to forestall our conversation, or maybe her nerves had driven her to a frenzy of activity.

We sat together and talked about our day. Then she said, "I know you say you need to hear the rest of the story." She had a speculative expression as she regarded me across the table. "You're not usually like this."

"Sorry, but—"

She held up her hand to stop me. "I've spent a lot of time thinking this over. I was searching my feelings, hoping the Sight would give me some direction.

"Thanks." I took a bite of strudel and smiled. "You must have been so relieved the war was finally over. But that bit about Kevin was kinda creepy. For a nice guy, he had a troubled soul, didn't he?"

Mum nodded thoughtfully. "Yes, a troubled soul."

"Is that what you meant when you said you had an uneasy feeling about him?"

"Yes, but he was quite likeable most of the time. He was charming and funny. He was always whistling little tunes. After Moira disappeared, those tunes turned sad. I didn't blame him. I was sad too."

"I can't whistle a note."

She smiled. "I'm afraid you get that from me." Her mood grew serious again. "I asked him once what tune he was whistling. He told me it was the story of his life. I never found out what he meant. So much happened so quickly after that."

"Go on. Please, I won't be able to sleep tonight if you don't."

"You might not sleep tonight if I do."

Chapter Thirty-Six

Christine—Greenock, Scotland
May 1945

A week later, Nurse Graham found me stocking shelves. "Chrissy, a letter came for you." She gave me a straight "no nonsense now" look.

"I've no idea why anyone would write to me here."

She had on her ward-nurse persona. "You're not trying to hide something from your parents?"

"No, Nurse, not at all. Let's open it and see who it's from." That seemed to satisfy her.

I tore it open. "It's from Kevin O'Brien." I read aloud, "Dear Chrissy, I won't be back till the 26th. That's a Saturday, and I know you'll be volunteering at the Y. I'd like to get my camera from you then. Can you bring it with you? Hope this letter makes it to you. I couldn't remember your home address."

"Well, that's all right." She looked relieved. "What camera is he talking about?"

"I'll show you." I walked her to my locker and pulled out

Kevin's camera. "He said he was afraid it might get lost or stolen. His da gave it to him."

"That looks very dear. I'm not surprised he feared it would be stolen." When she took it from my hand, something gave a metallic rattle. Nurse said, "It sounds like something's broken loose."

My heart raced. "But I haven't moved it. He set it right there. It hasn't left its place."

She handed it back to me, and I heard the rattle again.

"I don't know cameras well, but that doesn't sound right," she said.

"What should I do?" I was dismayed. "Kevin trusted me. I can't open it to see. He's got photos he hasn't developed."

"Why don't you nip down to Marks and Spenser? They do photo developing. They should be able to open it safely. Then you can find out what's rattling and get it fixed. Go ahead. I know I'd want to return it in good condition."

"Thanks, I'll do that."

She went back to her dispensary. I set the camera on the bench and reached for my coat and handbag. The edge of my coat swept over the bench. I turned just as the camera clattered to the floor.

"Noo." I sank to my knees. How in the world could I be clumsy enough to drop Kevin's camera? "Oh, God, don't let it be damaged." I lifted it onto my lap, and its back swung open.

"How could I let this—" A single metal ping sounded as something hit the floor. Soft sunlight filtered through the high windows, giving our little back room barely enough daylight to glint off a ring as it bounced under the bench. I scooped it up and squinted, focusing on the Celtic carvings and the sparkle of an inlaid emerald. It couldn't be, but warnings sounded in my head as I picked it up. "Moira's ring from her grandmother," I whispered.

I looked down at a single blue-black curl tied with a narrow blue ribbon. She might have given Kevin a lock of hair, but she'd never part with her grandmother's ring. But there it was in my hand. There must be an explanation.

Moira always said her family had passed the ring down from grandmother to granddaughter for generations. How many times had she noted with pride that it was only hers for safekeeping until she passed it to her own granddaughter? My fingers closed tightly around this precious remembrance of my friend. Still, it might mean Kevin was a thief, but it hardly proved anything more.

I looked at the camera in my lap. The door was still open. Why had Kevin lied about the camera? Something was terribly wrong.

My fingers closed around a bit of soft cloth, and I spread it on the bench in front of me. It was a woman's handkerchief with little pink roses embroidered around the edges. Inside were four curls of black hair, each tied with a blue ribbon. There was also another ring, a delicate gold chain, a small gold pin with a wee amethyst stone in the center, and a small pearl bracelet. I reached out to touch the pin and drew back my hand in terror. The curls and keepsakes—they belonged to other young girls. Not the kind of gifts a girl would give willingly. I felt cold at the realization that Kevin wasn't at all as he appeared.

Horror gripped my heart as I remembered the girls killed by the spy. They all had black hair like me, like Moira.

"God, no, how could he have been right here all the time?" I helped him woo Moira by coming along with them, making her feel safe. Afterwards, I went on walks with him. I'd comforted him in his grief at losing her. All the while, he was the person who had ended her life. The more I thought, the angrier I became. I carefully scooped up the hankie, taking care not to touch Kevin's keepsakes, and stuffed them all back in the camera, even Moira's ring and black curl.

Tears rolled down my cheeks. This was all that was left of the girls he'd murdered. He'd stolen their lives and their treasures.

I had a moment of sheer panic when I realized Kevin's plans

for me. My stomach roiled as I wondered, Did I ever tell him anything, even innocent information, he could pass on to the Germans? My mind raced over all the times he'd asked me questions. I shook my head slowly. No, I didn't think so.

I remembered my dad sitting at the kitchen table with his head in his hands and the pain in his voice over Operation Tiger, the dry run for D-Day where over 750 lives had been lost because one destroyer turned back with mechanical problems. I whispered one word: "sabotage." Hadn't Kevin told us he was leaving Greenock when that ship was in dry dock? I couldn't remember, but I had a strong suspicion our Kevin caused that catastrophe.

My fist pounded the bench. I'd known there was something wrong with the guy, but I'd ignored my instincts. I hated myself for letting this happen. The flame of anger was growing within me. I played back all the time I'd spent with him, seeing it now in a different light. I realized how he'd played off my sympathy. Moira trusted him, really cared for him. Kevin with his sweet ways, he'd killed my friend. I was sure now he was a murderer and a spy, but not for the Allies. No, he was an enemy. He murdered these other girls and helped the Germans kill how many of our men?

My uncle's words came back to me. "Keep your eyes open, Chrissy, and don't say a word to a soul. It's the only chance we have to catch the fiend."

MY THOUGHTS SPUN AHEAD of me as I ran down the crowded sidewalk to my uncle's station. *Well, you won't get away with this, laddie. I'm about to end your career.*

I nearly collided with my uncle as I came through the station doors. "Chrissy, lass, what's happened? You look so fierce. Are you all right?"

I had to make him take this seriously. "Uncle, I have something you and Inspector MacNeil need to see. Is he here?"

"Now, Chrissy, what is it this time?"

He was treating me like a child. I might have been wrong about Tom Gorsky, but I wasn't wrong about this.

Before he could dismiss me, I burst out, "I found Moira's ring. She never took it off. It's been in her family forever. And I found much more."

He grabbed both my shoulders. "We never told a soul it were missin', not even you." His smile lit up his face. "Ye may have cracked the case, lass."

Uncle motioned for me to follow him through a warren of desks to a small office. MacNeil sat with a pair of spectacles perched on his nose, reading what looked like typed pages. He looked up when we came in. "Ah, Christina Finlay. What brings ye here this afternoon?"

I handed him the camera. "Open the back." Uncle moved to stand closer as the inspector picked it up and flipped open the back. The contents spilled out onto his desk. Both men were momentarily confused.

I took a deep breath and launched into my explanation. "You remember my friend, Moira MacDonald, don't you?" A hint of accusation made my question sound sarcastic.

I could see by their frowns I'd offended them and reminded myself that I hadn't seen what was right in front of me either. "Sorry, of course you do."

My eyes filled with tears, and I blinked them back. It was harder than I expected to tell the inspector everything without crying. Uncle's expression was sympathetic. I took a deep breath. I wasn't going to cry.

"Right, Chrissy, take it slow."

"Her laddie Kevin still comes by my work for a visit, or sometimes we go for tea or a walk. He always seemed like he was having a hard time getting over losing Moira. Then he'd leave, saying he had business out of the area, and I wouldn't see him for days.

"He came by last week and asked me to keep this camera for him. He said he was afraid it would get lost or stolen where he was going, and he'd feel so much better if he tucked it away safe with me. A letter came from him to my work in today's post."

MacNeil used his own handkerchief to spread the contents out on the desk. He examined everything, touching nothing.

"You've handled these?"

"The ring fell out when I accidentally dropped the camera. That's when I saw the folded hankie. I opened it and found all those things. I realized what they might mean."

"Right, then. Your uncle says you're a smart lass, and I can see he's got the truth of it."

He moved the objects in the handkerchief with the end of his pencil. When he touched Moira's things, I said, "That ring belonged to Moira's grandmother. I know Moira would never give it to anyone. It was that precious to her. The rest . . ."

Once more MacNeil fished around inside the cavity and pulled out a single piece of folded paper I hadn't seen. No one was saying anything. When he unfolded the paper, I saw what looked like German writing with numbers.

"Radio frequencies." He started to gather things up. "This needs to go to the inspector general, Miss Finlay. Who knows about this?"

"Not a soul." I hesitated. "Nurse Graham looked at the letter from Kevin, and she asked me about it. I showed her the camera. Then she left."

"Good lass. Be especially careful from now on. Bide your tongue. Say nothing at all about this, not even to your parents." He looked up at me. "You said something about a letter. May I have that as well?"

I pulled it from my pocket.

"If I'm right, this Kevin O'Brien is a dangerous man, and you were smart to bring this straightaway to us."

He sat on the edge of his desk, leaning toward me. "Can you think of anything else about Kevin that would add to what you already told us?" I shook my head. I couldn't mention Operation Tiger. Da might get in trouble for talking about it. Instead, I said, "Kevin was always asking me about what my da does for Scotts. But I didn't tell him anything."

"We'll be in touch soon. Just need to put a few details together. If this Kevin should show up earlier than expected, do everything you can to avoid him. I think you know how dangerous he is." The inspector rose, indicating the interview was over.

All the way home I felt shaken. Not with fear, no, with a boiling anger. I should have listened to the Sight. I'd known something was wrong, but I'd pushed it off. Never again.

The very next afternoon, I was leaving Boots Chemist after work when Uncle approached me. "Chrissy, do ye have a few minutes?" My heart began to race, and I set my teeth. I'd been wondering how the police would catch Kevin but didn't expect to hear this soon.

Uncle's face was grim as we walked to a black police car parked at the curb.

"What is it, Uncle?"

He opened the door for me, and I slid into the front seat. I could hardly wait for him to get into the auto. I was hoping for news they'd caught Kevin, but Uncle wasn't smiling.

When he'd settled into the driver's seat, he said, "Lass, what I'm going ta tell ye is for yer ears only." I waited, feeling like he was stalling. I wanted to yell.

Finally, he said, "You gave us the first break we've had in your friend's murder. Not just hers, mind, but a string of killings across the country."

My stomach turned over. "All those little locks of black hair?"

Uncle nodded.

"And the jewelry?"

"His trophies most likely."

The horror of what I'd already concluded hit me again. "There were five curls."

"Right, and those wee treasures he's kept helped us piece together who this Kevin is." My uncle put his hand on my shoulder. "Now we have a real chance of catching him. We know when and where he'll be and, with your help, we can lure him into a trap. Make no mistake, he intends your hair to join the others."

I shuddered.

"Ye've done it, lass. Ye've found our spy. It's likely our Kevin is one and the same who's been giving inside information to the Germans. If we can catch him, we might break a spy ring."

"That's why he was here?" I remembered all the walks we'd taken along the quay and how interested he was in what my father did. "What can I do?"

"We want you to meet him at the Y on the 26th. We'll have men there watching you."

Fear gripped my heart, and I almost said, "No, I never want to see him again." Instead, I bit my lip, hoping the pain would steady me somehow.

Uncle was saying, "I was against this plan from the start. I couldn't live wi' myself if anything happened to ye. Scotland Yard thinks Kevin needs to see you at the meeting place. Feel he's in control. Mind, he's slipped through police fingers time and again. We can't take any chances. Not when we're so close to catching him. He thinks he's got another victim lined up. But, Chrissy, you can't tell anyone. We must catch this man. Can you do it, lass?"

"Aye," was all I managed. If my parents thought I was in any real danger, they'd never let me out of the house. Kevin would escape to kill again. Uncle looked me in the eye. I met his gaze without yielding.

"I believe you can," he said.

"I can't let him do this again. Not ever."

Wendy—Seattle
1968

"I'm shocked," I said. "I guess I wanted him to be innocent."

Mum's smile was sad. "I did too." She rose to go into the kitchen. But I followed her.

"Don't stop now. Did they catch him?"

She busied herself, avoiding my question.

"Mum?"

She stopped. "Okay, it's just"—she closed her eyes and took a deep breath—"not easy to tell." She sat at the table, and I did too. I waited a long, silent few minutes before she spoke.

Chapter Thirty-Seven

Christine—Greenock, Scotland
May 1945

Two days later, my uncle came for me after work. We met with some men from the inspector general's office and worked out a plan to lure Kevin away from the crowds. The inspectors assured me that at no time would I be alone with him and instructed me to tell him we needed to get the camera from my house.

Inspector MacNeil said, "Tell him it's only a short walk, and it will give you a chance to talk in private. Any lad would jump at the chance." I suppose he meant it as a compliment, but I was too frightened to acknowledge it. He added quickly, "We'll arrest him as soon as you both leave the canteen. Scotland Yard wants him out of the crowd. There are too many things that might go wrong with a bunch of people in our way."

"But I won't actually take his camera home?" I had no idea how I'd explain that to Mum or Dad.

"No, Kevin's camera will remain locked up at the station."

Uncle Angus laid his hand on my shoulder. "They'll always have a man watching over you. No worries, luv." But I did worry.

I was on edge all week. With the war in Europe ending earlier in the month, activity in town had increased. Ships were coming through for supplies and refitting before sailing home. The streets were full of servicemen on leave. I kept wondering if Kevin's face would pop up among the sea of unfamiliar faces.

I didn't sleep well. When I slept, I had horrible dreams about Moira's death or sometimes even my own, with one constant: Kevin O'Brien was always there. Saturday morning, I rose early. It was no use trying to sleep with Kevin's capture only hours away. My mind would race through potential scenarios of trying to trap him. I prayed for peace, but it was elusive.

Finally, I walked into town, hoping the exercise would quiet my nerves.

Greenock's Y stood in a small park near the town center. To me, it'd always been a friendly looking place. Not so now. With all the trees and shrubbery crowding close to the door, it appeared sinister. Its old stone walls and small windows made it oddly claustrophobic. I stopped before going inside. "It's all right," I whispered. This early no one would be here except the church ladies in the kitchen. The door closed with an echo behind me.

Still, I jumped when Mrs. Baily called to me, "There ye are, Chrissy, just in time. I need your help in the kitchen." *Not Kevin. Of course, it's not Kevin.* But my knees were wobbly all the same. I straightened and blew out a long breath. This was ordinary, familiar. On a Saturday, we always made enough food to feed a small army. It was all eaten by the end of the evening.

My mood lightened as I started putting sandwiches together. This was my place. I'd danced on these floors and made sandwiches in the kitchen for years. I had the home ground advantage. That steadied me.

As soon as the first lot of servicemen arrived that evening, we began our usual rush of activity. I was having trouble concentrating. My senses were overwhelmed looking for Kevin. Sailors from all the allied navies crowded the dance floor. The band was good, but I wouldn't be dancing tonight. Instead, I'd be bait for a very dangerous predator. Uncle's voice came to my thoughts. "Chrissy, I'll have lads round the room watchin' over ye." Still, no one stood out. There were always unknown faces, but everyone was in uniform, mostly Canadians. With the war over, an air of celebration filled the place.

A hand touched my back, and I spun around, but it was only Betts from work, who often volunteered with me. She nearly shouted to be heard above the noise. "Don't they feed them aboard ship? Can you get another tray of sandwiches from the kitchen?"

I smiled and nodded. I needed the distraction. *Get hold of yourself and stop being so jumpy.*

A lad called to me. "Hey, Chrissy, come on, let's dance."

"Can't right now. I'm on a sandwich run."

He screwed his face into a funny expression. "You're on a what?"

Nervous laughter bubbled up despite my mood. It was so loud. I wondered what he thought I'd said. I shouted, "I'm going for more sandwiches."

"Oh, you eat then." And he moved away to ask another lass for a dance.

I dodged dancing couples, making my way to the kitchen. As the door swung into place behind me, I stood for a moment with my eyes closed, soaking in the relative silence. I could still hear the band, all the talking and laughing, but the cooking was done so the kitchen was empty. I took a deep breath. *You can do this. You said you would, and you must. There's no turning back.* I scrunched my eyes harder as another fear hit me and said aloud, "If Da finds out, he'll kill me."

From the darkness someone whistled a slow, sad tune. It

stopped as Kevin stepped into the light. "Now why would your da ever want to kill such a beautiful daughter?"

My eyes popped open, and I put a hand on my heart. No need to hide my surprise.

"Kevin, you shouldn't sneak up on a girl like that." He stood near the blackout curtains. I knew the police were mostly out front or in the auditorium. They weren't watching the back door.

He strolled over with the expression of a man who has confidence in his charm. "I learn some very interesting things sneaking up on a darlin' like yerself."

"I'll just bet you do." I forced a smile. Kevin's dark auburn hair slid over his brow, giving him a boyish attractiveness. I could see how Moira had fallen for him. He wasn't that tall, but with my five-foot-two frame, he towered over me.

His good looks must have gotten him far with the lassies. I wondered how many times he'd had his way. Drat my light skin. I could feel heat coloring my cheeks. *Best not think; it'll show on your face. Play your part.* "Where did you come from? I've been watching for you all night." I didn't add, "and so have the police."

"Oh, I came in through the back way." He moved in close, pulling me into an embrace. My stomach lurched, and I swallowed back bile, commanding myself to hug him and pretend I was glad to see him. He tilted my chin up with one finger. His green eyes glittered with excitement.

"I've a sweet surprise for you." One of his hands wound its way through my long curls. I tried to smile, but all I could think was how much my skin was crawling. Kevin's lips touched my ear as he whispered, "What? Aren't you even curious?"

His expression turned tender. "Did I tell you how much I love your hair? Give me a brunette beauty every time, but your hair is so black. Look at the way it gleams in the light, every curl."

"Like Moira's hair," I said, remembering the five tiny locks of black hair I'd found in the camera, each tied lovingly with a ribbon. He leaned away, and I wondered if I'd thrown him off his seduction spiel. I saw it now. How every word, every movement was calculated to trap his victims in a romantic illusion.

I couldn't seem to catch my breath or get words to come out of my throat. I wanted to scream for help or scratch his eyes out and run.

I watched him catch himself after the shock of Moira's name. His face instantly became stricken with sadness. "Yes, our poor Moira. You and I, we've suffered her loss. It's time we move past that." As he spoke, his features softened, and he looked so innocent. "You've meant the world to me, Chrissy. I don't know what I would have done without you." He smiled. "I wanted to think of a surprise that would . . . well, you'll see."

I already knew what kind of sweet surprise he'd planned for me. But I said, "You just gave me a sweet surprise. Why would I need another?"

He leaned in to kiss my forehead.

Couldn't he read the lie on my face? I looked up into those green cat eyes. How could he look so good with the heart of a devil?

His next words snapped me back to the task at hand. "Did you bring my camera?"

Say it like you practiced. "With this lot here, not on your life. I left it at home where it's safe." I saw his face melt into a frown, so I added quickly, "I don't live far. We could walk up and get it, just the two of us." His smile returned.

"Darlin' girl, I'd like nothing better than to be alone with you. No need ta walk, though. I brought my new car."

I cast him a doubtful look. "You have a car? The government confiscated ours for the war effort, and I don't see them giving it back. How did you even get the petrol coupons?" But my thoughts were racing ahead. If he got me into his car, he could take me far from help. I'd be dead like Moira.

"And just look at your big brown eyes. Don't believe me, do you? I told you. Sometimes I work for the government."

I'll just bet he did. The question was which government?

"All right, I'll go get my coat." I turned to leave, but he grabbed my arm.

"Sure, and it's a beautiful night. You won't need a coat at all." Why was he trying to hurry me out? Did he suspect a trap or want to keep me from speaking to anyone?

Think. What would you say if you knew nothing of his intentions?

"Well, I'm not leaving it here. It came all the way from my aunt in Canada." The more I tried to get back to where people waited to help me, the more his grip tightened on my arm. In the past, he'd always been easygoing. This was a different laddie. He was in control.

His voice was calm but insistent. "It's all right, luv. We'll come back to get it after we go for my da's camera." He looked so concerned. "I'd be happier if I had it back with me."

I tried to show sympathy. "I understand." But I turned for the auditorium door, saying, "I think I left my handbag in the coatroom."

He stopped me. "Chrissy, I'm trying to tell you I don't have much time. Come on now, lass, your coat and handbag will be safe where they are. Can you come now? Can you do that for me?"

I turned back. "Of course." I hoped my uncle's men were wondering what was taking me so long and come to check. The knife we used to cut sandwiches was sitting on the counter next to Betts' sweater. I scooped it up with the cardigan. "I'll just bring my sweater then." It wasn't much, but even a small knife could be a weapon. I slipped it into my skirt pocket.

He smiled. He'd won. I was coming. We walked through the blackout curtains, down the dark hall to the back door.

He stopped me there in the dark hall, pinning me to the wall with his closeness. I thought I knew what he was up to, so I steadied myself as his lips covered mine. His kiss was tender. If I didn't know better, I'd think it was almost sweet. As he pulled back, he said, "Thinking of you here waiting for me has kept me alive the last few weeks."

I wasn't sure how to respond, so I forced a smile. He took my hand in his, giving it another tender kiss. Then he led me out the door. If I hadn't known better, I'd have thought he truly cared for me, just like Moira must have thought.

From the back door, a steep bank led up to a gravel drive that curved around behind the building. The sun had set, but I could see people at least fifty feet away. They were smoking cigarettes and talking. They didn't look like Uncle's men. Not a soul was close. My inner voice begged, "Please see me. I'm here with a murderer." But no one looked our way. Kevin had his hand on my back, guiding me up the path. Ahead, I could see the dark shape of a car. *Lord, show me what to do, please. If I get into that car, I'll be just as dead as Moira.* Where the hell were the police?

A surge of anger coursed through me, pushing all the fear away. I slipped my hand into my pocket. My fingers closed around the knife handle, and it gave me courage. Things hadn't worked out as we'd planned. If I was going to have to protect myself from this murderer, I was prepared to do it. Kevin wasn't getting me without a fight.

His voice came to me in the gathering gloom, so concerned and kind. Lies. "Are you all right, Chrissy? You seem so reluctant."

Please, God, help me.

The familiar whisper said, "You're not alone."

What should I do? I said the first thing that came to mind. "Is this how it was with Moira?"

He stopped and looked at me, his mask still in place. "Moira will always hold a special place in my heart, but I have you now."

Oh no, you don't. This won't end well for you.

I stopped, planting my feet firmly on the path. Carried away by a wave of rage, I let it have full rein. He turned back, not bothering to hide his impatience.

"So, what am I, Kevin, number five or six?"

He stood dead still then chuckled. "I've traveled all over and fancied other women, but no one like you, my darlin'." He took my arm and gently urged me on.

But I stopped again. "Did they all have black hair?" I couldn't stop. The words poured out of me. "Did you charm Moira too?"

He looked confused then feigned hurt. "You know how much I cared for Moira. What the bloody hell are you talking about?"

I don't think he realized how much he'd raised his voice. I saw heads swivel toward us. That was it. I needed a loud argument.

Kevin gripped my arm tightly and lowered his voice. "Well, if that's how you feel, I'll just get my camera and be done with you. Come on, Chrissy, you said you'd keep it for me, and now I want it back."

He was pulling me up the bank toward the road.

I raised my voice. "Well, Kevin, I'm not done with you." In rage I spit out, "Did you make Moira think you cared about her to get her alone and kill her when you were finished? Did you, Kevin? Did you?"

He still had a tight grip on my arm. "What the devil's got into you?"

It was like I stood outside my body watching myself in front of this man who I knew meant to kill me, and I couldn't stop challenging him. All at once I couldn't let him believe he'd fooled me. "I'll tell you what. There was an accident. I saw what's in your camera, and it's not undeveloped film."

He growled, his face full of unrestrained rage, pulling my face inches from his. He bared his teeth. "Those are mine."

I matched his tone. "You picked the wrong lass this time, didn't ye, my darlin' laddie?"

He stopped for a second, just staring at my face. His hand shot out. I flinched, but he didn't hit me. He reached out to grab my other arm, digging his fingers into the flesh, pulling me closer to the car. He was so strong.

Luckily, he didn't get hold of my hand. I slipped it back into my pocket. My skin was wet with perspiration, my fingers catching the edge of the blade then sliding up to grasp the knife handle. The time was now, or I'd lose my chance to use it.

I dropped Betts' sweater and swiped the blade across his wrist. He shrieked and let go of me. As I pulled away, I fell backward onto the grass, but he was on top of me, his hands groping for my throat, but I wasn't going to make it easy for him. As his fingers tightened their grip on my neck, I thrashed wildly.

Somewhere in my mind, a calm voice wondered if he'd gone mad. But I realized I'd pushed whatever shreds of sanity Kevin had left right out of him. I had just enough breath to scream.

Men were running toward us, their flashlights trained on Kevin, who was still braced on top of me. His head jerked up. When he looked back, his eyes radiated hatred. "I'll be seeing you again, my darlin' lass." His voice was casual. "You can count on that."

My breath caught for a second at the change in him, but then I recovered my wits and began screaming again, "Police. Help. Help."

Kevin was off me and making a dash for the car. I don't know where they came from, but men were on him before he could get the door open. He fell, his face forced into the gravel of the drive. Those snake eyes were trained on me. Even with a man's knee in his back to hold him down, Kevin managed a smile. I couldn't look away from Moira's killer.

He sneered, "I'll find you, Chrissy. I'll make you sorry."

I believed him.

My bravado gone, my knees gave way. Then my uncle's arms were around me. My body shook, but I didn't cry a single tear. Instead, I whispered into the soft wool of Uncle's coat, "That was for you, Moira."

Wendy—Seattle
1968

On my drive to school the next day, I kept thinking of her story. What happened after that? I could imagine Kevin standing trial as a spy and serial killer. He deserved to hang as a traitor. Or was he rotting in a UK prison? I spoke to myself. "Tonight. I'll find out the rest tonight."

After one class and a four-hour shift in the Humanities building, I left work to find Seamus coming down the path from the library. He hailed me with his usual casual charm. "And there's my darlin' girl."

His turn of phrase sent a shiver up my spine. I stopped short and watched him. Seamus didn't see John jogging down the path behind him.

As John approached, he said, "That's my darlin' girl."

Anger flared on Seamus' face as he turned. "Oh, and weren't you the one who threw her away?" His tone was light, almost teasing. But his words were venomous, and John didn't miss the jab.

Oh God, he'll probably hit Seamus.

John surprised me with the last thing I expected. He said, "I did, but I'll never make that mistake again." He walked past Seamus and put an arm around me.

For the first time, I saw how old Seamus must be. His lips tightened, and his expression grew hard, with deep frown lines. Then he turned on his heel and walked away.

Okay, what just happened? It didn't matter, I heard John promise to never leave me. I felt dizzy with happiness.

It suddenly hit me that I wasn't afraid of making the wrong choice. I'd made my choice. And so had John.

He was still looking after Seamus. "Did you see his face?" he said. "There's something not right about the guy."

His words were so reminiscent of Mum's feelings about Kevin,

I felt chilled to the bone. But I still defended Seamus. "I know him. He's maybe protective, but he's a good guy."

John got in my face. His tone became serious. "Don't be alone with him."

I nodded, my momentary happiness replaced with an ominous feeling. I was beginning to feel uncomfortable around Seamus, and that also reminded me of how my mum described her feelings when she was with Kevin.

I didn't know what the Sight felt like, but I had a growing compulsion to find out what happened to Kevin.

Chapter Thirty-Eight

Christine—Greenock, Scotland
May 1945

U ncle Angus took the knife from my hand. He looked at the bloody blade, pulled out his handkerchief and wound it around my palm. I couldn't take my eyes off Kevin as the police cuffed him. One of his hands was covered in blood.

"Don't worry, it's mostly his blood." I gave Uncle a crooked smile.

Uncle's expression sobered. His manner was very direct. "Your da was right about you." His eyes shone in the darkness as he gave me a hint of a smile, adding, "You're a brave lass and no mistake."

All the tension left me. "You're wrong, Uncle. I've never been more afraid in my life. That and I was so angry."

"You'll do, Chrissy, you'll do." He patted my back. "Let's get you home."

One of his men collected my things from the canteen. I watched Uncle wrap the knife in another handkerchief and give it to someone.

The police walked Kevin past us with his head down, his face blank. Kevin the madman was gone. Kevin the young Irishman was gone. He was a hollow man, beaten, captured. I almost felt sorry for him until he focused on my face. The change was instantaneous and pure evil. The Kevin I saw in that moment would haunt me the rest of my life.

His last words echoed in my thoughts. "I'll find you, Chrissy, and make you pay." I shivered again.

Uncle said, "I canna think we would ever have caught the maniac without yer help."

I nodded, not knowing what to say. When I found my voice, it sounded so small and weak. "I wasna brave one bit. He scared me to death."

"Well, that's what makes you sae brave, lassie."

Uncle's men opened the car door and pushed Kevin inside. By now, the people in the canteen were on the lawn of the Y, watching the police activity and speculating what it meant. They milled around in little clumps and whispered among themselves.

The car carrying Moira's murderer moved away down the drive. All the windows were dark, but the greater darkness was inside Kevin O'Brien.

My hand started bleeding, but there wasn't much pain. I think I was numb inside and out.

Uncle led me to his car. Someone handed me my things, and Uncle slid into the driver's seat.

As we drove away, I asked, "What happens now?"

"Can ye come down to the station tomorrow and make a full statement?"

"Will I have to testify?"

"I'm not sure. This is top level, and when Scotland Yard's involved, I'm not sure what to expect." I could just see his eyes, reassuring and kind, in the dark car. "Not to worry. We'll try to keep you out of this as much as possible."

Without thinking I asked, "Did Kevin sabotage the Scimitar?"

Uncle's eyebrows shot up, and he braked to a stop right there on Mount Pleasant Street. "And what do you know about that?" I was glad it was dark because heat flushed my face from my accidental admission.

"Sorry, Uncle. I overheard something and, well, I remembered that when the Scimitar came to port, that was one time Kevin suddenly disappeared."

He shook his head. "You don't miss much. Sure, you wouldn't like to work wi' me?" I heard a chuckle in his voice. Then he straightened. His voice held the authority of law. "Chrissy, this is top secret, so we still can't talk to anyone about it. D'ye ken? No, not even yer parents." He added with a half-smile, "Yer da would kill us both."

That was a huge relief. The last people I wanted to talk to about this were my parents. I was more afraid of their anger than Kevin's threat. No, I wouldn't tell them, not ever. "Aye, Uncle. You'd better let me out here. They'd surely have questions if you brought me home in a police car."

He chuckled. "Right you are, lass, right you are."

I slid out of the car, but before I closed the door, he said, "Tomorrow at half-past one at the station. We'll meet in MacNeil's office."

"Aye." I closed the door and waved goodbye. As he drove away, I turned to walk the rest of the way home.

When I came through our door, Mum said, "You're home early then, Chrissy. Och, what did ye do ta your hand?"

"Cut it on a sandwich knife."

"You should be more careful. Knives can be dangerous. We'll have a wee cup of tea. The scones are still hot." I realized how close I'd come to ending up like Moira and never seeing my mum again, but here I was alive with her and her smile that sweet. I bit my lip.

I'm so grateful, God, that I'm home safe. We talked about Mum's day and Grandma's health. Mostly I listened, soaking in the peace.

"Och, I almost forgot. A letter came for ye in the afternoon post." Mum retrieved it from the counter. It was from Margie Beckman in Canada.

With Russell lost to me, her letters had slowly stopped coming. It surprised me to get this one. I didn't open it until I was alone in my room. It read:

Dear Christina,

I'm writing to you at the request of my brother. He thinks you must have forgotten him long ago, but I told him we'd become good friends, and you weren't like that.

When he wrote to you that he'd found someone else, he was lying. His injuries were more extensive than he let on. The military doctor told him he'd be lucky to live out the year, so he made up the story of another girl so you wouldn't feel sorry for him. He wanted you to get good and mad so you could go on with your life.

Russell has never stopped loving you. He reads all your letters to me and keeps them with him. The thing is, a year has come and gone; and, besides being very lonely and miserable, he's doing much better physically.

A teardrop hit the paper and smeared the writing. I realized it was my tear, so I wiped my eyes and read on.

Last week, he went to a civilian doctor and had a full physical. To his complete surprise and relief, the doctor said he was perfectly fit and would probably live to be an old man.

We were all so happy until Russell realized he'd lost you forever. I told him I'd contact you and ask permission for him to write. Would you be willing to exchange letters again? It would make him so happy.

I crumpled the letter to my heart. "Russell." My heart's door opened once again.

Wendy—Seattle
1968

All day I thought about my mum's description of Kevin. I kept comparing her words to what I'd said about Seamus, my mind making connections I couldn't put aside. I rationalized that maybe all Irishmen shared some traits. I couldn't imagine Seamus with some evil, hidden side. Not Seamus. Not my friend.

Then the inner arguments began. Two young coeds had died recently. That reminded me of Kevin. Could Kevin and Seamus be the same person? An all-too-familiar whisper in my mind made wild accusations. "If Seamus really is Kevin, he could have strangled those two coeds."

It seemed ridiculous, but once my mind formed that link it wouldn't let go. I had to find out. Seamus was the right age, but that didn't make him guilty of being a serial killer. It didn't matter how I rationalized; the conviction grew.

Determined to learn what had happened to Kevin, I didn't wait for Mum to bring it up. I had to know Kevin's fate, but she was evasive. She moved from chore to chore with nervous energy.

"Really, Wendy, I don't want to talk about this. I can't. You don't know…all these years this fear's been there." She picked up a broom and began sweeping, and I followed her, asking question after question. She didn't answer. Instead, she spoke about her day and Heather's grades in school.

My throat tightened, and my voice sounded hoarse. "Don't leave me in the dark. I can't tell you why, but I need the whole story. You might think I'm imagining this…" Tears collected in my eyes. I cleared my throat and gave it one last try. "I don't think I have second sight. I just know there's a reason I need to know. Did you find out what happened to Kevin?"

Mum stopped with the broom poised in midair. "Not exactly."

Chapter Thirty-Nine

Christine—Greenock, Scotland
1945

I kept my appointment with Uncle at the police station right after church the next day. He met me at the door and walked me back to MacNeil's small office. The room was a drab grey with framed certificates on the wall. Other than a desk and several straight-backed chairs, it always looked empty. Today it was over-crowded with Inspector MacNeil sitting at his desk and another man I'd never seen before seated next to the wall. The stranger wasn't in uniform but dressed in a fine tweed suit that looked like it came from Savile Row in London. As Uncle ushered me into the room, both men rose.

My uncle said to the man I didn't recognize, "Christina Finlay, my niece." He gestured to the stranger. "This is Mr. Fenton of M-I5." I must have looked puzzled because he added, "British Security Service."

Inspector MacNeil said, "Please sit down, Miss Finlay." I sat in the chair offered and waited, my curiosity piqued.

Mr. Fenton cast a look at the floor as if he were contemplating the quality of my shoes. His attitude was that of any command authority, and I knew he must be deciding how much to tell me. Then he looked up at the other two men and back at me.

In a cultured English accent, he said, "What we have here is a very"—he paused—"ticklish situation."

"What, with Kevin?" I asked.

"Quite so. Our Mr. O'Brien has dropped a few highly placed names." He paused again, and I sensed he was weighing every word he spoke. "It appears he may have been a double agent."

I was grasping the arms of my chair, ready to jump at this self-important little man if he told me Kevin was going free. "You don't think he killed my friend and those other girls?" I sounded sarcastic but didn't care. Frustration and anger overwhelmed me.

"No, no, we're sure he's our murderer." Mr. Fenton shook his head. "No doubt about it. All the jewelry matched to his other victims." A smile flashed across his face, and I thought how incongruous his expression was. "You are a very lucky young lady. I'm sure you would have been his next target."

Uncle chimed in. "She was clever and brave." I must have been missing the intent of Mr. Fenton's comments, because my uncle sounded like he was coming to my defense.

I straightened my back. "Thank you, Uncle. But, if it's all right with you, I'd like to give my statement and go home."

"That's just it, Miss Finlay. Your statement won't be necessary."

I fairly jumped out of my chair. My eyes narrowed as I stared at this pompous Englishman. "Are you saying Kevin won't be punished for killing my friend? Not to mention the other lassies?"

He held up his hand. "On the contrary. Please be assured it's likely he will meet his end shortly. Just, shall we say, not publicly."

"Oh." No longer ready to explode, I let the air out of my lungs. "That's all right then." I looked at my uncle. "You no longer need me?" Right or wrong, my sense of justice for Moira's murder would be appeased as long as her murderer got his comeuppance. To tell the truth, I needed to know there was no way he'd come looking for me someday.

"You're quite wrong about that, Miss Finlay. We need your silence. If it were to get out that the British government recruited an agent from Ireland who turned double and began murdering young women . . ." He chuckled a little. "Well, it would be bad form, to say the least."

I got up. Since this pompous man and Kevin were the only men I'd ever met from MI-5, I began to have doubts about the future of our nation. But I didn't say what I was thinking—that time.

Nothing ever appeared in the papers about the murders or about the spy. It was as if the whole thing never happened. A few people had noticed me with my uncle after they captured Kevin. I told anyone who asked that I'd cut my hand, and my uncle had driven me home.

But I couldn't get Kevin's face out of my mind. I asked my uncle if he knew for certain that Kevin O'Brien was dead. He could never find out. It left me unsettled.

But my focus turned away from war and, as Nurse Graham suggested, I had to figure out what to do with the rest of my life. And then there was Russell. We corresponded again, and all the feelings I had finally tamped down flared to life. He wanted me. But not as a long-distance friend. Russell made it clear he wanted to marry me.

I remember visiting Grandma Cowan to ask her what I should do. How could I consider leaving my parents, my home, everything I loved?

Grandma said, "Whenever I'm faced with a question, and I can't find the answer, I open my bible and put my finger on the page."

"Oh, Grandma, what if it says something that doesn't make sense?"

"Well, I'm not saying it always works, but I pray first and most times the words give me clear direction." I was skeptical, but she finished with, "It's always best to follow your heart's direction." She took her bible from the kitchen table and handed it to me.

Another letter came from Russell asking if I would consider coming to Canada to discover if we both felt the same. I could see what life would be like on the other side of the world. He said he'd send an airline ticket if I agreed and promised we'd be well chaperoned. I was torn, my heart euphoric one minute and already homesick the next.

I knew one thing: I needed to make up my own mind before I spoke with my parents. Grandma's small bible sat on the bed next to me. I prayed for God to show me what I should do and opened it. My finger fell on Ruth 1:16. "For where you go, I will go, and where you lodge, I will lodge. Your people shall be my people and your God, my God." I had my answer.

But even after I left Scotland and traveled to Canada to marry Russell, I often found myself looking over my shoulder and wondering if Kevin had indeed met his end.

I kept my word and never told a soul. At any rate, who would have believed it?

Wendy—Seattle
1968

Mum's story kept me up most of the night. It was crazy to think Kevin and Seamus were the same person, but I noticed so many similarities between them. Could that be why I'd started feeling uncomfortable around Seamus?

I couldn't shake it. Despite the lack of proof, I feared something was wrong. Is second sight an unreasonable, overwhelming conviction that can't be ignored?

I groaned aloud. "Oh, God, I don't want the Sight."

Even though it had saved Mum's life on more than one occasion, it also caused her heartache. She said people were uneasy around someone who could glimpse the future.

I exhausted myself with worry, and finally, toward dawn, I drifted off to sleep. The next thing I knew, Mum was shaking my arm. "Wendy, come on, luv. Wake up. You'll be late if you don't hurry."

My eyes popped open. I couldn't afford to start the day late. My schedule included two classes, a two-hour shift in the Humanities building, and rehearsal.

The weight of foreboding stayed with me throughout the day. My thoughts replayed the news stories about the strangled coeds. I remembered seeing a picture of the victims in the paper. Both girls had black hair like Kevin's victims.

It was nothing but crazy to make connections between Seamus and those murders. The compulsion to discover the truth overpowered my fear that I might be right. If Seamus really was Kevin, Mum would be in danger. The question was, how could I find out without putting my own life at risk? After class, I dropped my books off at my car, analyzing the reasons I suspected him.

He offered friendship, but was that normal for a man of forty-something? Both John and my mum thought Seamus was hitting on me. At the time I'd protested, defending my Irish friend. I had to admit lately Seamus had been acting possessive around me, making me feel awkward.

Then there was the fact that he said he'd been all over Scotland during the war. That would be true of Kevin as well. And Seamus hadn't said he was in the fighting or even in the service.

I was walking back to work and stopped as I realized that once again I was comparing Seamus to my mum's stories about Kevin. *Oh, God, it's getting worse. I'm making the jump from suspecting him of being a serial killer from WWII to the coed killings in Seattle. I can't seem to let go of this obsession. If this isn't the Sight, I'm losing my mind.*

I said aloud to the deserted parking lot, "You can keep your

Sight. I don't want it." I would not surrender to unfounded fears about a man who might be innocent.

If I approached this logically, I might stop the feelings driving me to suspect Seamus of something terrible. Were the whispers my imagination or second sight or God? I had to think things through, and I needed to spend time with Seamus talking about his life. I thought of John's warning, but I'd spent plenty of time with Seamus and nothing bad had ever happened.

The Sight whispered, "You were never alone."

"That's right," I answered back. "I'll make it someplace with lots of other people around, just in case."

Between work and rehearsal, I walked to the library looking for Seamus, hoping to approach him on the pretense of apologizing for John's behavior. But Seamus wasn't there. I asked the librarian if she'd seen him.

"No, not today."

"Nann, what do you think of Seamus?" She stopped putting books away. I added, "Honestly."

She leaned in and lowered her voice. "He doesn't show up until you're on campus." Her frown deepened. "I shouldn't say this but . . ."

"Please, what is it?"

"I've seen him watching you from the balcony section. He'll put the odd book away, but his eyes never leave you until you come say hi." Her expression was intent. "If you were my daughter, I'd say be careful."

Her words left me shaken, but they didn't stop me from needing to know who Seamus was and what he was capable of.

I wondered if he might be having tea in the cafeteria. Not there either. Stumped for now, I walked to the theatre. It was too early for anyone to be there, but it would give me time to think. First, I checked my costumes in the greenroom. Everything was hanging ready for the final dress rehearsal tomorrow. A few soft lights shone on stage. Determined to settle my thoughts, I found a seat in the dark auditorium.

At first, I thought I was imagining someone whistling a sad tune. I sat up, straining to hear better. Seamus? Clutching the arms of my seat, I froze in place as the whistling floated to me through the darkness. I had the overwhelming conviction that if I paid careful attention, his own words would tell me what I wanted to know. It was time to discover the true Seamus.

A shadowy figure strolled down the aisle. "Wendy, is that you?"

I wanted to run for the door but remained in my seat. "Oh, Seamus, I was expecting Mrs. Wilson." His amiable smile faltered, and I added, "I'm glad it's you. I wanted to apologize for yesterday."

He gave a short, explosive laugh. "You mean for that big ape of a young man." He shoved his hands in his pants pockets. "Don't understand what you see in him."

The heat of defensive anger rushed through me. "And you weren't rude as well? You provoked him."

For a moment, his mouth flattened. Then he half smiled. "That I did. He's always with you. Watching over you. I can hardly get a minute alone to talk." He sounded jealous. I realized his attitude was all wrong. Could it be he hadn't offered me only friendship; could he be setting me up for some other reason? The whisper answered, "Seamus is dangerous." My hands felt clammy, and my heart sped up.

Now I understood why my mum didn't welcome the Sight. It was frightening. Was I losing my mind? I heard Mum's voice repeating what her Grandma Finlay had said. "It's like God pulls back the veil between Him and us to show us something."

I remembered the first time the whispers came to her. In Kirkcowan they floated on the breeze. When she was in danger from an unexploded bomb, the words yelled at her. These whispers scared me, but I needed their help.

Seamus scooted into the seat next to me. I changed the subject, trying to catch him off guard. In a lighter tone, I said, "There's another reason I should be mad at you."

"Me? What for?" His easy smile returned.

"I've got the tune you were whistling stuck in my head. What's it called?"

"*The Ballad of Kevin Barry*. The story of my life."

Kevin's very words to my mum. My heart stopped as my inner voice confirmed, "Now you know who Seamus is."

I was alone in the empty theatre with a killer. What should I do? I sent a desperate prayer to God. "If this voice is yours, Lord, help me like you helped my mum during the war. Show me what to say and do." Despite my earlier complaints, I hoped He wouldn't be silent.

"Wendy, what is it?"

I stood and gathered my things. "Not feeling well." I moved down the row away from him. He followed me, grabbing my arm. He was holding me so tight I cried out in pain. "Stop it, Kevin." A slip of the tongue, but a deadly mistake.

"Now there's a girl. So, yer Mum's told you all about me. Pity that. But she'll pay for her crimes." I struggled to pull my arm out of his grip. My friend Seamus disappeared, and the monster from World War II took his place.

"What crimes? You're the monster. How many lives have you taken?"

"All's fair in love and war, don't ya know." He leered at me. Seamus with his sweet, easygoing manner had disappeared. This man had a deep frown and blazing eyes. "And I loved them all before they were gone. All good girls, like you, like your mum."

"And the dead coeds, did you love them too?" Anger grew, pushing away my fear, giving me a quiet strength. I sounded more like Mum than me. Now I understood what she meant when she said her blood ran through my veins.

He scoffed at me. "Oh, and weren't they all yer fault? Had to blow off steam, didn't I? If you hadn't been so damn frustrating, I would have had you and your mum a long time ago." He winked. "And your little sister too. Though children aren't usually part of my appetite, I can make an exception to pay your mum back for helping MI-5."

I swung my free hand and slapped his face as hard as I could. And just as quickly drew back, horrified at what I'd done. What was I thinking? Even in the dark auditorium, the red imprint of my hand burned on his cheek. Kevin let out a low growl but cut it short as lights flicked on in the atrium, spilling into the auditorium seating.

He twisted my arm behind my back and pressed his face next to my ear. "Hear me. If you say one word, I'll kill whoever walks through that door." He pushed me back, throwing me off balance, and I landed hard in a seat. His eyes glittered in the half-light; his teeth were clenched, and the muscles of his jaw worked. "You'd better believe me." I nodded.

My drama professor, Mrs. Wilson, came through the double doors and flipped on all the seating lights at once. Only then did she notice us. "Here, what's this?"

Seamus didn't miss a beat. He turned to the drama teacher, as charming as ever. "Oh, the poor dear has a terrible headache. I fear she's under the weather."

Mrs. Wilson looked momentarily taken aback, but Seamus followed with, "I stopped by to see about volunteering in your drama program." I glanced over my shoulder and let out my breath as the cast members streamed through the door. My professor would be fine.

Her face was instantly aglow with pleasure. She moved toward him, hesitating only a moment as her eyes took in his cheek. I slid away. In one last look over my shoulder before I left through a side door, I saw Mrs. Wilson's meaty hand laid on Kevin's arm. I could see that he'd slipped into his role as faithful volunteer, and I knew he'd escape within minutes.

Outside, I could only think of one thing. Get away as fast as possible. It was the dinner hour, the campus deserted and security absent. I didn't want to waste time looking for a guard. As I ran to my car, the voice whispered, "Home."

I argued with the whispers. Shouldn't I call the police? I played out that scenario in my mind and decided it was pointless to think anyone would believe Seamus was a spy from the past. It would be his word against mine. Was I going to tell them that the Sight or God told me he was evil? I shook my head at how absurd that sounded, even to me. No, get home and call John. But first get my mum and Heather to safety.

That half-hour drive was the longest of my life. Every stoplight brought tears of frustration to my eyes. I kept looking in my rearview mirror, hoping to see John following me but afraid I'd see Kevin. Finally, I drove into my garage, thankful to be home. At least Seamus didn't know where I lived.

The small voice in my head whispered, "You knew you had a watcher."

All my life, my mother spoke about the Lord as a constant companion. Sometimes His words to her were frightening, but she never doubted that second sight was God talking, not after that very first time in Kirkcowan. I never understood till now. In the past it sorta freaked me out, but I was coming round to recognize that what I was thinking of as second sight might be God reaching out to me.

"If that's you, God, why didn't you tell me this earlier?" He didn't answer back. I realized I wouldn't have believed it. I found it easier to accept Mum's second sight. Nothing like that had ever happened to me. Did I have to come through this tough summer to be ready to listen?

I struggled with my feelings as I rushed up the six steps to the back door. I ran down the hall, past our bedroom doors and into the living room, scanning the open kitchen beyond. Heather was the first to see me. A bowl of SpaghettiOs sat on the coffee table in front of her. Her spoon stopped halfway to her mouth. "What's happened?"

My mum was in the kitchen, drying a frypan. Her mouth dropped open, and the heavy pan slipped to the floor with a loud clang.

"Mum, Seamus is Kevin. We need to get out of here. We don't have long." Neither she nor Heather moved. I looked from one to the other. "Hurry! He may be right behind me." Mum's face blanched, but she shut her mouth and moved toward my little sister.

"Hurry." I crossed the living room to the phone on the kitchen wall. John wouldn't doubt me. For once, I was grateful for his tougher side. I'd seen him intimidate people. And he always carried a large pocketknife.

Please, God, let him be home. My fingers were shaking so much I dialed the wrong number. I tried again. As the phone rang through, I heard Mum hurrying Heather to the back door. "Take the path to Roseanne's house, and don't come back till I come get you."

Heather resisted. "What's going on? Who's Seamus or Kevin? I want to stay."

They were out of earshot by the time John picked up the phone.

"Hello?"

"John, I need you. Seamus is coming to hurt us. No time to explain. I'm at home. Please help." I was counting on him.

Mum walked into the room to stand by the living room window. She drew back, putting her hand over her heart. "A car's coming up the drive." Without thinking, I hung up. She asked, "Are you sure this man's Kevin?"

"He told me as much. He says he's going to kill us." My throat closed around those last words. Panic filled me as I went to stand next to her. "You should have gone with Heather."

She grabbed both my shoulders, her eyes drilling into mine.

"It has to stop here." I gulped back a sob. Mom's voice was calm and firm. "I'm not going to spend the rest of my life being afraid Kevin will show up. If he's here now, we'll deal with him. I don't know how, but we will."

I bit my lip. "Mum, what would Chrissy do? Quick, what can we use as a weapon?" I scooped up a knife she'd left on the kitchen counter. It gave me an odd feeling to think Mum had done the same thing in 1945.

She retrieved her cast-iron frying pan and hefted it in her hand like a club. "Call the police." I could see brave Chrissy in my mum's expression.

I picked up the receiver. This time there was no dial tone. "Phone's dead." My voice quivered.

The whisper said, "You're not alone." Comfort and courage strengthened me.

I turned to tell Mom when she said, "Remember, we're not alone. God's with us." We took a silent moment, our gaze connected. Then I nodded.

"And John's on his way."

We heard footfalls on the steps that ran along the side of our house to our front porch. Too soon to be John. We turned to face the window as a dark shape scooted past to the front door. My gaze darted to the door handle, and I realized with heart-thudding panic, "I forgot to lock the door."

Mum shook her head. "It wouldn't matter. It wouldn't stop him."

The handle turned, the door latch released, and Kevin pushed the door with such force it banged against the wall. But when he stepped over the threshold, he said with a calm, pleasant voice, "Well, and aren't you both my darlin' girls?" He looked around. "And where's the wee girl?" His auburn brows rose in question. "Never mind, I'll see to her later."

Mum gave me a quiet smile, and I took courage; this was Chrissy, just like in her story. Her voice was calm with a hint of sardonic humor. "And where have you been these past twenty years?"

He laughed a little, and for a minute, I hoped Seamus had returned. "There you go again, surprising me with that nerve." But as his laughter faded, his tone flattened. "I almost died. They put me in solitary in Wakefield. The worst shithole in all of England. But after a few years, some bloke from the government needed a nasty job done and remembered me. You'd be surprised what governments will overlook for a man of my talents."

He turned his eyes on me. "What gave me away? I fancy we had a good friendship going."

"Your whistling."

He nodded. "I thought as much."

"Seamus was a friend. I want to know what made that song so important." I was counting on his love of self to buy us time.

"Do you? Haven't heard the story?"

"No."

Kevin's gaze was intense, searching me. "It's called the *Ballad of Kevin Barry*." He relaxed for a minute, adopting the casual stance of Seamus. "The bloke in the song suffered the same fate as me own da, killed by the English, he was." Kevin spat on the floor. "I saw it happen. And me only nine years old. They hanged him but didn't do it proper like. My da strangled to death."

"Oh, Seamus, that's awful." I hoped to keep Seamus with us as long as possible.

My hopes fell as I watched Seamus retreat behind a wall of anger. His body stiffened, and the hardness of Kevin returned.

Mum blurted into the explosive air. "Your mother, did she have black hair?"

A wicked grin spread across his face. "You have me figured out, do you? Well, you're right. A real beauty she was. She remarried, don't you know? Turns out my new da was the second son of an English lord."

His face crumpled into the expression of an angry child. "Said she had to do it to take care of me. I could have helped. How could she?"

I could see how this small lad had suffered. "That must have been terrible."

But it was Kevin's eyes that darted from Mum to me. His hand slipped to the back of his belt, and he drew out a large military-type knife. I flinched. My reaction seemed to please him. I searched for anything that would keep him talking. But Mum, bless her, spoke up.

"You sabotaged the Scimitar. All those men died." I caught the deadly tone of suppressed anger in her voice. "And Moira, my friend. She loved you."

"Right on both counts." Kevin looked pleased.

Mum said, her voice quiet but strong, "I stopped you. A mere seventeen-year-old girl stopped you." My heart jumped to my throat. She was making herself the target, drawing his attention away from me.

He growled again, fierce and low like an animal. He tensed, and I was sure he would spring at my mum with that knife. Without conscious thought, I lunged, pushing him back. Both our knives crashed to the floor, but he spun and kicked me in the stomach. I fell against the wall, gasping to catch my breath.

Stunned, I could only watch as Mum swung the frying pan. He saw it coming and put his arm up. The pan glanced off him. Before she could swing again, he grabbed hold of her wrist, his fingers digging in and twisting her delicate bones, forcing her to let go. The pan banged to the floor. Thank God, he let go of her and turned to me, pulling me up by my hair. He retrieved his knife and held it to my throat. I heard the back door swing open, and prayed I would hear John's voice.

Heather ran down the hall. "Stop." Her arms were swinging wildly, her voice shrill. "Don't hurt my sister."

If Mum hadn't grabbed her around the waist, she would have

charged right into me and Kevin. My little sister hissed, "We won't let you hurt her." I realized she said "we."

Kevin sounded amused at her vehemence. "Chrissy, all your girls have your same ridiculous disregard for danger. That suits me fine. What luck now I have you all together."

Heather's voice was full of conviction. "Let go of Wendy now, or we'll kill you."

It dawned on me she said "we" again. Kevin held me in front of him, but both our backs were to the front door. I shut my eyes. *Oh, God, let it be John.*

Kevin had all the power. His revenge was at hand. "Well, wee one, just in time to watch your sister die." I flinched as the knife broke the first layer of my skin, but he hadn't cut my throat yet. He must have decided to keep the pressure up. I knew he was enjoying himself. I caught the scent of English Leather—John's shaving cologne.

Mum did something completely unexpected. Her chin rose, and she said with authority, "Kevin O'Brien you are about to be judged for your crimes."

"You've got it all wrong," Kevin sneered. "You'll watch your children die, and I'll have some fun with you before I end your life." He put his face close to my ear. "At least this time your big ape isn't here to save you."

As Kevin drew back, I felt something brush the hair on the back of my head and slide into the space between us.

John's low voice sounded so close. "I wouldn't count on that, bastard. Move your hand even an inch, and it'll be your blood on the floor, not Wendy's."

Kevin stilled like a cat before it springs.

"Drop the knife."

To my surprise, it clattered to the floor. I moved away as quickly as I could. Heather threw her arms around me and buried her face in my sweater. The monster stood before us with John's large pocketknife held firm against his throat.

I turned to Mum. "Can you go to the bowling alley to call the police?"

Mum's eyes never left Kevin as she fished in her pocket and pulled out a coin. "Heather, you go. Dial the operator and ask for the police. Tell them our address and all that's happened." Heather looked from her face to mine. "It'll be all right. You can do this." With uncharacteristic compliance, Heather hurried down the hall to the back door.

Kevin's face paled, but his mouth twisted into an ugly smile. "Think the police will stop me from killing you? How did that work last time? I have important friends who need my talents."

I was flooded with rage and frustration. Kevin was going to stand there, wait for the police and take his chances. At that moment I wanted him dead or at least in some dark prison for the rest of his life. The last thing I wanted was his smug confidence that he'd get away with this and come back to kill us all later. A thought came to me. "You're not an American spy. Maybe in Britain they'd give you special treatment because your stepfather is a lord. Haven't you been in the U.S. long enough to know we don't give a rip who your stepfather is? No, we love the drama. Your picture will be in all the papers. That alone will make you useless as a spy. You'll be all over the cover of the *National Enquirer*. Don't you get it? You're news."

Mum joined me with a smug-sounding comment. "I'll tell everyone what you did during the war. You'll be famous. I may even make a bit of money off your story. Bring out the sad little Irish boy who saw his father hang. At the very least I'm sure you'll have lots of women sending you letters in prison."

He looked down his nose at us. "I'll have immunity."

Mum was on the attack again. "Think so? Maybe the British government won't want to claim you. It's sure to be a scandal when it comes out who's doing their dirty work.'

Kevin's face clouded, his eyes shifting from Mum to me. I could see the seeds of doubt we'd planted in his thoughts.

It happened so fast, if I'd blinked, I would have missed it. Kevin grabbed John's hands, pulling the knife away from his own neck, down to the left, twisting it backwards and thrusting the blade toward John's side.

John let go and spun out of the way. Now Kevin had the weapon. John stepped back, his concentration fully on the knife in Kevin's hand.

Mum pulled me out of the way as Kevin and John shifted side to side in a deadly dance to see who would take the advantage. My mother's living room wasn't crowded with furniture, but it seemed they had so little room to move. I wrung my hands as I watched. If I'd ever questioned the depth of my feelings for John, I knew now I couldn't see my life without him next to me. *Oh, God, help John.*

John fell into one of our kitchen chairs, but he was back on his feet in seconds. In one quick move, he pulled the chair forward. Kevin lunged, but John had it swinging in his direction, using it like a club. It came down with a terrible crack on Kevin's head.

Everything stopped as Kevin fell to the floor. His body was so still. The face that haunted Mom all those years stared up at us without recognition. I watched as the monster abandoned Kevin's body. Some part of me felt guilty for wishing he would die. This death was kinder than the ones I imagined. Maybe for the sake of the little boy who'd watched his father die, God had given Kevin this one last mercy. Already a pool of dark-red blood spread from the back of his head. John bent and checked for a pulse then looked up in surprise. "He's dead." He pulled back. His hands were shaking.

He staggered to me and pulled me into a warm embrace. "It's all right. He can't hurt you now." Ironically, he tried to comfort me when his face looked so stunned.

"John?" Mum spoke in her soft mother tone. "You need to sit down before you fall down." She guided him to another kitchen chair. That's where we were when Heather came running through the back door. She skidded to a stop next to Mum.

Heather's mouth opened and closed, but she didn't cry. "Is he?"

Mum's voice sounded flat with shock. "Yes. He can't hurt anyone ever again."

Oddly, I was a little sad for Seamus. He was the man Kevin might have been if things had been different.

We couldn't take our eyes off the body. I think we were all expecting him to rise up and attack us again. But he didn't. Mum used her mother's voice again to move us onto the porch to wait for the police, away from the monster on the living room floor. She started to cry and put her hand over her mouth. "I was always afraid he'd find me." She reached for John's hand. "Thank you for rescuing us."

The police came and a coroner and it seemed to take forever. Shaken, Mum did what she always did when she needed to clear her mind and keep from losing her cool. She passed out tea and cookies as if the police were all welcome guests in her home.

After we answered all the questions, John sat with me on the back steps. I couldn't take my eyes from him. "You came. I knew you would." My heart was so full. The words came on their own. "I love you."

John's eyes shone, reflecting his heart. He took my hand and brought it to his lips. "I love you more." Suddenly he looked so serious. "You went after a killer with nothing but a hunch? I'm thinking I should be concerned about your wild side." We laughed.

"Funny, I was counting on yours." I laid my head on his shoulder, soaking in the peace and offering a silent prayer to God: *Thank you for whispering to me, and I promise I'll never be afraid to listen to you again.*

The whisper came. "And you'll never be alone."

Return to Present Day

I closed the notebook and looked up to see Sheilla, a lone tear in her big blue eyes. Our tea was cold and our cookies uneaten. We still sat there together, Grandma on her rocker, Sheilla and I on the couch, boxes and packing laid aside while we walked the past together.

Mum gave an involuntary shiver. "Having Kevin come to the house was the most frightened I'd ever been."

"Me too."

I barely heard Sheilla say, "I'm not brave."

I shook my head, not wanting her to think we were any stronger than her. "We're not either. Things happen. You do what you can and have faith that God's got your back."

Mum reached for both our hands and gave a small squeeze. The silence hung in the air as she searched our faces, her eyes glistening with intensity. "It says in the Bible, 'Fear not for I am with you.'"

The whisper came to me one last time. "And I always will be."

Acknowledgments

Christine Finlay Beckman was part of our Scottish community here in the Pacific Northwest. She raised her family here and even became a part of the Seattle Highland Games Association. She was an extraordinary person who inspired not just me but many others.

Although 90% of this novel is based on the actual events of my mother's life growing up in Scotland during WWII, I used fiction to link her stories together and create the ending she feared most.

I believe we learn best from the accounts of ordinary people who find themselves in extraordinary situations and accomplish the impossible, and that life is much more than we can see from our human perspective.

I did so much research over the years of writing about Chrissy it's hard to remember it all. If you are interested in learning more about the historical events mentioned, visit my website: wendy-mutton.com. You'll find the tab for First Life has a research link and a place to leave comments.

If you enjoyed reading about Chrissy, I think you'll like my upcoming novel. *House on Latimer Square* is a pre-World War II historical saga with a supernatural twist. A story of courage, love, trust, and the willingness to do whatever you can to save the lives of others.

To my daughter Sheilla Christine Hagedorn, our cover designer: You amaze me with your creativity. I so appreciate your help and encouragement.

To my writing buddies Melva Timm and Liz Visser: I couldn't have written this book without you. Your critiques were always insightful. You encouraged, instructed, and enlightened me. You are both great writers and good friends. Thank you so much.

About the Author

Wendy lives in rural Washington State, with family close and her leading man, her husband John. Who's been a constant source of encouragement for over fifty-three years. Even with a seemingly ordinary past, Wendy has come to believe that life is much more than we can see from our human perspective.

House On Latimer Square

A Matter of Money

The Blue Finn Nightclub
Edinburgh, Scotland
March 1937

His luck was about to change. Laurie MacKenzie glanced at the gold engravings on his college ring. A graduation gift from his girl. University of Edinburgh, Class of 1937. He would rather have celebrated graduation with his mates in a lively Edinburgh pub, blow off some steam, but Marguerite insisted they meet at The Blue Finn Nightclub, a classy place. She wasn't the pub type, and anyway, wasn't this the life he dreamed of having? A smile spread across his handsome face.

He entered the lobby with a nod of appreciation. Even from the door, he could see the place was packed. The band played a favorite American song, *Pennies from Heaven*. The singer didn't sound like Bing Crosby, but it still put Laurie in the mood to dance.

He handed his fedora and overcoat to a redhead in the cloakroom. She smiled at him, her eyes traveling over his features. Laurie had a dusky complexion, an odd contrast to his sea-blue eyes. His dark auburn hair, a little on the long side, fell over dark brows. He raked his fingers through his hair and shrugged his new white dinner jacket into place. Laurie borrowed the money to pay for the jacket just to please Marguerite. He straightened his tie before stepping into the crowd.

Small lamps flickered from every table. His pulse raced as he caught sight of Marguerite and the way her pale blond hair shone in the soft lighting. He recognized two classmates sitting at her table. One lad leaned forward, saying something that made her laugh. He shook off a momentary stab of jealousy.

"Pardon me. Excuse me." Laurie maneuvered past dancing couples. She hadn't noticed him yet. He wanted to watch her face when she saw how he'd dressed for her. A hand touched his arm.

"Mr. MacKenzie?"

A young busboy stood at his elbow.

"That's me."

"A man at the bar gave me a note for you." The boy held up a folded cocktail napkin.

"Thanks." Laurie stopped to read the scribbled message before asking, "Which man?" But the lad disappeared into the crowd.

The note read: "Back door. Urgent. Rab." Although the hand bore no resemblance to that of Laurie's grandfather, there was always a possibility the old man had sent someone.

Laurie took one last look at Marguerite, wanting to ignore the note, but he doubted Rab would send someone unless he needed help. With a heavy sigh, he turned toward the kitchen.

He'd make this quick. She'd picked him, sure, but it wasn't wise to let his girl wait with so many other suitors ready to catch her attention.

"Where can I find the back door?"

The passing waiter pointed down a corridor to his left. Laurie trotted down the hall and through the doorway, his mind distracted with thoughts of Marguerite.

A hand reached out, spinning him around.

"What the hell!" He struggled to pull away. A large fist rammed into his nose. He might have fallen if his assailant's other hand hadn't grabbed his expensive dinner jacket. Another stunning blow landed just above his right eye. Laurie had been in a few fights and could handle himself, but the man's long arms held him like a rag doll. The massive hulk before him wore a suit stretched over bulging muscles. Laurie swung out wildly. He couldn't connect with anything solid. With surprising quickness, the bloke let go and landed three punches to Laurie's midsection, leaving him struggling to breathe.

He slumped to the ground. Time slowed. Sounds of a busy kitchen mingled with the hum of cars as they passed on the street, but no one was near enough to help. Not even an alley cat watched his beating. Still trying to breathe, Laurie squinted through already swollen eyes to see the face above him. The man's bulbous nose bent at an odd angle.

"Get on yer feet." Once again, giant hands took fistfuls of Laurie's lapels. The squashed nose loomed so close Laurie's eyes couldn't focus on it.

The big man growled, "You look like you can afford to pay." He released Laurie, sending him sprawling on the pavement. Laurie blinked up at the beefy face as the man spit out his words. "Toby wants his siller. I'll gi' ye a break the now. You don't want to make me do this again."

A wave of panic hit Laurie. His grandfather frustrated him, sure, but he'd do anything to protect him. "Rab. If you hurt him—"

"The old man's no been touched this time. Toby makes a point of knowing who he's dealing with, aye?"

Laurie lunged to his feet, throwing weight into a punch launched at the man's jaw. The giant stood his ground. Laurie's fist felt like it hit solid rock. With one punishing roundhouse blow, Toby's man sent Laurie back onto the cobblestones.

Laurie wiped a sleeve across his eyes. Blood and dirt smeared across the white fabric. "Look what you've done. This jacket's worth more than you are."

A heavy foot kicked him hard in the side, punctuating the disgust in the man's gravelly voice. "Tomorrow, mind, an' you better pay what you owe. Don't make me get rough." Laurie's attempt to laugh at the trite gangster imitation sounded more like a cough. It started a spasm of wheezing.

"Here, what's this?" A little man in shirtsleeves and an apron appeared from the club's back door with a bucket of kitchen scraps. As the alley filled with light, Laurie's companion melted into the shadows.

The little man dropped his pail, calling over his shoulder for help. Muscular arms supported Laurie as the kitchen worker sat him up.

"Are you all right, mate?"

Laurie squinted up at the work-worn face. He patted the little man on the arm. "No worries, you should see the other guy."

Milton Keynes UK
Ingram Content Group UK Ltd.
UKHW010639240424
441619UK00005B/440